The Language of Fruit

PENN STUDIES IN LANDSCAPE ARCHITECTURE

John Dixon Hunt, Series Editor

This series is dedicated to the study and promotion of a wide variety
of approaches to landscape architecture, with special emphasis on
connections between theory and practice. It includes monographs on key
topics in history and theory, descriptions of projects by both established
and rising designers, translations of major foreign-language texts,
anthologies of theoretical and historical writings on classic issues, and
critical writing by members of the profession of landscape architecture.
The series was the recipient of the Award of Honor in Communications
from the American Society of Landscape Architects, 2006.

THE
LANGUAGE
OF FRUIT

Literature and Horticulture
in the Long Eighteenth Century

Liz Bellamy

PENN

UNIVERSITY OF PENNSYLVANIA PRESS

PHILADELPHIA

Published by
University of Pennsylvania Press
Philadelphia, Pennsylvania 19104–4112
www.upenn.edu/pennpress

Printed in the United States of America on acid-free paper
1 3 5 7 9 10 8 6 4 2

A catalogue record for this book is available from the Library of Congress
ISBN 978-0-8122-5083-1

CONTENTS

Introduction

Discoursing with Fruit Trees

In his *Dialogue (or Familiar Discourse) and Conference between the Husbandman and Fruit-Trees* (1676), the horticultural writer and successful nurseryman Ralph Austen advises his readers that they need to "*discourse with Fruit-trees* having learned to understand *their Language.*" He argues that, although this language is not "Articulate and distinct to the *outward sence of hearing* in the sound of words," trees nonetheless "speak plainly, and distinctly, to the *inward sence, the understanding.*"[1] This book can be read as a response to Austen's injunction, since it aims to discourse with fruit trees, understand their language, and recognize how they communicate with our inward sense. It will explore the meanings of fruits and fruit trees by considering how they have been represented in texts across a period stretching from the Restoration to the Romantic era, or, roughly, from Ralph Austen to Jane Austen. The focus will be on how poets, playwrights, and novelists have deployed fruit in their works, and how they have responded to changes in cultivation techniques, the range of available varieties, and mechanisms for the exchange and distribution of fruit.

Of course, literary depictions cannot be read as direct and unproblematic reactions to developments in fruticultural practice. Fruit has so many symbolic associations that its portrayal is inevitably inflected by inherited topoi, cultural resonances, and stories, which all shape how it is perceived and how it functions within a text. Representations are also influenced by cultural codes embedded within the formal conventions of different genres or discourses. These factors of stasis or tradition interact with horticultural innovations to ensure that change is interpreted through a lens of inherited assumptions. To achieve Austen's aim of allowing fruit to speak directly to our understanding, we need to explore the meanings accruing to fruit in the early modern period and how these meanings are articulated within a range of forms. This will involve not only the biblical sources that feature in Austen's dialogues, with the story of the fall and the erotic fruit imagery of the Song of Solomon, but also the classical texts that constitute the other pillar of the iconographic repertoire of English literature. Works by writers such as Virgil, Ovid, and Horace are full of fruit metaphors and references and were widely translated and adapted in the early modern period.[2] Robert Appelbaum has highlighted the potency of myths of plenty and tales of the abundant fruits of the Land of Cockaigne and these have roots in both the Garden of Eden and classical stories of the Golden Age.[3] These sources will be considered alongside more practical tracts and treatises on techniques of fruit cultivation, exploring the relationship between symbolic and horticultural frames of reference. As the title page to Austen's *Treatise of Fruit-Trees* (1653) exemplifies, works on agriculture and gardening frequently incorporate biblical or classical references, or both (Figure 1).[4]

Fruit is freighted with symbolism derived from its physical form and its origins in sexual reproduction as well as its literary heritage. Its swelling and ripening can represent female fecundity and fruitfulness as well as male sexuality and tumescence. Sexual maturity or availability can be expressed in terms of ripeness and those who have not reached this condition may be identified as green or unripe fruit. The loss of virginity is suggested by the plucking and biting of fruit, particularly the cherry, and some of these associations have continued to the present day. Particular body parts can be identified with specific fruits: female buttocks and breasts with peaches and melons; male genitals with pears, plums, and nuts, as well as with wrinkly dried fruits such as apricots and raisins. The literary representation of fruit can thus be explored as an aesthetic negotiation of the links and boundaries between the figurative and the quotidian, inherited allusion and contemporary change at a time when Britain was developing the characteristics of a consumer society and an exchange economy.

The many references to fruit in literary texts indicate its importance in early modern society. Ken Albala suggests that Renaissance writings on health and regimen manifest "a fear of fruits bordering on the pathological," yet the centrality of orchard fruits within British cuisine is evident from early modern cookbooks, with numerous recipes for stewing and baking but also pickling and preserving apples and pears, as well as hardy stone fruits like cherries, plums, and damsons.[5] These were the staple products of the early modern English orchard, along with nuts such as walnuts and filberts.[6] Whether eaten raw, cooked in pies, or used as an ingredient in chutneys, preserves, sauces, and stuffings, fruits and nuts provided important nutrition and variety in a

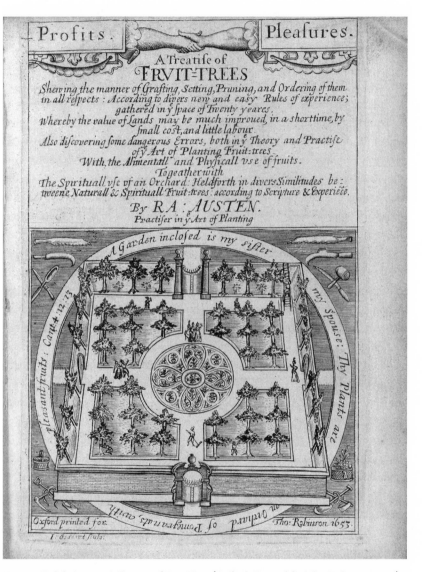

Figure 1. Ralph Austen, *A Treatise of Fruit-Trees* (Oxford: Printed for Tho. Robinson, 1653), title page, showing the significance of biblical references within practical gardening tracts.

frequently monotonous diet.[7] Although fruit was consumed by all social classes, the apples and pears produced in British orchards were a particularly significant component of the diet of laborers. The pears grown in Britain up to the nineteenth century were largely the starchy warden type that were rich in carbohydrates and therefore provided a vital source of energy prior to the widespread cultivation of the potato.[8] In addition, apples were made into cider and pears into perry. Farmers and landowners would often maintain an orchard to produce the warden pears, cider, and perry, which were central to the sustenance of their live-in servants. The cultivation of large quantities of orchard fruit did not just provide a desirable addition to the table; it was regarded as essential to the continuing health and prosperity of the nation. It was portrayed in works on horticulture and political economy as a patriotic duty, notably in the years of the Commonwealth and the Restoration when the country was recovering from the environmental and economic devastation of the English Civil War.[9]

Trees bearing "orchard fruits" were not confined to orchards in the early modern landscape but were dispersed throughout gardens, fields, and hedgerows. John Beale notes in *Herefordshire Orchards* (1657) that "in most places our hedges are inriched with rowes of fruit-trees, pears, or apples, Gennetmoyles [a cider apple], or crab [apple] trees."[10] Pruning and other management techniques could increase the quality and quantity of the yield, but they were far from essential since these trees could survive and flourish completely untended. In contrast, more delicate "wall fruits," such as peaches, nectarines, and apricots, were not completely hardy in Britain, so they needed to be grown against a wall with a south-facing aspect to produce fruit that was suitable for human consumption. The orchards of the husbandman might contain one or two apricot or peach trees in a particularly sheltered corner, but horticultural guides tend to dismiss such produce as not worth the effort of the practical farmer. In the seventeenth century, wall fruits were primarily associated with the walled gardens of more prosperous landowners. The fresh fruits supplied to the kitchen and table were prized luxuries and the difficulties involved in picking, transporting, and storing them reinforced their special status compared to the more resilient and durable apples, pears, and nuts that connoted a homely diet.[11] Fruit thus encompassed both the hardy and abundant orchard crops consumed by the lower classes and the delicate produce of the kitchen garden, reared with intensive labor and care for the tables of the affluent, furnishing metaphors that could be appropriated for the representation of different social groups.

The early modern period saw a sustained increase in the number of orchard and wall fruits cultivated in Britain, as new varieties were developed by growers or introduced by plant collectors like the John Tradescants (Elder and Younger) in the seventeenth century and Sir Joseph Banks in the eighteenth. Harriet Ritvo suggests that whereas there had previously been a trickle of new domesticates, "in the seventeenth and eighteenth centuries that trickle became a torrent."[12] John Parkinson lists twenty-one different varieties of peach in his 1629 *Paradisi in Sole Paradisus Terrestris* (Park-in-Sun's Earthly Paradise), commenting that "Their varieties are many, and more knowne in these dayes then in former times" (580). Some of the new fruits were hardier than their predecessors and more able to withstand the British climate, some had new flavors or culinary applications, and some had different flowering and fruiting patterns, making it possible to extend the period of harvest. This was part of a growing enthusiasm for the cultivation of out-of-season fruits in the hope of limiting the period in which fresh fruits were unavailable. Improvements in the technology of hotbeds and the subsequent development of hothouses were likewise associated with the drive to extend the fruiting season and these innovations eventually encouraged attempts to cultivate more exotic fruit trees, such as the subtropical citrus. This culminated in the eighteenth century in the production of tropical fruits such as pineapples and mangoes. There was thus a progressive extension of the types of fruit that could be raised in Britain, as well as improvements in cultivation techniques and fruticultural equipment, with increasing emphasis on human intervention and the control or mastery of nature.

These developments form a backdrop for the composition of the poems, plays, and novels of the long eighteenth century, but there are also significant changes within literature, with shifts in the way different genres use fruit and the kinds of fruit depicted. For example, the country house poetry of the seventeenth century heralds the expanding range of produce available within the kitchen garden as a manifestation of natural abundance and the providential ordering of society.[13] The description of Eden in Milton's *Paradise Lost* not only reinforces the connections between fruit, temptation, and sexuality, but also evokes the sensual pleasures of eating fashionable wall fruits and represents gardening as the ultimate gentlemanly recreation.[14] The georgic poetry of the early eighteenth century draws on Virgil and Horace to celebrate the virtuous innocence of rural retirement through the cultivation of orchard fruit, but it does so with an emphasis on the labor required to ensure a successful crop at a time of concerns about food security. The various poetic genres adopt distinct perspectives and represent different fruits, but their common preoccupation is with fruit that can be plucked from the tree or bush, whether in the georgic orchard, the walled garden of the country house, or the distant forests of the Amazon or Caribbean. This is very different from the fruit that is incorporated into the plays of the Restoration and eighteenth century. Since drama tends to have a metropolitan outlook and setting, fruit is depicted as part of a system of commercial exchange, bought from a professional vendor rather than cultivated for personal consumption. In particular, plays contain recurrent references to the oranges that were imported from Europe and especially Portugal and sold to the audiences within the playhouses by "orange wenches." The purchase and consumption of these fruits is sometimes dramatized in the action on stage, and oranges and other bought wares dominate the fruit symbolism within the texts, emphasizing ideas of fungibility and commodification rather than the natural abundance at home or abroad that is celebrated within poetry.

Oranges likewise feature, along with orchard and wall fruits, in the novels of the eighteenth century, but the preoccupation is increasingly with domestically produced rather than imported fruits. By the end of the century, oranges have been displaced by pineapples as the most prominent and culturally resonant literary fruit. Their cultivation within hothouses represents human control of nature, and the greenhouse, or "forcing house," provides a space for the interrogation of conflicting visions of social change. The humble crops of the orchard are contrasted with the valuable produce of the hothouse, while the abundance of nature is juxtaposed with the labor and ingenuity required to raise crops that are fundamentally unnatural. The various literary genres therefore focus on different kinds of fruits, as well as on different aspects of the production and distribution process, from the evocation of abundance of seventeenth-century poetry, through the imported and commodified wares of drama, to the orchards of eighteenth-century georgic, and the artificial hothouse fruits of the Romantic novel.

Representations of domestic fruit-growing can invoke the conventions of pastoral tradition to portray fruitfulness as a manifestation of natural abundance or divine providence. The produce of the hedgerow and orchard sustains the working man, falling into the hands of the laborer or poet without effort or expenditure. Yet this image is countered by the association of fruit with complex and costly cultivation methods. Wall fruits and exotic fruits are identified as luxuries, raised with difficulty within the walled garden, the hotbed or hothouse, or imported through commercial exchange. The topos of bounty is therefore challenged not only by a topos of labor, drawing on the development of increasingly sophisticated horticultural technology and economic networks, but also by the imagery of a postlapsarian world and the conventions of the georgic genre. Literary critics have emphasized the dominance of pastoral modes in Renaissance writing on the countryside as a manifestation of the uneasiness with the portrayal of labor and suggested that this was challenged by a resurgence of georgic from the late seventeenth century.[15] This study will focus on fruit to explore the tensions between these conflicting representational repertoires in horticultural as well as literary texts, showing how the language of fruit negotiates concurrent ideas of pastoral prelapsarian plenty and georgic postlapsarian labor. At the same time, it will use the representation of imported and exotic fruits to discuss themes of commodification and colonialism and their intersection with inherited associations of gender and sexuality.

The exploration of these issues will require breadth of coverage in terms of both chronological span and the variety of discourses and genres, necessitating rather more detailed accounts of the texts and sources than would be expected in works with a more limited timeframe or generic range. This approach is designed to clarify the evidence and arguments for the nonspecialist reader, appropriating horticultural works and concepts for students of literature, and making literary works and concepts accessible to garden historians. It is also in line with the reappraisal of the role of plot and story that has been a feature of recent critical theory.[16] Although the scope of the study is wide, encompassing different genres and periods, the focus is specific, since the central concern is with how fruit is represented and how it is used to explore ideological issues, whether with regard to gender, class, race, the function of the market, or humanity's place in the natural world.

The argument presented here crosses disciplinary boundaries, encompassing the study of agricultural and horticultural literature and food history, as well as literary criticism and theory, so its debts to existing works are widespread and extensive. The late twentieth century saw the emergence of scholars from a range of backgrounds who shared an interest in agrarian discourse and the connections between technical innovations and writings on landscape and the land, many of the most prominent of whom contributed to the collection of essays titled *Culture and Cultivation in Early Modern England*.[17] In the twenty-first century, the insights and approaches developed with respect to agricultural literature were extended to English garden theory, with studies by such critics as John Dixon Hunt, Rachel Crawford, and Rebecca Bushnell. While Hunt shows how certain high status horticultural works provide a schema for understanding relationships among the human, the natural world, and the divine, Crawford discusses agricultural and horticultural treatises and identifies a growing concern with contained spaces, which she also discerns within a range of written forms.[18] Rebecca Bushnell's *Green Desire: Imagining Early Modern English Gardens* evaluates the influence of gardening tracts and treatises on a range of readers, including the humble housewives and husbandmen to whom many of the practical works are addressed.[19]

This interest in the cultural functions of horticultural discourse has been accompanied by developments within literary studies which have culminated in the emergence of what has become known as "ecocriticism." This uses literary texts to explore relationships between human culture and the natural world, and fruit clearly has a crucial place in a theoretical perspective which focuses "on the material interactions between humans and nonhumans related to gender, race, and class."[20] Yet much of the criticism drawing on ecocritical approaches is primarily interested in literary representations of flowers, whether blooming in Renaissance gardens, the tropics, or hothouses. In this book, I will argue that readings of this floral symbolism need to be supplemented by understanding of the place of fruit within orchards, gardens, the tropics, hothouses, and literature. As a natural product of human intervention that is freighted with symbolic associations, fruit subverts unproblematic binary oppositions of nature and art, agriculture and industry, and nature and culture that have been articulated in some ecocritical theory.[21] As a comestible rather than an object of purely aesthetic appeal, fruit's iconographic functions are significantly different from those of the flowers that are also produced within gardens and greenhouses.

Many of the works self-identifying as ecocriticism in the twenty-first century have focused on seventeenth-century poetry, and particularly *Paradise Lost*, which has been analyzed as a response to "an environmental crisis of unprecedented proportions" in early modern England.[22] Drawing on critics such as Diane McColley and Ken Hiltner, who have challenged readings of *Paradise Lost* as inherently misogynistic, these studies have developed the idea of Eve as "the 'genius loci' of Eden" and related Milton's text to attempts to create an environmental paradise within England.[23] Similarly, both Jonson's "To Penshurst" and Marvell's poetry have been subjected to ecocritical scrutiny, resulting in their appropriation as green texts.[24] All these studies and approaches have been invaluable in refining the arguments and readings presented here, but the focus on fruit will enable consideration of how the green impulse is manifested across a range of genres and periods, looking at Restoration drama and the Romantic novel, as well as the estate poetry of the seventeenth century and the georgic of the eighteenth, to evaluate the impact of inherited topoi and formal conventions in shaping literary responses to practical and environmental change.

Ecocriticism has only been acknowledged as a discrete entity relatively recently, but its roots can be discerned in a long-standing preoccupation in literary criticism with the depiction of nature and relationships between human-kind and the environment. Researchers working in the seventeenth century have shown how literary representations of the natural world responded to the emergence of the New Science and the epistemological developments that culminated in the founding of the Royal Society. Studies of eighteenth- and nineteenth-century literature have analyzed the impact of the revolution in scientific knowledge, which culminated in binomial nomenclature, the system of naming organisms developed by Carl von Linné, or Linnaeus, in his *Species Plantarum* of 1753. These accounts are informed by the concept of cultural history articulated in Michel Foucault's *The Order of Things*, which highlights the role of classification in the emergence of the modern episteme. Harriet Ritvo theorizes the relationship between humanity and nature, and of the wild and tame, that followed the development of scientific taxonomy, as well as the introduction of new varieties from places that were increasingly subject to colonial control. Alan Bewell emphasizes the overtly sexualized nature of the discourse of Linnaean botany and Amy King explores the role of this discourse in the development of the nineteenth-century novel, showing how popular botanical understanding provides a vocabulary for conveying the sexual element of courtship and marriage that was acceptable within polite literature. Sam George considers the implications of the discourse with reference to literary representations of female botanizing, and Deidre Lynch discusses the significance of what she identifies as Jane Austen's "Greenhouse Romanticism" and the preoccupation with plant imagery derived from the hothouse rather than the field.[25] Taken together, these works could perhaps be classified as a genus of "taxonomic criticism," and identified as part of the family of ecocriticism.

This study will end around the point where King and Lynch begin and will focus on fruit rather than flowers. It will explore scientific change through

developments in fruticultural technology, but it will suggest that these innovations need to be appreciated within the context of the existing tradition of
iconography. New ways of understanding and classifying the world and new
techniques for producing and sourcing fruit are initially perceived through,
and incorporated into, an established repertoire of images that provide a
framework for discussions of such things as gender difference and female
sexuality, ideas of natural and unnatural cultivation, and the opposition of
domestic and foreign goods. In her contribution to discussions of the theoretical
approach known as new formalism, Caroline Levine has argued that it is not
inherently reactionary to emphasize the cultural significance of forces of stasis,
and indeed that it is necessary to recognize how these forces function in order
to implement change.[26]

Another theoretical perspective, related to ecocriticism but gradually
developing its own autonomous identity, is the approach combining concern
for the environment with awareness of the legacy of colonialism known as
"postcolonial ecocriticism." Richard Grove's mighty *Green Imperialism* argues
that ecological awareness developed alongside colonial expansion as early
settlers sought to ameliorate environmental problems on the tropical islands
they colonized. Far from simply imposing a purely destructive "environmental
imperialism," they combined new scientific methodologies with the understanding of the landscape of the indigenous communities in an attempt to
assuage the impact of humanity on an environment that was apprehended
through ideas of the Garden of Eden. More recently, Graham Huggan and
Helen Tiffin have discussed the relationship between postcolonial and ecological approaches and analyzed how they are manifested in a range of literary,
largely fictional, texts, principally from the twentieth century.[27] One of the
works of postcolonial ecocriticism that is particularly relevant to the present
study is Beth Fowkes Tobin's *Colonizing Nature: The Tropics in British Arts and
Letters, 1760–1820*. Tobin explores the way tropical plants are represented in
the art and literature of the colonizers, to reveal a "trope of bounty" that functions to deny the agricultural labor and technology of the colonized.[28] My
argument will draw on biblical and classical sources to consider the origins of
this trope and its significance in relation to representations of domestic fruit
production as well as the portrayal of imported or foreign fruit.

A further aspect of cultural inquiry that has informed the current study is
the discipline of food history, which has grown rapidly in recent years, pio-
neered by Ken Albala, Robert Appelbaum, and Joan Fitzpatrick. These critics

have stressed the importance of rituals of consumption and the representation of food, including fruits, in Renaissance writings.[29] Although they are principally concerned with a slightly earlier period to that considered here, the anxieties that they identify, about fruit in general and green fruits in particular, persisted into the eighteenth and even the nineteenth centuries. They provide an additional set of associations, derived from cookbooks and medical treatises, which interact with literary iconography and horticultural codes.[30] They also provide a valuable reminder that for all their symbolic resonances, the fruits produced in the early modern period were above all a source of sustenance, nutrition, and pleasure for a hungry and rapidly expanding population.

The main focus of this book will be the representation of fruit within literary texts, genres, and horticultural discourse from the long eighteenth century, but the study of these constructions provides significant insights into the practicalities of cultivation and consumption. While not a master narrative, the account of what actually happened in the gardens and orchards of the past represents an important chapter in the story of how people thought about fruit and its production and formulated it in language and images. The book will use existing studies of garden history to provide the backdrop against which the fruit drama unfolds.[31] It will also draw on accounts of individual fruits and individual texts, such as Fran Beauman's encyclopedic history of the pineapple and Appelbaum's reading of the representation of the forbidden fruit in *Paradise Lost*.[32] These works will facilitate the conversation with fruit trees recommended by Austen to expose the shifts in their ideological and metonymic significance, while consideration of literary representations and semantic codes will illuminate aspects of fruit cultivation, distribution, and consumption.

Before analysis of the early modern texts, however, Chapter 1 will explore some of the most resonant fruit stories from the Bible and classical literature. These traditions furnish recurrent tropes, images, and characters, but they also lead to the emergence of the contrasting genres of pastoral and georgic, which provide divergent conventions and structures for writing and thinking about fruit. Both biblical and classical writings are concerned with fruits from the subtropical climates of the Middle East and the Mediterranean, but material from the medieval period indicates how these stories and genres were appropriated into English literary tradition and adapted to the colder temperatures and limited produce of the British Isles. The interrogation of fruit myths in Chapter 1 will therefore establish the literary context for the central study of the portrayal of fruits within early modern literature. It will trace the ancestry of fruit associations, such as the identification of fruits with ideas of gender and sexuality, and tensions between conflicting concepts of abundance and labor.

The second chapter will consider how fruit and fruit trees are represented in works providing advice to gardeners, as writers develop discursive conventions to frame practical instructions or more philosophical horticultural precepts. The emphasis on the production of orchard fruits in the tracts and treatises of the seventeenth century is gradually diversified from the Restoration to the eighteenth century, with increasing stress on techniques for raising subtropical wall fruits, such as nectarines, apricots, and peaches, and ultimately exotic fruits like oranges and pineapples. This chapter will analyze how fruit growing is represented within these works, looking at the practical advice proffered, but also at how this is expressed within a conceptual framework that is itself shaped by mythic and iconographic connotations and ideas of the effects of fruit on the constitution of the individual and the state.

This exploration of horticultural discourse will be followed by a series of chapters looking at how fruit is represented within the literary genres of seventeenth-century poetry, Restoration drama, eighteenth-century georgic, and the Romantic period novel. The narrative will contain a large cast of literary fruits, which will be introduced through analysis of poetry, depicting the abundant produce of aristocratic gardens and the fruit-rich paradisal landscapes of tropical islands or paradise itself. As the story develops, however, three central characters will increasingly come to the fore: the apple, the orange, and the pineapple. The apple is on the stage from the start of the story and continues throughout the drama as a symbol of natural abundance, simplicity, and English integrity. As a rustic and self-effacing figure, it tends to hover in the wings, until its big scene which comes in the account of eighteenth-century georgic. The orange makes a relatively early appearance as a visitor from overseas, associated with trade and exchange in Restoration theater, but it is some time before it can be naturalized as a British resident. The pineapple has a late but dramatic entrance as a cosseted and an exotic child of indulgence, epitomizing extravagant luxury in the novel. All these fruits have their part to play. By focusing on literary texts from the seventeenth to the nineteenth centuries, and looking at the genres of poetry, drama, and the novel, this study will expose the symbolic versatility of fruit, showing how it can signify the homely and exotic, the domestic and imported, and the hardy and the frail. It will indicate how these symbolic representations are informed by changing concepts of gender, class, and national identity.

Some of the genres and texts have been extensively scrutinized in recent decades. Country house poetry from the seventeenth century and georgics from the eighteenth have been read as manifestations of very different visions of the emergent British polity, with some critics emphasizing their endorsement of the dominant ideology and others identifying more subversive strands.[33] The novels produced after the outbreak of the French Revolution have been subject to similarly conflicting interpretations.[34] The purpose of this book is not to rehearse existing readings of the political significance of individual texts and genres but rather to indicate how ideological debates can be illuminated by acknowledging the changing practical and metaphorical functions of fruit, as literary symbolism responded to technological developments and diversified the class and gender implications of inherited iconographic codes. This will generate some reflections on the nature of representation and the terms of its negotiation of shifts in cultural practice and formal and symbolic conventions.

The literary chapters are organized generically but with a rough chronological structure. Chapter 3 considers seventeenth-century poetry, looking at descriptions of fruit growing not only in the gardens of the nobility but also in more exotic locations. Chapter 4 explores fruits within the largely urban environment of Restoration drama, while Chapter 5 returns to the countryside to assess the georgic poetry of the eighteenth century. Chapter 6 examines the geographically expansive landscapes of fiction, showing how fruit figures in texts that encompass the country and the city. The analysis combines canonical texts and authors with the less familiar, encompassing poets such as Edmund Waller, John Philips, and John Armstrong, as well as Marvell, Milton, and Gay; playwrights like Charles Sedley, Susanna Centlivre, and Colley Cibber, as well as Congreve, Wycherley, and Behn; novelists such as Mary Robinson, George Walker, and Amelia Opie, as well as Smollett, Charlotte Smith, and Austen. The aim is to show how literary genres responded to social and iconographic developments by exploring responses from across the cultural spectrum, covering both quotidian and egregious works.

The generic division of this material, despite the chronological nature of the development of fruit production, draws on recent theoretical studies that have been characterized as new formalism. Works such as Caroline Levine's

Forms: Whole, Rhythm, Hierarchy, Network have emphasized the role of genre and other aspects of form in shaping how literary texts respond to cultural change, challenging the hegemonic status achieved by historicist approaches in recent decades. Levine argues that "literary forms and social formations are equally real in their capacity to organize materials, and equally *un*real in being artificial, contingent constraints."[35] Although innovations in patterns of production and the discourses within which these were disseminated inevitably influenced how fruits were conceptualized, these developments were perceived and depicted through the distinct conventions of genre and form, as poets, playwrights, and novelists responded differently to the challenges posed by the evolving social, economic, and symbolic functions of fruit. The formulation of these responses was shaped and conditioned by what Levine has termed the "affordances" of the forms in which they worked, just as innovations in fruit production were mediated through established horticultural assumptions and techniques, as well as through iconographic associations. The following chapters will show the importance of specific fruits within particular genres and will identify the significance of fruit production, distribution, and consumption both within and between different literary forms. Although this book contains separate chapters on the biblical and classical context, horticultural writing, and the principal literary genres, it is not aiming to hierarchize discourses or genres or to provide a study in influence. It does not attempt to prove that literary works were influenced by classical sources, by horticultural texts, by the determining conventions of literary genre, or even by a combination of all three. Rather, it is positing a more integral relationship, arguing that fruit is inevitably, inherently, and incessantly conceptualized in simultaneously symbolic and practical terms in both gardening works and literary texts.

Chapter 1

"I Am the True Vine"

The Uses of Fruit in Biblical and Classical Tradition

And when the woman saw that the tree *was* good for food, and that it *was* pleasant
to the eyes, and a tree to be desired to make *one* wise, she took of the fruit thereof,
and did eat, and gave also unto her husband with her; and he did eat.

The story of how Eve ate the forbidden fruit reverberates through the writings
and iconography of late medieval and early modern Britain to the extent that
it is perhaps no exaggeration to say that all textual acts of fruit consumption
echo Eve's calamitous bite. Although the King James Bible was only available
from 1611, its account of the fall is virtually identical to that in the Geneva Bible
of 1599, which in turn closely resembles the fourteenth-century Wycliffe Bible.
At the same time, English translations of writers like Virgil and Ovid were
bringing classical works to a wider audience, and with them an alternative
repertoire of fruit symbolism, providing a framework through which social,
economic, and scientific changes could be apprehended and represented. The
cultural connections of fruit are such that an apple is never just an apple and
an orange is never just an orange, whether in country house poetry or in tracts
on improving techniques of husbandry.[1] This chapter will therefore outline
some of the most significant fruit-related stories from biblical and classical
tradition. It will show how, like tender fruits, these myths were gradually
naturalized and appropriated during the medieval period and absorbed into
English literary and cultural tradition, shaping the perceptions and representations of the early modern period.

From the late twentieth century, new historicist and cultural materialist
approaches to literature have emphasized that cultural artifacts need to be

interpreted in the context of competing discursive constructions of the world, as responses not so much to historical events as to the codes and conventions for the representation of those events. The portrayal of fruit in poetry, drama, and fiction needs to be set alongside the development of horticultural writings, from the humble practical gardening guides to the more philosophical disquisitions on human intervention in the natural world. In the twenty-first century, ecocriticism has challenged the emblematic and allegorical readings of early modern texts, and, although individual critics like Diane McColley have provided sensitive interpretations of the symbolic associations of writers like Milton and Marvell, the general tenor of this theoretical approach has been to emphasize the extent of literary engagement with scientific innovation and empiricism. This book aims to draw on both new historicist and ecocritical approaches, exploring how literary texts engage with a range of fruticultural discourses and respond to changing conceptions of the natural world; at the same time, however, it will attempt to emphasize and reestablish the centrality of the mythic and iconographic resonances which have perhaps been neglected in recent years. Biblical and classical stories have shaped the way individuals and communities saw fruit, and the genres and forms within which those fruits were portrayed.

Fruit is significant in Genesis even before the events of the fall, and critics have explored how the relationship between humankind and nature is conceived in the prelapsarian world. Harriet Ritvo has shown that the story of creation manifests a taxonomic impulse, as the central categories of the physical world are established, although she notes that these categories "have been both refined and contradicted" by subsequent scientific developments.[2] In chapter 1, God tells Adam and Eve, "Behold, I have given you every herb bearing seed, which is upon the face of all the earth, and every tree, in the which is the fruit of a tree yielding seed; to you it shall be for meat" (1:29). In chapter 2, the garden is described as containing "every tree that is pleasant to the sight, and good for food" (2:9) and Adam is required to "dress it and keep it" (2:15). Leah Marcus distinguishes between the first chapter of the story, which emphasizes "human *dominion over* nature," and the second chapter, which "emphasizes human *responsibility for* nature."[3] Alastair Fowler argues that dressing and keeping implies fairly minimal maintenance and thus stands in contrast to the situation after the fall, when Adam is sent forth "to till the ground" (3:23), suggesting more arduous labor.[4] Yet in William Lawson's horticultural treatise, *A New*

Orchard and Garden, probably first published in 1618, shortly after the King James Bible, the chapter devoted to the correct method of pruning fruit trees is titled "Of the Right Dressing of Trees."[5] Lawson may be referencing Genesis, or the King James may be following contemporary horticultural usage, but it indicates that, rather than denoting the general care and oversight suggested by "keeping," "dressing" has a specific meaning and involves the skilled labor of pruning. Even within the prelapsarian garden, a degree of husbandry is required, but this is presented in positive terms. The relationship between humanity and nature is fundamentally harmonious, as the tree is not damaged when the fruit is plucked, and human work takes the form of pruning and other types of maintenance that help to sustain productivity.

It is following the intervention of the serpent in the third chapter that fruit acquires an alternative symbolic repertoire, connoting destructive desire that causes the expulsion of humankind from paradise and brings death, sin, and pain into the world (3:16–19). Eve is motivated by appetite. She sees that "the tree was good for food" and is "pleasant to the eyes," but her actions are also associated with hubris and vanity for she recognizes that "it was a tree to be desired to make one wise." The serpent argues that the tree can turn mortals into gods, so the consumption of the fruit is a consequence of pride and social aspiration. Yet the gendered connotations of the story are implicit rather than explicit within Genesis. Despite pinning the blame on Eve as soon as he is confronted by God (Genesis 3:12), Adam eats the fruit when Eve gives it to him, without requiring the persuasions and blandishments that are introduced into later versions of the story, such as those within the English mystery play tradition or in Milton's *Paradise Lost*.

The early fifteenth-century carol "Adam Lay Ybounden" includes no mention of Eve:

> Adam lay ybounden, bounden in a bond,
> Four thousand winter thoughte he not too long;
> And al was for an apple, and apple that he took,
> As clerkes finden writen, writen in hire book.
> Ne hadde the apple taken been, the apple taken been,
> Ne hadde nevere Oure Lady ybeen hevene Queen.
> Blessed be the time that apple taken was:
> Therfore we mown singen Deo Gratias.[6]

The carol indicates that the source of the story is the Vulgate Bible, the "book" that is identified with the "clerkes," or clerics, and draws on the medieval concept of the *felix culpa* [happy fall] to celebrate Adam's consumption of the fruit as a glorious event that made possible the life of the Virgin Mary. In a detailed study of images of the fall and their significance in *Paradise Lost*, Diane McColley suggests that most Renaissance representations show either Adam taking the fruit first or Adam and Eve acting simultaneously, while the illustrations in English Bibles "either place blame squarely on Adam . . . or else represent an entirely mutual fall," in line with the doctrines of Calvin and Luther.[7] A fifteenth-century decorative roof boss in the East Nave of Norwich Cathedral shows both Adam and Eve accepting fruit from the serpent,[8] and in a sixteenth-century depiction by Lucas Cranach the Elder, it is not entirely clear whether Adam is passing the fruit to Eve or she to him (Figures 2 and 3).

The connection between fruit and sexuality is signaled in Genesis when Adam and Eve attempt to cover their nakedness, recognizing that knowledge of good and evil involves the identification of the human body with sin and shame (3:10). God reinforces this connection by punishing Eve's disobedience through the pains of childbirth as well as subjection to patriarchal authority (3:16). Adam's penalty is that he will have to endure physical labor to produce food "in the sweat of [his] face" (3:19), for the fruits of the postlapsarian world need cultivation, rather than just the dressing and keeping required in the prelapsarian world. However, the consumption of the fruit leads to the acquisition of knowledge of good and evil and thus the possibilities of moral choice. And as "Adam Lay Ybounden" explains, it enables the revelation of divine love by necessitating the life and sacrifice of Christ. The Genesis story therefore contains the essence of the two competing concepts of fruit, which are invoked in subsequent literary tradition. The trope of abundance draws on the image of the prelapsarian world and represents fruit as freely available, needing only to be plucked from trees that God has provided and human beings maintain. It suggests an egalitarian and sustainable world where people can live in harmony with nature. The trope of labor, by contrast, is predicated on a postlapsarian world of sinful sexuality. Successful fruit production depends on human endeavor and crops are proportionate to the amount of effort expended. Implicit within this association of fruitfulness with labor input is the potential for the accumulation of wealth, an unequal distribution of property, and thus the development of exploitative relationships between individuals and between humanity and nature. In this world, fruit consumption functions as a reminder

Figure 2. Decorative roof boss from the East nave of Norwich Cathedral, Norfolk, depicting Adam and Eve taking fruit from the hands of the serpent. Photograph © Julia Hedgecoe.

of humanity's fallen condition and of the sexual knowledge that is a consequence of the fall, thus reinforcing the botanical significance of fruit as the product of sexual reproduction.

The Book of Genesis does not specify the type of fruit growing on the Tree of Knowledge, although the fruit in the Talmud has been identified variously with the grape, the fig, and wheat.[9] The ancient Jewish text, the Book of Enoch, includes a description of the Tree of Knowledge as "like a species of the tamarind tree, bearing fruit which resembled grapes extremely fine; and its fragrance extended to a considerable distance," while Jewish folk tradition

Figure 3. Lucas Cranach the Elder (1472–1553), *Adam and Eve* (1526). While grapes grow around the tree, the fruits on the tree are clearly apples (*Malus pumila*). © Samuel Courtauld Trust, Courtauld Gallery, London.

frequently identifies the pomegranate as the forbidden fruit (1 Enoch 31:4). The identity of the fruit was a subject of intellectual debate in the early modern period. Henry Butts, in his 1599 regimen, argues that the forbidden fruit "was not an Apple but a Figge," while Georg Andreas Agricola, in his *Philosophical Treatise of Husbandry and Gardening* (1721), evaluates the contending claims of the fig and apple and concludes that "the *Forbidden Fruit* was a certain sort of *Apple*."[10] The tree depicted in Lucas Cranach the Elder's *Adam and Eve* (1526) is clearly an apple (Figure 3) and various commentators have reiterated the suggestion in the *Oxford English Dictionary* (*OED*) that the association with the apple comes from postclassical Latin tradition and may derive from a punning connection between the Latin words *malum*, meaning apple, and *malum* from *malus*, meaning evil. It may also draw on the golden apples of the Hesperides and the apple of discord within Greek mythology. The apples in the Norwich roof boss are depicted in gold (Figure 2), inviting the assimilation of biblical and classical traditions. However, as definition 2a of the 1933 edition of the *OED* suggests, the word *apple* was often used generically to refer to "any fruit or similar vegetable production" and was "from the earliest period, used with the greatest latitude." Early references within English literature to the forbidden fruit as an apple, such as in "Adam Lay Ybounden," may thus signify an unspecified fruit rather than what we regard as an apple (*Malus pumila*).

The other named tree within the Garden of Eden is the Tree of Life, the fruits of which provide an antidote to the Tree of Knowledge. God explains that the expulsion of Adam and Eve from paradise is primarily a preventative rather than a punitive measure, to ensure that they are not able to eat the antidote and regain the eternal life that has been forfeited. The sanative and redemptive qualities of one tree are balanced by the destructive properties of the other, with the Tree of Life providing a symbol that could later be used to represent Christ within the exegetical tradition. The Genesis story therefore endows fruit with a range of complex and contradictory associations. It invokes a time of innocence, when humans lived in harmony with nature, without labor and without sin; it supplies an explanation for the origins of labor in the world; it functions as a metonym for female frailty, temptation, and sexuality; it signifies the moral autonomy of humankind; and it represents the possibility of new life and redemption.

The Song of Solomon provides a different concept of the relationship between fruit and sexuality, and it can be read as a fruit-based celebration of the eroticized body. A male and female speaker discuss their work in the vineyards and orchards, using fruit and fruit trees as images and analogies for their passion. The female speaker declares, "As the apple tree among the trees of the wood, so *is* my beloved among the sons. I sat down under his shadow with great delight, and his fruit *was* sweet to my taste."[11] The male speaker responds, "The fig tree putteth forth her green figs, and the vines *with* the tender grape give a *good* smell. Arise, my love, my fair one, and come away" (2:13). Despite the anxieties about the consumption of green fruit expressed in classical medical discourse, here greenness is associated with wholesomeness and sexual availability, with the female speaker noting that "our bed *is* green" (1:16). In the fourth chapter, the male speaker compares his beloved to an enclosed garden: "A garden inclosed is my sister, my spouse; a spring shut up, a fountain sealed. / Thy plants *are* an orchard of pomegranates, with pleasant fruits" (4:12–13). The enclosed garden symbolizes the female body, containing choice fruits and spices. The gate is locked, suggesting virginity, but it is ready to be unlocked, by the key of the male beloved, at which point the spring and the fountain will burst forth, in an outpouring of female desire. The final consummation is conveyed by the female speaker in images of fruit consumption, as at the end of chapter 4, she exhorts: "Let my beloved come into his garden, and eat his pleasant fruits" (4:16), to which the male speaker replies, "I am come into my garden, my sister, my spouse" (5:1). Elsewhere in the Song of Solomon, consummation is signaled through the flowering of the pomegranate, as the female speaker declares, "Let us get up early to the vineyards; let us see if the vine flourish, *whether* the tender grape appear, *and* the pomegranates bud forth: there will I give thee my loves" (7:12). The flowers will be followed by fruits which will develop and swell like the blossoming love between the two speakers. The sexual symbolism is explicit. The female body is an enclosed garden that the male lover desires to enter, and sexual consummation is portrayed through images of flowering pomegranates and eating fruit.

The lovers share a mutual wish to taste the fruits of love. The female beloved is the garden containing the fruits and the fruit that is ripe for consumption, and she is herself a consumer of fruit. The positive terms of this portrayal are in striking contrast to the condemnation of sex as sinful in the Genesis story, and feminist readings have highlighted the redemptive nature of the celebration of female sexuality and desire that is contained in the verse.[12] The very different fruit narratives of Genesis and the Song of Solomon furnish a range of images that can be deployed in later texts, either to celebrate female beauty or to develop misogynistic constructions of female sexuality, or as a combination of the two. The latter is exemplified in the objectification of the blazon tradition, in which individual features of the female beloved are represented through similes establishing connections with material forms, including fruits such as cherries and strawberries.[13] The Genesis story can be used to censure women who are active consumers of fruit rather than the passive consumed, and the equation of consummation with consumption can endow sexual imagery with cannibalistic overtones. This range of symbolic functions was further extended by subsequent interpretations of the texts.

The Song of Solomon was well known in the medieval period in the Latin Vulgate version, often referred to as The Song of Songs, and many literary texts exploit its symbolism, particularly in references to the enclosed garden, or *hortus conclusus*. Yet as Ann Matter has shown in her detailed analysis of medieval commentaries, Christian exegetes were reluctant to accept that the song was an evocation of secular and human love and instead developed a series of allegorical readings which interpreted it as a symbolic anticipation of the events of the New Testament. For example, the flowering of the pomegranate is read not as sexual climax but as a symbol of the Virgin Mary, and thus of purity and virginity; the *hortus conclusus* is a metaphor for the church or another symbol of the Virgin Mary.[14] The fruit garden is thus a locus for the expression of highly charged erotic desire that is simultaneously representative of transcendent chastity.[15] The significance of the garden within Western culture has long been recognized,[16] but its symbolic associations are inscribed, reinforced, and complicated by the distinctive iconography of fruit in both Genesis and the Song of Solomon. Within prelapsarian Eden, fruit symbolizes divine benevolence and an innocence in which humankind lives in harmony with nature that can provide for all needs. At the same time, the story of the forbidden fruit connects desire and disobedience with female aspiration. The Song of Solomon develops the association of fruit consumption with sexuality in poetry that draws on sensual imagery to celebrate mutual, physical love. Yet the reluctance of clerical commentators to embrace this reading of the text led to the appropriation and reclamation of fruit symbolism, which was endowed with connotations of purity and virginity. This draws on the redemptive qualities of the Tree of Life but conflicts with the biological facts of the horticultural function of fruit.

The importance of viticulture in the Middle East is evident in the recurrence of vines and vineyards as symbols in both the Old Testament and the New

Testament. For example, the Song of the Vineyard in the Book of Isaiah (5:1–7) recounts how the "well-beloved," representing God, creates a vineyard, "in a very fruitful hill." He fences, tends, and guards it and even makes a winepress in anticipation of all the grapes that the vines will produce. Yet the harvest is meager, since "ten acres of vineyard" only produces "one bath" of wild grapes (5:10). A bath was the equivalent of about eight gallons, whereas ten acres should produce around four thousand gallons of wine, raising the question of why the crop was so poor. The keeper of the vineyard could not have done more, and yet the grapes turn out to be bad. The subsequent discussion exposes the metaphor in explaining that "the vineyard of the LORD of hosts *is* the house of Israel, and the men of Judah his pleasant plant" (5:7). God shows his disappointment at the failure of the men of Judah by laying waste to the vineyard, declaring that "it shall not be pruned, nor digged; but there shall come up briers and thorns" (5:6). The song seems in some ways to recapitulate the story of the fall, in that God is initially presented as providing a fruitful home for humanity or, in this case, the people of Israel, but this is converted to a much more inhospitable environment when they show themselves to be undeserving. God "looked for judgment, but behold oppression; for righteousness, but behold a cry" (5:7).

In the New Testament, Christ appropriates the symbol that in the Old Testament was associated with Israel, declaring "I am the true vine."[17] He develops the metaphor to explain "my Father is the husbandman. Every branch in me that beareth not fruit he taketh away: and every branch that beareth fruit, he purgeth it, that it may bring forth more fruit." (John 15:1–2). As in the Song of the Vineyard, God is the viticulturist, responsible for nurturing the vine of Christ to encourage the fruit of discipleship. Yet once again there is a suggestion of ruthlessness in the construction of the role of the husbandman, since he is prepared to prune away the branches that do not bear fruit, and the withered branches will be cast into the fire and burned (15:6). But the principal function of pruning is to increase yields, providing an oxymoronic metaphor of destruction and creation, death and renewal, in line with the mythic tradition identified by Sir James Frazer in *The Golden Bough* (1890). Only if the branches are cut back and the old wood destroyed will the vine bring forth plentiful fruit, rather than just a few wild grapes. Both speakers in the Song of Solomon describe working in the orchards and vineyards, so the celebration of fruit as a symbol of prelapsarian plenty and natural abundance is juxtaposed with the identification of fruit production with skillful labor. Fruit consumption can be used to connote sexual consummation, but fruitfulness also symbolizes the word of God, who is represented as the consummate gardener.

The volume of references within the Old and New Testaments shows the continuing significance of fruit within the culture of the Middle East and the Levant (Figure 4), and the imagery within classical literature suggests that it was of comparable importance in the Mediterranean. A similar ambivalence to that which characterized the biblical stories is discernible in the classical tradition, with fruit represented as both a natural product and a consequence of human labor. On the one hand, there is the idea of a Golden Age of plenty, comparable to the Garden of Eden, in which fruit is freely available without the effort of cultivation. But on the other hand, the world is portrayed as having declined from this Golden Age so that successful fruit production requires both labor and knowledge. The description of the home of King Alcinous in Homer's *Odyssey* has provided a source for many subsequent literary representations of idealized landscapes of abundance, including many examples of seventeenth-century country house poetry, yet the passage exemplifies the complexity of classical fruit imagery.[18] Since the focus of this study is the early modern period, classical texts are cited through popular early modern translations wherever possible, and, although Homer's account is often identified as a description of "the garden of Alcinous,"[19] George Chapman's influential 1616 version translates this as "a goodly orchard-ground . . . of near ten acres," emphasizing this as a landscape of production rather than just a pleasure ground, and highlighting the centrality of fruit. This orchard is circled by a "lofty quickset" or hawthorn hedge, like the orchards of early seventeenth-century England,[20] and within this is found:

High and broad fruit trees, that pomegranates bore,
Sweet figs, pears, olives; and a number more
Most useful plants did there produce their store,
Whose fruits the hardest winter could not kill,
Nor hottest summer wither. There was still
Fruit in his proper season all the year.
Sweet Zephyr breath'd upon them blasts that were
Of varied tempers. These he made to bear
Ripe fruits, these blossoms. Pear grew after pear,
Apple succeeded apple, grape after grape,
Fig after fig came; time made never rape

Figure 4. Wall painting from the west wall of the north side of the tomb of the
Egyptian administrator Nakht and his wife Tawy, TT52, in Sheikh Abd el-Qurna,
part of the Theban necropolis, dating from the eighteenth dynasty (c. 1543–1292
BCE). The facsimile was painted at the tomb, probably around 1909–10, by
Norman de Garis Davies, director of the Graphic Section of the Metropolitan
Museum's Egyptian Expedition. The painting shows the grape harvest and wine
production, highlighting its importance within Egyptian culture, and is on view at
The Met Fifth Avenue in Gallery 135. CC0 1.0 Universal (CC0 1.0) Public Domain
Dedication.

Of any dainty there. A spritely vine
Spread here his root, whose fruit a hot sunshine
Made ripe betimes; here grew another green.
Here some were gathering, here some pressing seen.
A large-allotted several each fruit had;
And all th'adorn'd grounds their appearance made
In flower and fruit, at which the King did aim
To the precisest order he could claim. (7:156–74)

In his notes to Chapman's translation of this passage included in his anthology *The Country House Poem*, Alistair Fowler reads this as an image of supernatural abundance, arguing that "in the Earthly Paradise, seasons are simultaneous, so that all fruits are available in various stages of ripeness."[21] Yet the language of the passage emphasizes human rather than divine activity. Although fruit is available "all the year," and can withstand the temperature extremes of both winter and summer, the profusion is identified with a good planting and stocking policy, rather than with the earthly paradise of a magical Golden Age. It is the range of types and varieties of plant, combined with the Mediterranean climate, that ensures that fruit of some kind is always available, while each individual plant fruits "in his proper season." One tree blossoms as another bears fruit; individual trees do not blossom and fruit simultaneously, as in the classic image of supernatural plenty derived from the habits of the citrus. The succession of fruits is thus achieved by working with nature rather than through a distortion or subjugation of nature, or through the prelapsarian state of perpetual fruitfulness suggested by Fowler. Each plant is carefully cultivated in its own spacious "several," a term referring to an enclosed pasture as distinct from a common field, with the aim of creating "precisest order." This connects the productivity of the land with human intervention and the agricultural innovation of piecemeal enclosure. The language of Chapman's translation emphasizes that the succession of fruits is the result of choosing a good range of varieties and implementing modern husbandry techniques, combined with a benevolent climate, to ensure "the precisest order." The Golden Age is therefore located within the domesticated environment of the orchard and connected to human intervention and the trope of labor, rather than natural fecundity and the trope of abundance. King Alcinous is constructed as the skillful husbandman working in his orchard, rather than the idle aristocrat enjoying the fruits of the garden.

In contrast, the grapes, figs, and apples described in the *Idylls* of Theocritus (c. 283–246 BCE) and the *Eclogues* of Virgil (c. 44–38 BCE) function as metonyms for natural bounty and an essentially benevolent world. They are part of a fertile pastoral landscape within which the songs and rivalries of the shepherd poets are played out. They grow unbidden and unassisted, manifesting abundance that can be appropriated to embody divine providence in Christian tradition. While Virgil's shepherds lament the fragility of the pastoral landscape, the threat to the life of ease is human and political, rather than natural, and focuses on the dangers of dispossession from the land, not the challenges posed by the

Figure 5. Detail from a manuscript of Virgil's *Eclogues and Georgics*, created in Germany or Austria c. 1473. The illustration shows a man picking grapes, accompanying the Second Georgic. © British Library Board.

land.[22] The celebratory tone of the evocation of rural ease therefore enhances the political critique by emphasizing the benefits of the life that is revealed as under threat. This is very different from the image of the countryside presented in Virgil's *Georgics* (29 BCE), which uses the trope of labor to highlight the human effort required to maintain the productivity of the land. The four books of the *Georgics* provide practical advice on plowing, planting, raising cattle, and keeping bees, with the second book devoted to the best techniques for the cultivation and propagation of grapes and other fruits. The poet opens with the declaration that he will sing of Bacchus and invites the god of wine to join him in treading grapes to produce the next vintage (Figure 5). In Dryden's 1697 translation, the poet exhorts the "Learned Gard'ner" to "mark with care"

> The Kinds of Stocks, and what those Kinds will bear:
> Explore the Nature of each sev'ral Tree;
> And known, improve with artful Industry:
> And let no spot of idle Earth be found,
> But cultivate the Genius of the Ground.[23]

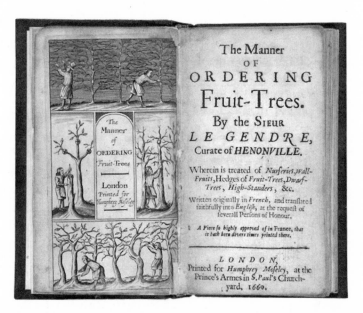

Figure 6. Title page illustration for John Evelyn, *The Manner of Ordering Fruit-Trees* (London, 1660), a translation of Robert Arnauld d'Andilly, *Manière de cultiver les arbres fruitiers* (Paris, 1653). The illustration shows the pruning and grafting of fruit trees.

Successful fruit cultivation comes from the knowledge as well as the industry of the husbandman, and the poet challenges the idea of natural abundance by emphasizing human intervention. Detailed instructions are given for grafting and inoculating trees, on the grounds that fruit trees that have been grafted are superior in both flavor and yield to those that grow naturally (2: 47–60).

Grafting and inoculating involve cutting a slit into the bark of a young trunk and inserting material from a different variety or species, which will then be able to draw sustenance from the root stock (Figure 6). This is a form of asexual propagation and is effectively a cloning technique, without the possibilities for hybridizing that occur when plants are raised from seed. It means that it is possible to grow a heavy cropping or tasty fruit on the roots of a hardier, often wild plant, and this process continues to be used to the present day—for example, with the grafting of dessert apples onto crab apple or dwarf stock to make smaller, more manageable trees. But Virgil goes much further than this to suggest some rather bizarre combinations, such as grafting walnuts onto the arbutus and apples onto plane trees. These would not work since it is only possible to graft successfully using different species of the same genus and this has led twentieth-century commentators to argue that the *Georgics* cannot have been intended as a practical agricultural guide.[24] Yet Dunstan Lowe suggests that while "it is undoubtedly no longer possible for any critic to see the poem as a straightforward celebration of the rustic life," its account of grafting is in line with a long tradition of interest in this process. Lowe argues that "Roman writers of all periods show a consistently positive attitude towards grafting."[25] This is in contrast to biblical injunctions against the use of "mingled seed" (Leviticus, 19:19) and "divers seeds" (Deuteronomy, 22:9). It is also strikingly different from later representations, which associate the techniques with miscegenation and unnatural sexual practices.[26] Moreover, despite the recent critical emphasis on the satirical aspects of Virgil's text, it is clear that the vast majority of writers of the early modern period, whether literary or horticultural, regarded it as a serious work of practical information. It is also a celebration of rustic life, but, in contrast to the pastoral genre, the pleasures of this life are located in physical work.

Book 2 of the *Georgics* describes the agricultural riches of Italy (2: 136–50), and while there are references to the Golden Age stereotype of twice-fruiting trees (2: 150), the primary emphasis is on the skill and labor that are required to maximize the benefits of the natural abundance and to ensure its continuance. As well as descriptions of the best techniques for pruning, grafting, and inoculating (2: 73–82, 362–70), there are detailed accounts of the importance of identifying the right soils for the right plants (2: 226–58, 298–314) and knowing the right time to plow and plant (2: 315–45). The farmer's life is not entirely conceived as a postlapsarian struggle against the elements, however, and Book 2 culminates in a paean to the happy "Swain" who, in Dryden's rendering, "Receives his easy Food from Nature's Hand." Rural life is described in terms of innocent simplicity, away from the luxuries and decadence of urban living, as well as the tensions of civil strife and the demands of humble petitioners.[27] References to "homebred Plenty" and "easy Food" are juxtaposed with acknowledgments that this can be a life of toil and deprivation. The happy Swain lives simply, but at the same time he is not constructed as a simpleton, with praise of his understanding of the study of agriculture and theology, subjects which are viewed as inseparable.[28] Book 2 ends with the farmer enjoying a "holy-day" and offering libations to Bacchus, but this is constructed in very different terms from the rural ease that is a way of life for the shepherds in the *Eclogues*.[29] The farmer of the *Georgics* participates in festivities after he has brought in the year's harvest of fruits and corn, relishing his holiday precisely because it marks a cessation of the toil that characterizes his way of life.

Horace's Second Epode opens with lines that Henry Rider translates in 1638 as:

Blest is the man, who, free from molestation,
(As were the mortals antient nation)
With his owne oxen tills his country ground,
From all usury unbound.[30]

The poem describes georgic activities of cultivating vines, raising cattle and sheep, collecting honey, and grafting fruit, followed by an itemization of the fresh local foods that can be enjoyed in the countryside, including pears, grapes, sweet wine, fresh fish and shellfish, olives, salad, and lamb. The farmer is presented as outside the system of commodification symbolized by the bonds of usury and economic exchange. He has a chaste wife and sweet children who are identified as the preserve of inhabitants of the countryside. As such, the poem provides a classic articulation of the country/city opposition and constitutes a key source for English country house poetry.[31] Yet the poem is ironically subverted in the final four lines as we discover that this praise of rural retirement has been articulated by Alphius, a money lender, and, as such, a representative of the corruption of urban life. He decides to move to the country during the Ides, which occurred on the thirteenth or fifteenth of the month, but he changes his mind a fortnight later, at the start of the next month. This suggests that the appeal of a country life is transitory (116). Ruralist nostalgia and images of fruitfulness and abundance are portrayed as pipe dreams of the urban classes and thus as a joke. Yet Horace's account is often used in early modern literature as a source for celebrations of rural society without reference to the ironic coda, as in Abraham Cowley's 1650 translation, for example, which omits the concluding quatrain.[32]

Perhaps the most fecund source of classical fruit references is Ovid's *Metamorphoses*, a compilation of transformation stories derived from Greek and Roman myth and adapted for an emergent Roman Empire that was anxious to match its political and military power with cultural capital. Like the Bible, it begins in a prelapsarian world, with an account of the first Golden Age, when "Springtime lasted all the yeare" and the earth yields its fruits "untoucht of spade or plough." Golding's 1567 translation describes how

Men themselves contented well with plaine and simple foode,
That on the earth of natures gift without their travail stoode,
Did live by Raspis, heppes and hawes, by cornelles, plummes
    and cherries,
By sloes and apples, nuttes and peares, and lothsome bramble
    berries.[33]

The fruits identified in the original Latin are arbutus, strawberries, red mulberries, cornel berries, and acorns (1:104–6). Golding adapts and extends this
list to represent fruits that would be known to his English readers and would
be regarded in the sixteenth century as natural products, capable of growing
in the orchard or the hedgerow without human intervention. The Golden Age
is used to connote the hardiness and simple abundance of the orchard, rather
than the luxury of the walled garden, with the emphasis on the familiar instead
of the exotic, and the diet of the laboring class, rather than the elite. In both
Ovid's portrayal and Golding's translation, the proliferation of more desirable
fruits is associated with the degeneration of society from its egalitarian origins
and the displacement of the trope of abundance by the trope of labor. The
mechanism for this change comes from a fruit-based narrative, the myth of
Proserpine, which Ovid had previously used in his *Fasti*, an account of Roman
customs and mythology structured around the calendar.[34]

Proserpine is a Roman version of the Greek goddess Persephone, the
daughter of Ceres (Demeter) and Jove (Zeus), who is abducted by her uncle,
Dis (Pluto), king of the underworld. *Metamorphoses* describes how she is
snatched while gathering violets and lilies in a meadow, emphasizing her
innocence and youth.[35] In her despair, Ceres "curst all lands," saying that they
were "unworthy of the fruites bestowed them upon" and "marrde the seede,
and eke forbade the fieldes to yeelde their fruite" (5: 473–79). The world, which
was perpetually fruitful, is rendered barren and dead. When Ceres eventually
discovers her daughter's fate, she persuades Jove to force his brother to give
her back, but he will only do so on the condition that Proserpine has not tasted
any food while in the underworld. Unfortunately, while straying in "Plutos
Ortyard," she picked "a ripe Pownegarnet" and "tooke / Seven kernels out and
sucked them" (5: 530–32). This means that Proserpine cannot come back
permanently, but Jove agrees that she can spend half the year with her mother
on earth and half below ground with her husband. While her daughter is away,
Ceres mourns, rendering the fields bare and barren, but as soon as Proserpine

returns, everything becomes fruitful once more, providing an etiological account of the changing seasons.[36]

This story has invited comparisons with the Judeo-Christian account of the fall, since both narratives focus on female fruit consumption to explain how the world has fallen away from a state of plenty and perpetual fruitfulness. After the biblical fall, the land is cursed by God so that humankind is forced to eat the herbs of the field, which can only be raised in the sweat of man's face; after the abduction of Proserpine, the land is only fruitful for half the year. In both instances, the trope of abundance is replaced by the trope of labor. Yet there are significant differences as well as similarities between the two stories, particularly in terms of the role of gender. The events of the fall result from feminine weakness. Eve is motivated not only by appetite but also by a desire to rise above her station. In the story of Proserpine, by contrast, events are precipitated by the male. The loss of a golden age in which fruit and crops are available throughout the year is a consequence of the concupiscence of Dis/ Pluto and "the ravishment / Of Proserpine against hir will" (5: 427–28). Proserpine eats the seeds of the pomegranate, but she does so because she has herself been plucked and consumed against her will and before she has attained true ripeness. The description of her straying "rechlessely from place to place" in the underworld (5: 531) and sucking on the seeds rather than eating them, suggests a listlessness that is very different from evocations of appetite or desire. She is characterized as a child, crying for the loss of her flowers as much as for the virginity they represent and, in emphasizing her youth and innocence, Ovid highlights her status as victim. She is simultaneously identified with the fruit that is consumed and with her own consumption of fruit, in paradoxical imagery that is later exploited in the comic drama of the Restoration. Her ambivalent position is reinforced by Jove's verdict that she must fulfill the roles of both child and wife. She spends half the year as the fruit of Ceres, symbolizing the reproductive function, and half the year as the seed that is buried beneath the ground. Her incarceration with her older husband suggests sexual compulsion and elides the consumption of pomegranate seeds with rape rather than with consensual consummation.

Metamorphoses contains many stories which feature acts or threats of male sexual violence, and in the tale of Pomona and Vertumnus this is again connected to fruit. Pomona is the goddess of orchards and her name is used in horticultural writings on fruit cultivation, such as John Evelyn's 1664 *Pomona* and the *Herefordshire Pomona* (1878–84), while poetic celebrations of fruitfulness frequently invoke Pomona's harvest. Golding's translation suggests:

> There was not to bee found
> Among the woodnymphes any one in all the Latian ground
> That was so conning for to keepe an Ortyard as was shee,
> Nor none so paynefull to preserve the frute of every tree.
>   (14: 623–26)

Pomona carries a "shredding hooke" for pruning and grafting, inserting slips from heavily fruiting varieties into trees with stronger root stock (14: 629–32), showing her arboricultural skill but also a preoccupation with asexual methods of propagation. She has no interest in sexual passion; her orchards are her "love and whole delyght." To exclude neighboring satyrs, the embodiments of predatory male desire, "shee walld her yards about" (14: 635–41). She is a garden enclosed like the female beloved in the Song of Solomon, reinforcing the connection between the walled garden and female virginity. But whereas the female voice in the Song is anxious to let her beloved into the garden and release the fountains of passion, Pomona wants to keep everybody out. The orchard is her refuge against threatening masculinity.

Ovid's story tells of how Pomona is courted by Vertumnus, the god of seasons. Because the seasons change, Vertumnus is protean and appears to Pomona disguised as a variety of rural workers, including a mower, a gardener, and a fisherman, but he eventually gets to talk to her in the guise of an old woman (14: 647–63). In praising her fruits, he develops the classical trope of the marriage between the vine and the elm, drawing on the practice in Roman orchards of planting vines between heavily pruned elm trees so that the trailing branches of the vines can be twined around and supported by the trunks of the elms. The Latin phrases of "nupta vitis" and "marita ulmus," the wedded vine and the husband elm, were common representations of conjugal harmony in classical literature.[37] The frail and feminized vine requires the strength of the male elm, and the disguised Vertumnus invokes this image to exhort Pomona to marry him (14: 670–78). The beldame's appeal ends with a fruit version of the carpe diem tradition, as she warns Pomona to seize the moment, lest the frosts and winds of spring blight her blossoms and prevent her chance of becoming fruitful (14: 761–62). Vertumnus resumes his normal shape as "a lusty gentleman" and although "He offred force," now "no force was needfull in the cace" since "shee beeing caught in love with beawty of his face, / Was wounded then as well as hee, and gan to yeeld apace" (14: 769–71). Pomona succumbs voluntarily, perhaps influenced by the arguments in favor of marriage proposed by the beldame, but Vertumnus was prepared to use force if Pomona had refused. The story develops the association of fruit with ideas of femininity and weakness implicit in Genesis, but it combines these with the suggestions of male violence inherent in the story of Proserpine. Women are weak vines, requiring support from the male elm, and they are also blossoming fruit trees whose principal concern should be to safeguard the buds that will form the fruits that will justify their existence. Their fruitfulness is therefore constructed as an argument for the acceptance of male dominance.

The apples of the Hesperides appear only briefly in *Metamorphoses*, but other sources connect them to a range of different myths. The Hesperides are Nymphs of the Setting Sun who live on an island at the far western edge of the ocean. With the help of a dragon, they guard a famously beautiful garden of the gods, which contains trees that produce golden apples. Like the fruits of the Tree of Life, these apples convey immortality, leading Walter Raleigh to draw a comparison between the Garden of the Hesperides and the Garden of Eden.[38] "Hesperian" becomes a standard adjective in English poetry to convey the beauty and desirability of fruit, and it is particularly used for oranges growing in exotic locations, giving them mythic connotations. One of the labors of Hercules involves stealing an apple from the Garden of the Hesperides and some accounts identify the "apple of discord" as one of the Hesperian fruits. This is inscribed "For the most beautiful," and is thrown by Eris, the Goddess of Strife, among the guests at the wedding of Peleus and Thetis.[39] The competition it precipitates between the rival goddesses Hera, Athena, and Aphrodite ultimately leads to the long years of suffering of the Trojan War, reinforcing the identification of fruit with the destructive power of female vanity.

Classical literature provides a range of stories and symbolic associations, as well as a series of generic forms, which contain assumptions about fruit cultivation and relationships between people and nature. Pastoral assumes a world of natural abundance, connoting a rural life of ease and idleness in contrast to the corruptions of urban living. The suffering of this life is located exclusively in the prospect of its loss, through the specter of dispossession. In georgic, rural life is described in terms of hard physical toil, but it is constructed as healthy and innocent precisely because of this. The cultivation of vines and orchard fruits involves not only the sanative labor of digging and planting but also the exercise of skill in tasks such as pruning and grafting. The representation of fruit within classical myth perpetuates the association with sexual activity of biblical tradition, but the stories of Proserpine and Pomona contain suggestions of male violence that reorient their gender politics and ideological implications. The portrayal of women as weak and fallible consumers of fruit is supplemented by images of women as the fruits that are consumed in metaphors for sexual consummation and sexual assault.

The Renaissance is often identified as the period that drew its iconography from classical sources, but the influence of the classics on fruit imagery is already evident in the Middle Ages. Chaucer's "Merchant's Tale" provides a useful case study of how classical allusions are elided with biblical references and appropriated within vernacular tradition, to provide a complex iconographic repertoire for subsequent literary texts. The narrative exploits the tensions between the different representational codes, exemplifying the ambivalence of fruit symbolism; it also manifests a domestication of biblical and classical imagery. Despite the notional location of the tale in Lombardy, it shows how fruit narratives from the Levant and the Mediterranean are adapted to the more challenging growing conditions of medieval England. The story concerns a lecherous old knight, Januarie, who marries a young wife "fresshe May."[40] He is particularly fond of taking May into his private garden to perform "thynges whiche that were nat doon abedde" (2051). The garden is a *hortus conclusus*, "walled al with stoon," and the link with the Song of Solomon is made explicit when Januarie incorporates various quotations into his own love song to May, telling her "How fairer been thy brestes than is wyn!" and "The gardyn is enclosed al aboute" (2138–45).[41] Notwithstanding the tradition of medieval exegesis, Januarie clearly regards the Song as an erotic rather than a spiritual dialogue, and this is reinforced by the narrator's invocation of romance and classical tradition in the comment that neither the author of the erotic *Romance of the Rose*, nor Priapus, the phallic god of horticulture, could do justice to the beauty of Januarie's garden (2032–37). Myth functions to emphasize the sexual aspects of the fruit symbolism of the tale, and, as the narrative unfolds, mythic references are deployed to modify the gender politics of the biblical allusions. Laura Howes argues that walled gardens and parks represent the restricted role of married women in the medieval period,[42] but in "The Merchant's Tale" the ideas of female constraint and confinement are subverted through the reader's knowledge that May is planning to use the garden to cuckold the obsessively jealous and now blind Januarie. May can be equated with the impermeable integrity of a walled garden, but she has given the "clyket" (key) to the "smale wyket" (gate) of the *hortus conclusus* (2045–46) to another man. Her enclosed garden suggests the passion of the female voice in the Song of Solomon, rather than the supreme chastity of the Virgin Mary, but without the fidelity of the former.

The account of the garden as an earthly paradise harks back to the Merchant's suggestion that a wife is a "paradys terrestre" (1332) and Januarie's claim that a man's wife is "his paradys" (1821), but, given that the Merchant has characterized his wife as "the worste that may be" (1218), the reader is invited to interpret these claims ironically. The sensual imagery of the Song of Solomon is juxtaposed with the idea of Eden, a paradise destroyed by the female appetite for prohibited fruit. This connection is further reinforced when May declares that she "moste han of the peres that I see." She "so soore longeth . . . To eten of the smale peres grene" that she "moot dye" if her wish is not fulfilled. May enforces her words with the exclamation "Allas, my syde!" adding that

> a woman in my plit
> May han to fruyt so greet an appetite
> That she may dyen but she of it have. (2329–37)

The implication is that her appetite is a consequence of pregnancy, which causes women to experience a desire for fruit. This draws on the contemporary belief that pregnant women could be afflicted with pica, a disruption of the appetite, leading to cravings for unsuitable foods. The mother and child could be endangered if the foods were consumed, but also if the cravings were thwarted.[43] May is not pregnant, and she longs for fruit of a different kind to the "smale peres grene."[44] The scene takes place on 8 June when even early ripening varieties of pear would have been very "smale" and very "grene." Medieval writings on health are full of warnings about the dangers of consuming unripe fruit, so the pears would have been identified by readers as unhealthy, manifesting a dangerous female desire.[45] Amy Tigner suggests that the pears represent female genitalia, but they are conventionally identified as phallic in popular culture, and this association makes more sense in the context of Chaucer's tale.[46] In an anonymous lyric, "I Have a New Garden," dated to the early fifteenth century, the narrator gives a fair maid a graft of his pear tree and "by that day twenty weeks / It was quick in her womb."[47] In "The Merchant's Tale," May's lover

Damian is hiding in the branches of the tree. The pears provide a metaphor not only for the appetite associated with May's mythical pregnancy but also for the fruition of her affair with Damian. She is attempting to taste the forbidden fruits of illicit sexuality, in front of the literally blind eyes of her husband, and the lexical connection between Damian and demon reinforces the link to the Genesis narrative, with Januarie and May as debased versions of Adam and Eve and also perhaps Joseph and Mary.

Bruce Rosenberg argues that the pear-tree episode is an ironic parody of the "Cherry Tree Carol."[48] The song is based on an incident in the Gospel of Pseudo-Matthew (20), which is dramatized in "The Nativity" in the N-Town Cycle, and four versions are recorded in Francis James Child's *English and Scottish Popular Ballads* (1882–98). They describe Mary and Joseph walking through an "orchard good" (54a), a "garden gay" (54b and c) or "gardens cool" (54d) when Mary expresses a desire for some cherries from a tall tree. In versions 54a and 54d, Mary asks Joseph to pluck her a cherry "for I am with child," reinforcing the idea that pregnancy causes a craving for fruit, while in 54b her words "O gather me cherries, Joseph, / they run so in my mind" suggests that this craving can become obsessive, in line with concepts of pica. In 54c, Mary requests the cherries to give to her child. Joseph's response is similar in all versions; he replies, as 54a phrases it, "with words most unkind": "Let him pluck thee a cherry / that brought thee with child." At this point, either the child in Mary's womb (a, b, d) or Mary herself (c) asks the cherry tree to bow down so that she can reach the fruit, and when it does so, Joseph recognizes that the child is indeed the son of God. All versions begin with the words "Joseph was an old man," reinforcing the link with Chaucer's story of Januarie and May, but while the bending of the cherry tree demonstrates Mary's innocence, May is intent on precisely the act of which Mary has been falsely accused. She requires human assistance to obtain the fruit she claims to crave, since divine aid is unlikely to be forthcoming. She clambers into the pear tree on the back of the husband she is cuckolding, ostensibly to pluck real fruit but actually in pursuit of forbidden fruit. The fruit symbolism therefore emphasizes her culpability, as an Eve rather than a Mary figure.

These biblical references are, however, combined with classical mythology, which complicates the gender dynamic and moral implications of the tale. The scene is witnessed by Pluto and Proserpine and, while their story involves female fruit consumption, Chaucer's Merchant narrator acknowledges its association with men's sexual violence rather than with women's sexual weakness. He introduces Proserpine as "queene Proserpyna / Which that he [Pluto] ravysshed out of [Ethna] / Whil that she gadered floures in the mede" (2229–31). As in *Metamorphoses*, the references to picking flowers signals Proserpine's youth and innocence and the Merchant invites us to read Claudian for further details of Pluto's attack, including "How in his grisely carte he hire fette" (2232–33). Pluto and Proserpine are now a married couple and their responses to events in the garden show their entrenched gendered perspectives. Pluto sympathizes with Januarie and is determined to restore his sight so that he can witness his wife's infidelity, but Proserpine sides with May (2258–60). She not only ensures that May has a "suffisant answere" when she is charged with infidelity, but also that the same is true for "alle wommen after" who are "in any gilt ytake" (2266–68).

Although May is clearly the guilty party, the presence of Proserpine invites the reader to view her infidelity with indulgence. Januarie is deluded, in line with the *senex amans* tradition of satirizing dirty old men who marry young wives with ridiculous expectations of the pleasures of matrimony. He marries so that he can indulge in unspecified, unconventional sexual acts without facing divine retribution, on the grounds that "A man may do no synne with his wyf" (1839). He is also presented as physically repulsive. On his wedding night, he covers May with kisses and "rubbeth hire aboute hir tender face," with "thikke brustles of his berd unsofte, / Lyk to the skyn of houndfyssh, sharp as brere" (1823–27). After laboring at his marital duties until morning, Januarie sits in bed, croaking a love song while "The slake skyn aboute his nekke shaketh" (1849). May has been selected by Januarie as his chosen wife and given no say in the matter and, as Howes suggests, the reference to Pluto and Proserpine indicates that she has been compelled to marry against her will.[49] Thus while May's longing for the forbidden fruits of adultery is presented as transgressive and associated with the idea of female weakness enshrined in the Genesis story, compounded by the mendacity of her assumed pregnancy and her apparent desire to humiliate her husband, the juxtaposition of this story with references to the violently deflowered Proserpine suggests that these feminine failings need to be set in the context of a prevailing environment of male sexual violence and forced marriage. The exotic pomegranate that tempted Proserpine is replaced by a small green pear. As the following chapter will indicate, pears were associated with the diet of the laboring class, so the reorientation of the fruit to the produce of the English orchard may signal May's humble origins and aspirations, and as an unripe fruit it constitutes a potential threat to health. As such, May's longing is unnatural, except that, rather than representing a true object of feminine desire, the fruit is part of a scheme of deception, symbolizing a woman's ability to evade male control that the story suggests is universal.

Like Chaucer's tale, Sir Thomas Malory's *Morte Darthur* manifests the medieval preoccupation with the physiological consequences of fruit consumption, combining its medical and symbolic connotations. After the completion of the grail quest, and as the Fellowship of King Arthur's knights is coming under strain, Queen Guinevere decides to hold a "pryvy dynere" in order "to shew outward that she had as grete joy in all other knyghtes of the Rounde Table as she had in Sir Launcelot" following his departure from court.[50] The queen invites twenty-four knights and provides "a grete feste of all maner of deyntees." Among the guests is Arthur's favorite nephew, Sir Gawain, who "loved well all maner of fruyte, and in especiall appyls and pearys" (590). This preference is sanctioned by the concept of the humors at the heart of medieval medicine. Because "Sir Gawayne was a passing hote knight of nature," the consumption of fruit would help to balance his "choleric" constitution, since apples and pears were considered cooling foods, particularly when consumed raw. Galen's *On the Power of Foods*, written around 180 CE and drawing on earlier writers such as Hippocrates, emphasizes that different kinds of apples have different properties, but that "harsh apples can be employed when the stomach is weak because of hot bad temperament."[51] Guinevere therefore "lette purvey for hym all maner of fruyte."

Sir Pyonell, who "hated Sir Gawayne," poisons some of the apples, but the fruit is eaten by Sir Patryse who "swall sore tylle he braste" and "felle downe suddeynly dede amonge hem" (590–91). This incident precipitates the sequence of events that culminates in the disintegration of the Fellowship of the Round Table and the death of Arthur, and it is probably no coincidence that the initial cause of dissension is an apple. While Guinevere is not responsible in the sense that she does not personally administer the poison, the use of the apple as the "fatal fruit" invokes the fall and connects the coming catastrophe to ideas of female temptation and sexual transgression. The poisoned apple implicates Guinevere as an Eve figure whose actions initiate the loss of the idealized community of Camelot and destruction of the homosocial bonds by which it has been maintained. Yet the symbolic associations of the apple with concepts of death and female desire are juxtaposed with references to more positive properties of fruit and particularly its importance in mitigating the excesses of a passionate disposition. Sir Gawain associates consumption of the fruit with his "condicion" and Sir Patryse takes the fruit because he is "enchaffed with hete of wyne." Fruit could be sanative if the right fruits were consumed by people with the right constitution, but the fruits also had to be in the right condition. In his commentary on *The Seven Books of Paulus Aegineta*, Francis Adams cites a passage from Athenaeus, quoting the Greek physician Diphilus from the third century BCE that "green and unripe apples are unwholesome and unsavoury, swim in the stomach, form bile, and occasion diseases. Of the ripe, such as are sweet are more wholesome and more laxative from having no astringency; the acid are more wholesome and constipating, but such as have also a certain degree of sweetness become more delicious, and are at the same time stomachic from having some astringency."[52] Similar arguments are still being propounded at the end of the eighteenth century. *The Universal Family Physician and Surgeon*, a compilation of medical advice drawn from the publications of Hugh Smythson, Samuel-Auguste Tissot, William Buchan, and Bryan Cornwell, argues, "Good fruit is an excellent article of diet but the greater part of what is used in this country by the lower orders of the people, is mere trash. Fruit should be eaten in the early part of the day, when the stomach is not loaded with food, and it ought never to be eaten raw till it is thoroughly ripe."[53] Green fruits symbolize individuals who are "unripe" and sexually immature, but they also represent a threat to the healthy constitution.

English literary texts of the early modern period draw on such physiological concerns, along with biblical and classical stories and generic conventions, to develop a repertoire of images by which fruit can be portrayed as wholesome or unwholesome; green and unripe, ripe for plucking, or overripe; symbols of female sexual frailty, male sexual violence, or natural sexual gratification; manifestations of the abundance of divine providence; or products of intensive human skill and labor. But these figurative functions were neither static nor backward looking, as they could be appropriated to fit the requirements of individual texts and individual genres, as well as adapted in the light of changes in horticultural practice and theory. Chapter 2 will consider the terms of the discussion of fruit cultivation through analysis of gardening handbooks from the seventeenth to the nineteenth centuries, to show not only how the various horticultural discourses deployed and appropriated the inherited tradition of imagery but also how they manifested changing ideas of individual fruits and fruit in general in the light of changing production techniques.

Chapter 2

"A Chiefe Meanes to Enrich This Common-Wealth"

The Language of Fruit in Horticultural Literature

Throughout the seventeenth century, British farmers and landowners were urged to plant fruit trees on their land. The cultivation of orchard fruits was represented as a patriotic duty that would enhance the wealth of the nation and the health of the people. Starting with John Taverner in 1600, a series of writers on agriculture and horticulture emphasized the significance of apples and pears not just as an element of the national diet but as the raw material for the manufacture of cider and perry, in rhetoric combining agrarianism with physiology. While Taverner stresses, at the start of the century, that "cider and perry is very wholesome for the bodies of natural English people," in 1664 John Evelyn expresses the hope that by encouraging the planting of fruit trees the author will be able to "obtain some grateful admittance amongst all Promoters of Industry," and Moses Cook argues in 1679 that the art of raising fruit trees has "ever been esteemed amongst the truly Noble, Wise, Ingenious and most refined Spirits of the World from Age to Age."[1] These works were part of the dramatic expansion of publishing that followed improvements in printing technology, leading to the identification of early modern Britain as an essentially literate and print-based society.[2] This chapter will consider how fruits and their cultivation are discussed and represented in a range of tracts and treatises dealing with matters fruticultural. These constitute an alternative tradition to the classical, biblical, and physiological sources analyzed in Chapter 1, but not one that is entirely autonomous and discrete. The language and imagery of horticultural discourse were inflected by inherited iconographic resonances at the same time as they responded to changes in the technology of fruit production. Allusions to the Garden of Eden, or to "Hesperia and Thessaly," rub shoulders with descriptions of soil types, root stocks, and plow and spade designs, along with discussions of the healthiness or otherwise of different types of fruit, manifesting the indivisibility of mythic and technical frames of reference.[3]

Works on agriculture and horticulture have been scrutinized in recent decades as part of the new historicist emphasis on competing discursive constructions of the world. Rebecca Bushnell has developed the horticultural implications of the expansion of works of popular instruction in early modern England and uses William Eamon's term "secrets book" to describe the practical gardening guides that address a readership of housewives and husbandmen as well as humbler professional and recreational gardeners.[4] These "common gardening manuals" are often miscellaneous in their contents and organization, but Bushnell discerns a gradual movement toward a more systematic treatment of knowledge from the sixteenth to the late seventeenth century, as gardening becomes more professional.[5] Despite the manuals' emphasis on practical husbandry, they include reflections on nature and art, and on "the role of pleasure, profit and contemplation" that become central to later garden theory.[6] John Evelyn remarks in his *Elysium Britannicum* that he does not "pretend . . . to write to Cabbage-planters; but to the best refined of our nation who delight in Gardens," and John Dixon Hunt invokes these words to explore works written to the best refined readers by Samuel Hartlib, John Beale, and Stephen Switzer, as well as by Evelyn.[7] Hunt suggests that these writers develop a philosophy of gardening based on the scientific principles that informed the founding of the Royal Society, but they also introduce wider questions about relationships among the individual, nature, and God, as well as about the significance of horticulture in shaping concepts of national identity. Rachel Crawford has likewise located constructions of the nation in diverse discourses of the land, including responses to parliamentary enclosure, writings on landscape design, and works on kitchen gardens, to contend that these works show an increasing interest in the confined prospect and the enclosed space that has a corollary in the development of literary forms.[8] The horticultural books explored in this study address gardeners from across the social spectrum, from "Cabbage-planters" to "the best refined," and the arguments will be informed by the work of Bushnell, Hunt, and Crawford, as well as by recent approaches to agrarian discourse and garden history.[9] The analysis will principally concentrate on works produced from the Restoration to the Romantic period but will argue that these need to be understood in the context of inherited concepts of fruit cultivation and fruit symbolism, from earlier horticultural works, but also from medical discourse, myth, and literary tradition. Individual discourses and genres have discrete representational codes and conventions, but the boundaries are at least semipermeable. This study suggests that it is important to recognize the extent of intellectual osmosis and the continuing conversation that is conducted between works from different times and with different constituencies.

Ken Albala has identified growing xenophobia in dietary tastes in the seventeenth century, as traditional concepts of healthy and unhealthy foods were supplanted by an emphasis on the sanative properties of domestic produce.[10] Albala has related this to a decline in the authority of classical medical sources, but it can also be connected to the rise of mercantilism and the idea that the strength and wealth of the nation are derived from maximizing consumption of domestic goods (such as cider and perry) and minimizing foreign imports (such as wine). In *Certain Experiments*, Taverner grounds his argument for increased production of orchard fruits in the claim that farmers could dramatically reduce their use of malt by producing cider and perry rather than beer for their servants. They might even be able to sell any surplus liquor for a profit, benefiting both the farmer and the state, by making more malt available for export and strengthening the balance of payments. This view of the economy was systematized by Thomas Mun in 1628 and was widely adopted through the seventeenth and into the eighteenth century so that luxury was increasingly defined in terms of consumption of foreign goods. This encouraged the identification of foreign goods as physiologically and politically bad, through a semantic connection between the constitution of the individual and the constitution of the state. By extension, domestically produced orchard fruits are regarded as natural, wholesome, and healthy. Nationalistic rhetoric thus informs a wide range of publications in which horticultural advice is incorporated into the emergent discourse of political economy, exhorting farmers and landlords to greater fruit production.[11] This political preoccupation in turn informs ideas of the wholesomeness of fruits, with the promotion of the health benefits of apples, cider, and perry, and the denigration of imported wines and exotic fruits as suitable only for the inhabitants of the countries in which they were produced.

Critics and historians have associated various horticultural works produced in the 1650s, 1660s, and 1670s with the prevailing political situation and attempts of the Commonwealth or Restoration governments to repair the economic and environmental damage from civil war.[12] An increased interest in husbandry and rural affairs has also been discerned among those aristocrats who retired to their estates during the years of conflict. Yet it is striking how many of the texts on fruit cultivation produced in the second half of the century incorporate the language of earlier books and pamphlets; sometimes entire tracts of text are reprinted within a later work. In reading the ideological significance of horticultural or agricultural works, the cultural historian must acknowledge the fundamentally cannibalistic nature of the English publishing industry in general, and didactic writing in particular, in the seventeenth and eighteenth centuries. This is one mechanism by which changes in practice were mediated by forces of stasis embedded within discourse and literary form, and the ideological implications of the process of representation will form one of the persistent themes of this study, by means of the example of fruit. Thus, while political developments such as the founding of the Georgical Committee of the Royal Society (1664) had a practical impact, for example by encouraging the planting of fruit trees,[13] the discursive framework in which this project was formulated has roots in earlier writings. Joan Thirsk has indicated how the agricultural tracts of the sixteenth and seventeenth centuries combine information drawn from personal experience and experiment with material from classical sources such as Cato, Varro, Columella, Palladius, Xenophon, and Virgil.[14] Graham Parry argues that despite the practical emphasis of John Evelyn's *Sylva*, published in the year of the founding of the Georgical Committee, "the treatise is shot through with visions of England as a paradise of noble groves, that elevate the souls of the fortunate men who dwell among them" and Amy Tigner has emphasized the pervasiveness of images of the Garden of Eden in works by Royalists and Protestant reformers alike.[15] Restoration literature on orchard cultivation is inflected by practical precepts and mythic resonances from classical and biblical tradition, but it is also indebted to more immediate forebears, such as Taverner and others at the start of the century and perhaps beyond. Key ideas and turns of phrase are incorporated into later works, with contrary political perspectives and readerships.

Gervase Markham's *The English Husbandman* (1613) is explicitly addressed to "the plaine russet honest Husbandman," who has no title but "goodman," and Markham suggests that this is "a title . . . of more honour and virtuous note, then many which precede it at feasts and in gaudy places."[16] Yet the identity of the intended audience is more equivocal than these initial assertions might imply. The first part of Markham's work explores plow designs and techniques for arable agriculture, suggesting a reader who is actively engaged

in the practicalities of cultivation, yet the subsequent account of the construction and maintenance of an orchard incorporates descriptions of how the
proprietor could build "some curious and arteficiall banqueting house" or
include "any quaint fountains or any other antique standard" (35). Likewise,
William Lawson's *A New Orchard and Garden* (1618) presents the orchard as
a paradise that can be adorned with flowers, borders, mounts, a "dyall" or
clock, walks, mazes, butts or bowling alleys, conduits and rivers and topiary,
as well as fruit trees (56–59). Thus despite the emphasis on the rusticity of
the husbandman, and McRae's argument that "writing towards the lower
socio-economic orders gradually became the norm" for English husbandry
manuals in the early modern period, these works are not directed at individuals who are purely concerned with subsistence and practical agriculture.[17]
The orchard is presented as a predominantly productive space, but the
husbandmen addressed by Markham and Lawson can afford to use it as a
landscape of pleasure which "delights all the senses" and shows the benevolence of God (56). The orchard is the Garden of Eden, the husbandman is
Adam, and Lawson acknowledges the biblical injunction to "dress and keep"
the garden (Genesis 2:15) by titling a chapter devoted to pruning: "Of the
right dressing of Trees" (32–34).

Markham's orchard is divided into four sections, which he recommends
planting with apples; pears and wardens; quinces and chestnuts; and medlars
and services. Yet while these hardy fruits are the staple products, he suggests
that if the orchard has a wall, it can be used to cultivate a few soft fruits,
including cherries, almonds, figs, plums, and grapes on north-, east-, and
west-facing walls, and apricots, verdochio [greengages], and peaches on the
south-facing wall (36). Attempts had been made to grow these last three in
England since the Middle Ages,[18] but they required special care and protection
from the weather, especially given the challenging climate of the mid-
seventeenth century when the "Little Ice Age" meant that temperatures
reached historic lows.[19] Horticultural literature of the period contains considerable debate over whether it is worth the effort to cultivate such fruits,
and Lawson is one of many writers who recommends sticking to "Fruit-trees
most common and meetest for our Northern Countries: (as Apples, Peares,
Cheries, Filberds, red and white Plummes, Damson, and Bulles [bullaces],)
for we meddle not with Apricockes nor Peaches, nor scarcely with Quinces,
which will not like in our cold parts, unless they be helped with some reflex
of Sunne, or other like meanes" (3). He subsequently argues that trees are

damaged by being grown against a wall and one so treated will not "live the tenth part of his age" (8).

Studies of garden history, literature, and relationships between the two have emphasized the steady expansion of plant varieties cultivated in Britain from the seventeenth century, as new and often exotic species were introduced. This has been read in the context of the development of British colonial power, and the domestication and classification of exotics has been identified as a mechanism for conceptualizing and legitimizing the control of the colonial center.[20] Harriet Ritvo argues that the incorporation of tropical species into gardens was facilitated by scientific developments that engendered a stronger sense of human control of the natural world, as well as by increased political influence in the supposedly "wild" parts of the world from which these species came.[21] The arguments presented here will draw on these readings and show the ideological significance of the cultivation of increasingly exotic fruit, but it will place the colonial appropriations within a longer tradition of introductions and fruit movements, the desirability of which was the subject of continuing debate. The celebrations of new and unusual varieties that have been connected to attempts to re-create Eden within Britain can be juxtaposed with a counter discourse, challenging their physical and economic viability in terms that can be deployed in literary texts to question the colonial project. In the eighteenth and nineteenth centuries, these debates focused on the cultivation of the orange and the pineapple, but in the seventeenth century "Peaches, Nectellings, Apricocks and all sorts of such kinds of Fruit" are causing similar concerns, and in *The Epitome of the Art of Husbandry* (1669), Joseph Blagrave discourages their planting since they require "extraordinary attendance."[22] Other texts express similar sentiments but include brief instructions on the cultivation of such fruits nonetheless, casting the resistance as a residual discourse in the face of the reality of expanding introductions.

When horticultural guides refer to such kinds of fruit, it is always stressed that they can only be produced in a protected, walled environment and the disagreements over whether the husbandman should attempt their cultivation is associated with a lack of consensus over how the orchard should be bounded. Markham suggests that orchards can be enclosed "either with a stone or bricke wall, high strong pale, or great ditch with a quicke-set hedge" but recommends that "the wall is best and most durable" (34–35). Lawson, however, argues that "of all other (in mine owne opinion) Quickwood and Moats or Ditches of water . . . is the best fence" (14). The description of an orchard in Abraham

Cowley's Latin poem *Plantarum* (1668), translated by Nahum Tate (1708), describes how:

> Hedges instead of Walls this Place surround,
> Brambles and Thorns of various Kinds abound,
> With *Haw-thorn*, that does Magick Spells confound.[23]

The triplet functions to reinforce the density and impenetrability of the hedge, while the reference to the folk myths associated with hawthorn (or quickwood or quickset) reminds the reader of its magical protective properties and is reminiscent of the description of the "lofty quickset" surrounding the orchard of Alcinous in George Chapman's 1616 translation of *The Odyssey* (7: 155). But horticultural and aesthetic considerations aside, the high cost of bricks in the early modern period meant that most orchards belonging to husbandmen would have been hedged rather than walled. These would therefore have been principally devoted to the cultivation of hardy fruit rather than wall fruit, as shown by recent research on the fruits grown in Norfolk orchards from 1632 to 1800. Of 664 fruit trees, there were 366 apples, 143 pears, 55 plums, 63 cherries, 34 walnuts, and 3 quinces.[24]

This list is reminiscent of the fruits identified in Golding's 1567 translation of Ovid's *Metamorphoses* as characteristic of the "plaine and simple foode" produced without "travail" in the Golden Age, but it is also in line with the mercantilist emphasis on the domestic production of staple commodities associated with supporters of the Commonwealth and the scientific agriculture of the "New Husbandry."[25] Samuel Hartlib's *Designe for Plentie by an Universal Planting of Fruit Trees* (1652) incorporates earlier writings from a range of hands, developing suggestions from Taverner and Lawson that Parliament should legislate for the compulsory planting of "wholesome" fruit.[26] The emphasis on "wholesome" fruit shows the continuing resonance of the dietary advice of writers such as Galen, Athenaeus, and Paulus Aegineta, in translations of whose works it signifies foods that are nutritious and beneficial to health, and for Hartlib it means specifically "Apple, Peare, Walnut and Quince" (4). Hartlib's work is short and polemical, combining public political discourse with practical horticultural advice, and in his epistle "To the Reader" he refers to Ralph Austen's work, *A Treatise of Fruit Trees*, which would be published the following year, as a source of further information. This identifies the planting of fruit trees as "a chiefe meanes to enrich this *Common-wealth* . . . as that we should not need to bestow our monies for *French Wines* or the like, having *Liquors,* (*Cyder, Perry, Cherry-wines &c.*) as good, or better, made of our own fruits."[27] The economic arguments for the expansion of fruit production are supplemented by detailed advice on when and where to plant fruit trees, grafting, pruning, and how to maximize the physical benefits of fruit consumption. This practical information is juxtaposed with a section on "The Spirituall Use of Fruit Trees," essentially a compilation of fruit-related Bible quotations reinforcing the symbolic as well as the economic importance of fruit during the Commonwealth.

While the spiritual elements were expanded in the 1657 *Treatise,*[28] they were entirely omitted from the 1665 edition, which has a pragmatic and scientific focus in line with the more secular cultural environment of the Restoration. Instead, the initial account of practical husbandry methods is followed by a reprint of Austen's 1658 *Observations upon some parts of Sir Francis Bacon's Natural History,* detailing experiments in planting, feeding, grafting, and pruning. The earlier editions were dedicated to Hartlib, a noted supporter of the Commonwealth, but the 1665 edition is addressed to Robert Boyle, whose involvement with the Royal Society encouraged association with the ideological values of the Restoration settlement. Indeed, Michael Leslie suggests that Austen excised the spiritual material at Boyle's behest.[29] The practical sections of the *Treatise* are primarily concerned with the cultivation of apples and pears for the manufacture of cider and perry, with some information on cherries, plums, walnuts, and quinces, and a few references to more delicate fruits, such as "Aprecots, Peach, Nectarine, Vine-tree &c."[30] Austen suggests that these can be grown next to the house and the branches trained through the windows to benefit from the warmth of the fires.[31] But the main focus is on what Austen describes as "the *courser, and harder kindes of fruits*"; as the marginal heading suggests: "The courser fruits very profitable."[32] The 1665 *Observations* notes that: "*Aprecots, peaches* and such like cold fruits will scarce ripen but against a *south wall;* they have need both of the direct and reflex beams of the Sun: And it were more practised to set some other *choice kinds of fruits* upon a *South-wall,* (as the *great Burgamet, Sommer Boncriten, Green-field Pear,* and other special kinds) this would advantage them greatly, not only in bigness, but also in their early *ripeness and goodness of tast.*"[33] Bergamot, Bon Chretien, and Green-field are all varieties of dessert pear, recommended in John Evelyn's *Kalendarium Hortense* (1664) as being in their prime in September.[34] Austen's suggestion that the cultivation of these orchard fruits would be a more appropriate use of a south-facing wall than would the nurturing of temperamental stone fruits like peaches and apricots reinforces the promotion of the planting of fruit trees as a national duty and a means of increasing the nutritional resources of the state, rather than as a way of producing luxury products for the gentleman's table. This is represented as a means of assisting "Poore People" and delivering them from "*Idleness, Beggery, Shame,* and consequently, *Theft, Murther,* and (at last) *The Gallowes.*"[35]

Austen endorses not only the patriotic rhetoric of earlier texts, but also their tendency to associate the consumption and cultivation of orchard fruits with those that he denominates "the Vulgar."[36] Many writers reproduce Taverner's assurances that cider and perry "will warme the stomacke even like white wine and tast as pleasantly," yet there is little evidence that these beverages were widely consumed by the wealthier classes. John Beale explains in *Herefordshire Orchards* (1657) that "Pears make a weak Drink fit for our *hindes,* and is generally refused by our Gentry, as breeding Wind in the Stomack," and refers to "the Masculine Qualities of Cyder" (2, 3). Taverner suggests that cider and perry are particularly appropriate for "such as do labor and travell [work]," as well as being suitable "to furnish ships for long voyages by sea" and claims to know many men "that have 12 or twenty persons uprising and downe lying in their houses" who can supply all their domestic alcohol requirements. These, like Beale's "*hindes,*" are the living-in servants whom Ann Kussmaul has denominated "servants in husbandry," reinforcing the idea that the husbandmen to whom the tracts are addressed may be producing fruit for consumption by their household rather than necessarily for themselves.[37] Recent research in East Anglia suggests that cider was not produced commercially until the eighteenth century, reinforcing its association in these seventeenth-century texts with the rural domestic economy rather than the market.

The practical sections of Austen's work furnish the metaphors of his *Spirituall Use,* although the complexity of the analogy ensures that some parenthetical exegesis is required. Austen explains: "As I have planted many *Naturall Fruit-trees* for the good of the *Common wealth,* so also I have taken some *Spirituall Cyences, or* Grafts from them (I meane severall *Propositions* drawne from *Observations in Nature*) and bound them up in a bundle, and sent them a broad for the good of the *Church of God:* And if men will accept of them, and be willing to engraft them in their owne *Gardens,* (their hearts and minds) by the Husbandmans watring of them by his Spirit, they will grow, and blossome, and beare much good fruit, here and for ever."[38] The horticultural/religious observations are cuttings for the readers to graft into their hearts and minds, enabling them to produce spiritual blossoms and fruits from the gardens of their souls. This process will be overseen by God who, in line with the Song of the Vineyard (Isaiah 5:1–7), is the *"Great Husbandman"* who provides the spiritual rain that will help the grafts to grow.[39] The image draws on Austen's identification of the fruit tree as a metaphor for, as well as a subject of, his text; both have leaves and the knowledge of good and evil which Austen seeks to convey is a direct consequence of the consumption of the forbidden fruit. Yet the *Spirituall Use* is also identified with the antidote to the fall. A prefatory letter in the revised edition of 1657 comments that "as we have all felt the misery following of our eating the forbidden fruit, we may eat now of this Tree of life."[40] Austen's reflections are presented as fruits with redemptive power, appropriating the role of Christ within the exegetical tradition.

The cultivation of orchard fruit is associated with rural farmers and laborers but provides a metaphor for personal improvement that is applicable to all readers. Lawson's *New Orchard and Garden* uses pruning as a metaphor for spiritual rejuvenation and Austen draws on the biblical ambivalence of fruit by highlighting the positive connotations of the "Tree of Life" rather than the negative implications of the "forbidden fruit."[41] Tigner suggests that Austen wants to return England to its Edenic origin by propagating the tree that was associated with the fall.[42] He distinguishes between the "lower and inferior labour" of tilling the ground to which Adam was consigned after the fall, and the cultivation of fruit trees in which he was employed "*in time of his Innocency.*"[43] John Salkeld's *Treatise of Paradise* (1617) similarly explains that the work of Adam and Eve in the Garden of Eden, far from being "a toile or affliction of the body," was "a recreation and reioycing of the will and minde."[44] Unlike other forms of agricultural activity, fruit cultivation can be related to the trope of abundance rather than the trope of labor, despite the associations of the latter with the forbidden fruit and the consequences of the fall.

The "Epistle to the Reader" in *The Fruiterers Secrets* notes the efforts that have been made to increase fruit production among "all degrees," indicating the general relevance of the work, and Robert Appelbaum has identified similar claims to a socially diverse readership as a recurrent feature of early seventeenth-century cookery books.[45] Yet *The Fruiterers Secrets* distinguishes between the motives of "the common sort" who plant fruit trees "for profit, and for the better reliefe of their family" and "the better sort" whose labor is "for their pleasure, & in that they doe delight to see the worke of their owne handes prosper, as also to eate the fruite thereof."[46] Labor is a practical necessity but one that can be constructed as innocent and healthful recreation. While Markham's chapters on grafting are addressed to the husbandman who "must raise every thinge from his owne indeavours" rather than to "great persons" who "buy their fruit trees ready grafted," Parkinson claims that although the "Nobility and better part of the Gentrie of this land" tend to buy their fruit trees from professional nurserymen, yet "many Gentlemen and others are much delighted to bestowe their paines in grafting themselves, and esteem their own labours and handie worke farre above other mens."[47] Parkinson provides information on the cultivation and usage of a wide range of orchard and wall fruits. The frontispiece depicts a pineapple growing at the center of the Garden of Eden (Figure 7), but Parkinson's section on "Pine Apples" relates to pine cones rather than ananas (600). The pineapple at this period is associated with a prelapsarian paradise rather than with the practicalities of cultivation in Britain.

As indicated above, most husbandmen could only produce tender wall fruits on a very limited scale because of the prohibitive cost of bricks, but building the wall was only the start of the trouble and expense of this form of fruit cultivation. Wall fruits were commonly shaped into fans or espaliers, necessitating regular pruning, support for the branches, and protection against pests and frosts. The large-scale domestic production of wall fruits like peaches and nectarines therefore tended to be associated with the extensive walled gardens of the nobility and wealthy gentry, where there were the facilities and staff to maintain walls and protective structures and provide the "extraordinary attendance" the plants required.[48] Smaller scale production was, however, possible by planting a few peach or apricot trees against a south-facing wall of a house so that clergymen and prosperous farmers could join the growing vogue.[49] In Jane Austen's *Mansfield Park*, Mrs. Norris recounts how her late husband, the parson, enjoyed cultivating an apricot, planted against the stable wall.[50]

The works of political arboriculture, which address the "plaine English Husbandman" and advocate the cultivation of orchard fruits for the sake of the public weal, can therefore be juxtaposed with an emerging tradition of writings discussing fruit production as a refined hobby rather than a means of subsistence. Some of the latter continue to address the husbandman, but this is increasingly used as a flattering reference to virtuous recreational labor, shorn of connotations of low social status. The changes in the significance of the term "husbandman," and in the anticipated audience for horticultural

Figure 7. John Parkinson, *Paradisi in sole paradisus terrestris* (1629), Frontispiece. The image depicts the "vegetable lamb of Tartary" as well as the pineapple growing in the Garden of Eden, perhaps suggesting that both plants had semi-mythical status at this time. Wellcome Library, London. Wellcome Images. Faithfully reprinted from the edition of 1629; London: Methuen, 1904. Facsimile of original engraved title page. Copyrighted work available under Creative Commons Attribution only license CC BY 4.0 http://creativecommons.org/licenses/by/4.0/.

works, are signaled in the naming and, particularly, the renaming of gardening books. Markham's *English Husbandman* was reissued in 1695, long after his death, as *The Compleat Husbandman and Gentleman's Recreation or, the Whole Art of Husbandry* and continued to be reprinted under this title well into the eighteenth century. The observations included in John Worlidge's *Systema Agriculturae* (1669), *Vinetum Britannicum* (1676), and *Systema Horticulturae* (1677) were similarly compiled by a group of booksellers into the posthumous volume *A Compleat System of Husbandry and Gardening; or, The Gentleman's Companion, in the Business and Pleasures of a Country Life* (1716).

The definition of the leisure gardener was progressively extended to include prosperous professionals, members of the commercial classes, and above all clergymen, as shown in the proliferation of books and pamphlets like John Laurence's *The Clergyman's Recreation* (1713), reprinted in 1719 in a compendium titled *Gardening Improv'd*, alongside *The Gentleman's Recreation* and Charles Evelyn's *The Lady's Recreation*. The preface describes how gardening has "of late Years become the general Delight and Entertainment of the Nobility and Gentry, as well as Clergy of this Nation," and the frontispiece to the 1717 edition shows the gentleman and his family enjoying the pleasures of the fruit garden (Figure 8).[51] At the same time, advice was available for urban residents from works like Thomas Fairchild's *The City Gardener* (1722), reissued in 1760 as *The London Gardener*. Fairchild established a nursery at Hoxton and was well known for his innovative work in developing techniques for rearing exotic fruit. His introduction notes "the general Love my Fellow-Citizens have for Gardening" and explains that the aim of his book is to ensure that "every one in *London*, or other Cities . . . may delight themselves in Gardening, tho' they have never so little Room, and prepare their understanding to enjoy the Country, when their Trade and Industry has given them Riches enough to retire from Business" (6–7). The reference to "Fellow-Citizens" rather than to gentlemen anticipates a prosperous, mercantile, urban audience and, instead of assuming his readers have access to extensive acres, Fairchild includes advice for those with small and shady plots or even balconies. Of course, in addressing citizens who are making their fortunes in the city before retiring to the countryside, and "Persons of Quality" obliged by "publick Affairs" to be in town, Fairchild is not encompassing "every one," and even his advice for the cultivation of plants in pots on balconies involves the expense of bringing plants to London in the spring and returning them to the country, or to nurseries like his own, for the winter (7, 61, 64–65). His writing is, however, infused with the belief that

Figure 8. John Laurence, *The Gentleman's Recreation: or The second part of the art of gardening improved*. Frontispiece to 1717 edition, showing the gentleman and his family enjoying his fruit trees. © British Library Board.

gardening is a moral occupation, associated with the contemplation and rural retirement eulogized in classical tradition, but it is an activity whose pleasures require cultivation. The businessman must learn the delights of gardening and relaxation in anticipation of his eventual retreat to the country. The horticultural literature therefore suggests a shift toward fruit cultivation as a recreational activity that is gradually extending through the social classes.

The emergence of gardening as an elite activity has tended to be identified in horticultural histories with the period of the Commonwealth when Royalist aristocrats retreated to their estates and turned their attention to plants rather than politics.[52] Yet works such as Parkinson's *Paradisi in Sole* (1629), with advice on wall fruits, walls, and other garden features, suggest earlier roots, and it is possible to distinguish a growing separation between mercantilist and more recreational writings. The former works tend to emphasize the labor involved in fruit production, but they justify it on the grounds of the public good; the latter represent labor as a good in itself, benefiting the health and well-being

of the individual. These horticultural tracts therefore anticipate the development from pastoral to georgic, which critics have located in the poetry of the
eighteenth century.[53] Moreover, while mercantilist tracts prioritize the production of orchard fruit, with relatively scant consideration of wall fruit, the
opposite pertains in recreational works. But once again these are broad, general
patterns rather than clear distinctions. In his 1665 *Flora, seu, de Florum Cultura,*
which presents itself as an updated version of Parkinson's text, John Rea argues
in his address "To the Reader" that "Apples are fruits fitter for Orchards than
Gardens." Yet he goes on to acknowledge that "some choice kinds may conve-
niently be planted in large Fruit-Gardens, either in Bushes, or on North-walls,
which ought not to be left naked" (209). There is a role for the gentleman in
the cultivation of unusual or particularly delicious varieties, even though he
is not concerned with the production of those "courser" apples used for cider
or as a staple of the rural diet.

Distinct literary and horticultural traditions are discernible but with considerable overlaps; works on orchards include references to gardens and vice
versa, and the boundaries between spaces and discourses are not always clear.[54]
There are, nonetheless, differences in the characterization of orchard and wall
fruits both between and within texts, which are significant for representations
in the various literary genres. While advice on the cultivation of orchards
invokes nature, emphasizing the importance of maximizing the inherent
productivity of trees, discussion of walled garden horticulture stresses not just
the improvement of nature but also the distortion of its patterns and processes.
Such manipulation is required to rear plants not naturally able to endure the
harsh climate of seventeenth-century Britain, but it also provides an opportunity to display human ingenuity and control. Gardening manuals celebrate
the science and skills involved and Rebecca Bushnell has shown how they
"impel the reader to find his or her pleasure in overcoming nature."[55]

The hot bed was central to this project. At its most basic, it was a frame
containing manure, which gave out a steady heat as it rotted, warming the soil
and encouraging early germination.[56] These had long been used to extend the
period in which fresh produce was available and thus limit the "hungry gap,"
but the desire for out-of-season fruit was increasingly associated with the
luxurious appetites of the elite and a wish to subdue nature. Ralph Austen
provides instructions for the construction of a hot bed, which he recommends
for forcing "Cherries, Strawberries, and other Fruits."[57] The cultural significance
of forcing techniques is shown in the literary use of the production of winter

fruit as a type of adynaton, or impossible task. It is deployed by Boccaccio, in both *The Decameron* and *Filocolo*, as part of "rash promise" narratives, in which the heroine attempts to get rid of an unwanted suitor by demanding a garden of fruit and flowers in January.[58] In Christopher Marlowe's *Doctor Faustus* (1592), the metonym of out-of-season fruit displays the unnaturalness of Faustus as he instructs Mephistopheles to procure grapes for the pregnant Duchess of Vanholt "in the dead time of winter and in the month of January."[59] As Eamon has indicated, Giambattista della Porta's *Magia Naturalis* (1558) was widely available in translation in early modern England and included chapters on such subjects as "How to procure ripe fruits and flowers before their ordinary season" and "How we may have fruits and flowers at all times of the year" as examples of natural magic.[60] Amy Tigner has noted the connections between science and magic in the Renaissance garden, and while many of the magical effects described by della Porta would nowadays be ascribed to science, they reinforce the association of out-of-season fruit with the realm of the supernatural and therefore unnatural practices.[61]

The cultivation of soft fruits, stone fruits, and out-of-season fruits strengthened the concept of gardening as a leisure activity and a means of indulging the luxurious tastes of an elite that sought a mastery of nature associated with magical control and esoteric knowledge. In mercantilist discourse, the mean husbandman raises apples and pears that will help to feed the hunger and slake the thirst of his laborers; the gentleman husbandman of the recreational tradition cultivates wall fruits, such as apricots, peaches, and nectarines, and forces fruit out of season to provide luxuries for his table. Of course in practice, production of both orchard and wall fruit was an increasingly commercial enterprise as more fruit was supplied by professional growers and many farmers and large houses sold fruit onto the local market.[62] Malcolm Thick has traced the progressive expansion of market gardens, particularly in the area around London, in the second half of the seventeenth and the early eighteenth centuries.[63] Some of these professional gardeners published their own books of horticultural advice, but, like Fairchild, they tend to address an audience of amateur gardeners and emphasize the recreational application of their occupation.

The late seventeenth century saw a growing interest in developing the potential of the hot bed to nurture delicate and exotic plants, particularly the citrus. Food historians have traced the gradual spread of oranges from southern China, where they are thought to have been cultivated as early as 2400 BCE, to North Africa and Rome, reaching Spain by the eighth century. There is evidence of orange trees in France in the fourteenth century, and Charles VIII constructed an orangery at the Château d'Amboise at the end of the fifteenth century.[64] The orangery subsequently became a feature of French aristocratic architecture, culminating in 1686 in the completion of the orangery at the Palace of Versailles, designed by Jules Hardouin-Mansart and which was large enough to hold 3,000 trees. John Evelyn claims that the first English orangery was created by Sir Francis Carew at Beddington in Surrey in the early seventeenth century and orange houses spread through the gardens of the nobility in the course of the century.[65] Citrus trees had a particular fascination at a time when gardeners were preoccupied with manipulating nature, since they themselves appear to subvert the natural pattern by blossoming throughout the year and producing flowers and fruits at the same time, furnishing a particularly resonant literary image.[66] Abraham Cowley's 1668 *Plantarum* depicts a quarrel between Flora and Pomona over who shall be associated with the orange tree, with each goddess reinforcing her claim by accusing the other of sexual laxity (4:381). Gillian Riley suggests that Gerolamo dai Libri's depiction of a lemon tree in *The Virgin and Child with Saint Anne* draws on the association of citrus fruit with fecundity, as well as the significance of lemon juice as an analgesic in childbirth (Figure 9).[67]

It would be a mistake, however, to assume that the construction of orangeries in Britain was necessarily connected to the production of oranges or, at least, of oranges as we know them, since the orange tree is depicted in most works as a source of flowers rather than fruit. While Parkinson includes "orenges" in his list of fruit trees in *Paradisi in Sole*, he distinguishes between the orange trees in warm countries which "groweth very high" and the domestic trees which "riseth not very high." He explains that the orange "beareth in the warme Countries both blossomes and greene fruit continually upon it, and ripe fruit also with them for the best part of the yeare," with the implication that this is not the case in cold countries like Britain (584). Nicholas de Bonnefons argues that Orange Trees "serve rather for curiosity than for profit."[68] The argument between Flora and Pomona over who can lay claim to the orange tree in Cowley's *Plantarum* is in the volume titled "Of Flowers," and concludes with the judgment that "Such fragrant Fruits as these may Flowers be call'd / And henceforth with that Name shall be enstall'd" (4:381). This shows the preoccupation with ordering and classifying that culminates in the development of the Linnaean system in the eighteenth century and makes it clear that

Figure 9. Gerolamo dai Libri, *The Virgin and Child with Saint Anne*, 1510–18. The lemon tree symbolizes perpetual fruitfulness, and lemon juice was used as an analgesic in childbirth. © National Gallery, London.

the orange is regarded as a flower. Other works reach a similar taxonomic verdict. Rea's *Flora* is divided into three books—*Flora* (flowers), *Ceres* (annual plants raised from seed), and *Pomona* (fruits), with the account of *Mala Arantia* in *Flora*, in the section on "Greens," covering evergreen shrubs, such as laurel and bay. Rea explains: "The *Orenge-tree* considered as it groweth with us, may more fitly be placed among the *Greens* than with the *Fruits*; for that all the benefit it affordeth us, consisteth in the beauty of the ever-green leaves and sweet-smelling flowers, the fruit in our cold Countrey never coming to maturity. Orenge-trees in Spain and other hot Countries grow to tall and fair trees, but with us seem no other than shrubs" (16). John Gibson notes in 1691 that many of Sir William Temple's "orange trees, and other greens" have been given to Temple's brother, indicating that Gibson, like Rea and Cowley, identifies orange trees as greens, providing foliage and perhaps scent during the winter months, but not as a source of fruit.[69] This explains the absence of light and ventilation in seventeenth-century orangeries, since they were designed to keep plants alive during cold weather, rather than to promote fruit production (Figure 10).[70]

Even when fruits were produced, these did not resemble our idea of an orange. Samuel Pepys first encountered an orange tree in 1666 and he describes how he "pulled off a little [fruit] by stealth (the man being mighty curious of them) and eat it, and it was just as other little green small oranges are; as big as half the end of my little finger."[71] Even if Pepys had been blessed with exceptionally large fingers, this small green orange was very small indeed. Most of the other fruits were presumably larger, but even these were probably more like kumquats than modern oranges and, as Billie Britz suggests, this may have been typical of home-produced fruits.[72] This could elucidate Gibson's widely quoted but otherwise slightly mystifying account of how the gardener at Beddington gathered "at least ten thousand oranges" in a single year, since this may be plausible if the fruits were similarly diminutive.[73]

There is evidence to indicate that the produce of British orangeries remained small even after the horticultural innovations that have been heralded as enabling the cultivation of dessert fruits. In 1724, Philip Miller quotes Richard Bradley, the first professor of botany at Cambridge University, who claimed that orange trees planted following his directions will set fruit "about the Bigness of a Musquet-Ball" (i.e., one to two centimeters in diameter). Miller clearly regards this as an achievement and explains that while the bitter Seville orange tree "will come to Maturity with us," the sweeter and more popular

Figure 10. "Oranje-stoove," unsigned engraving from Jan van der Groen, *Den Nederlandtsen hovenier* (Amsterdam: Michiel Groot and Ghisbert de Groot, 1683).

China orange "never makes a handsome Tree, but is always inclining to look sickly, and seldom bears Fruit in Perfection." He concludes that, "altho the fruit does not ripen with us so well as in *Portugal* and *Spain*; yet they serve for many Physical Uses; and the Flowers here are more valuable than the Fruite."[74] The primary purpose of the trees is therefore decorative, but the fruits can have a medicinal ("Physical") function. Parkinson had previously described how orange flower water can "prevent or . . . helpe any pestilential fever" and the rinds, when "candid with sugar," can "helpe to warme a cold stomack, and to digest or breake winde therein" (586). In 1732, Robert Furber produced a series of hand-colored engravings from paintings by Pieter Casteels titled *Twelve Months of Fruit*, showing the fruits that would be available in each month. There are 364 different varieties of fruit, including peaches, nectarines, and even a pineapple, but no oranges, and no oranges are listed in Furber's *Catalogue of Great Variety of the Best and Choicest Fruit-Trees That Best Thrive in our Climate of England* (1727).

Oranges were nonetheless very familiar fruits in the early modern period through imports from Portugal and Spain, the hard skins enabling them to withstand the rigors of transit. William Carew Hazlitt's nineteenth-century *Gleanings in Old Garden Literature* claims that the first oranges arrived in Southampton in 1290, and that in 1480 it was possible to buy ten oranges for a silver penny.[75] Thomas Dawson's *A Booke of Cookerie* from 1620 contains recipes "To boyle a Capon with Orenges and Lemmons," "To make a Sallet of Lemmons," and "To make a pretty dish with Dates and the juyce of two or three Orenges."[76] The toughness of eighteenth-century orange skins is evident from a recipe for candied orange peel from 1737, which requires that the peel be rubbed with salt, soaked in water for two days, and then boiled in several changes of water before being put into the syrup for candying.[77] By comparison, a modern recipe involves simply cutting up the peel and boiling it in syrup for forty-five minutes. In the Restoration, oranges were dispensed to theater audiences by female itinerant sellers and John Rea's 1665 account in *Flora* notes that, "although the Tree be rare and strange to many, the Fruit is common and well known unto all" (16). The importation of fruit continued into the eighteenth century, with Miller noting in 1724 that China oranges are "propagated in *Portugal* and *Spain*, which now yearly furnishes us so plentifully with those Fruits."[78]

Grapes were also imported and Parkinson describes the "great, long and round white boxes, containing halfe an hundred weight a peece" which were used to transport them (564). Gervase Markham suggests in his *English Husbandman* that vines should be grown "more for delight, pleasure, and prospect then for any peculiar profit," since any grapes cultivated in Britain will not be suitable for wine, and recommends that if any grapes are produced they should be dried in bunches before the fire "for a fruit-dish at our Tables."[79] Here and elsewhere the term "fruit dish" seems to be used to refer to a dish of dried fruits, such as currants and raisins, rather than a bowl of fresh fruit, and it is possible that we underestimate the extent to which fruit was consumed in cooked or dried form in the early modern period. The preference for preserved wares perhaps goes some way to explain the apparent dissonance between rates of consumption and the near pathological fear of raw fruit identified by Ken Albala within writings on health and regimen. The English appetite for dried fruits was widely recognized, with the Venetian ambassador reporting in 1628 that the English "consume a greater amount of currants than all the rest of the world" and that "men have been said to hang themselves because they have not enough money to buy them."[80] References to eating apples, pears, grapes, and peaches in literary texts, diaries, and letters may relate to dried or semi-dried forms and it is clear that people carried around cooked apples for a snack, although this is represented as a sign of low social class.[81]

The sources surveyed here suggest that British orange trees in the seventeenth and even the early eighteenth century were primarily decorative. Any fruits tended to be small, green, and bitter, and suitable for medicinal and culinary purposes rather than as a dessert. Albala notes in relation to France that "the medicinal use of oranges ... seems to have followed the courtly fashion for orangeries" and this observation can perhaps be explained by the fact that French oranges, like the English ones raised in similar conditions, were not suitable for any other function.[82] So while orchard fruits were identified with the laboring classes, and wall fruits like peaches and nectarines were associated with the country house and the cult of the gentleman husbandman, oranges suggested warmer climes but also foreign imports and consumer society. While exotic, they were not obtained from the New World but from neighboring European powers. This made them reasonably affordable and available, particularly in London where they were sold alongside other confectionary. They therefore had very different connotations from the produce of either orchards or kitchen gardens. Their foreign origins are symbolized by their sun-like skins, while the ability to bear blossoms and fruits simultaneously invokes a mythical Golden Age or prelapsarian world before the advent of seasons. But the identification of oranges with the theater raises a contrary frame of reference, suggesting concepts of commodification and sexual availability. As will be seen in Chapter 4, the importance of oranges in the rituals of playhouse attendance in the Restoration is manifested in the orange references within the plays.

From the late seventeenth century, however, there were rapid advances in horticultural techniques, often originating in the Netherlands, to encourage orange and lemon trees to produce genuinely edible fruits.[83] Buildings were designed that could deliver the required levels of heat and light. The former was made possible by better stoves and greater understanding of the temperatures needed by different plants. In place of the previous methods of controlling temperature by seeing if a damp cloth went stiff with frost and then bringing in a bucket of hot coals, there were increasingly sensitive thermometers to measure ground and air temperature, as well as the introduction of adjustable heating systems.[84] Some houses had under-floor heating and some included a series of rooms with different degrees of heat, known as "succession houses," in recognition that "the various classes of vegetables have their various temperatures in the air in which they can thrive best."[85] Greater acknowledgment of the importance of light in the life cycle of fruit trees led to the inclusion of more windows, with opening lights to provide ventilation.[86] Advances in glass manufacture, particularly in France, culminated in the production of plate glass from 1688, but the panes were small and expensive, not least as a result of punitive British taxes from 1696 to 1851. The light, well-ventilated houses with effective temperature controls that were required to raise citrus trees successfully were therefore only within the means of the wealthiest in early eighteenth-century Britain. Jan Woudstra has traced the development of the orangery at Hampton Court Palace, as the basic glass cases were replaced by a sophisticated greenhouse, highlighting the vast costs of building, maintaining, and running this grand edifice.[87]

Yet as technology improved, with greater understanding of how the needs of the plants could be met most effectively, there were some opportunities for those of more limited means to engage in hothouse cultivation. Clergymen and gentleman gardeners could raise a few orange or lemon trees in pots, putting them outside in the summer and into the stove in the winter, even if they did not necessarily succeed in getting them to flower or fruit. Bradley introduced Dutch cultivation techniques to Britain and disseminated them through his extensive publications. His *General Treatise of Husbandry and*

Gardening was brought out in installments between 1721 and 1723, in a collected edition in 1724, and a revised edition in 1726. The 1726 edition includes a chapter espousing "A Method of Meliorating Orange-Trees in England so as to make them thrive and bear more profitable Fruit than has yet ripen'd with us by ordinary practice." Miller's description of Bradley's musket ball oranges should, however, be borne in mind in reading this account.[88] Bradley acknowledges that "though we have several very fine Orangeries in *England*, which produce Abundance of Fruit," nonetheless "that Fruit has not always the Advantage of sufficient Nourishment from the Tree" (2: 366). His suggestion that his methods will yield fruit that is "profitable" may relate to the first definition identified in the *OED*, as something "that yields advantage or benefit; useful, valuable," rather than the second meaning, "That yields financial profit; lucrative."[89] English oranges may have been useful in cooking or for medicinal purposes, particularly when candied through being boiled in sugar, but they were not sufficiently large, sweet, or juicy for consumption or sale as fresh fruit in the early eighteenth century.

Henrik van Oosten suggests in *The Dutch Gardener: Or, The Complete Florist* of 1703, in a section titled "A Particular Account of the Nursing of Lemon and Orange Trees in a Northern Climate" that "the Stove or Winter-house, ought to be handsomely contriv'd to the end that the Master or Proprietour when he sits in his Pleasure-house, may not only entertain himself with the Sight of the Trees, but enjoy their agreeable smell through open Windows."[90] The hothouse is identified as part of a landscape of pleasure, gratifying the senses of a proprietor defined by leisure rather than healthful labor, and a source of pleasurable sights and smells rather than kitchen produce. In a chapter on "Ornaments and Decorations for Balconies, and the Outsides of Windows in large Streets" in *The City Gardener*, Fairchild comments, "If one was to have a Pyramid of Shelves to be cover'd with Pots of blossoming Orange-Trees, with Fruit upon them, intermix't with Mirtles, Aloes, &c. for Variety-sake, it would be extremely beautiful for the Summer."[91] He suggests that these orange trees could be brought to the site when in flower and then returned to the garden in August "to be taken Care of for the Winter at the usual Price," indicating that commercial hothouses such as his establishment at Hoxton were available for overwintering plants, making it possible for individuals to enjoy the benefits of exotic plants without the costs of maintaining their own hothouses (65). But the benefits are clearly identified by both van Oosten and Fairchild as a floral display with ornamental fruit rather than a harvest of edible produce.

Thus, although many of the horticultural works produced in the late seventeenth and the eighteenth centuries include sections on the cultivation of citrus fruits, often in the form of an appendix or addendum to a reissue of an earlier work, the idea of orange trees as foliage plants persists well into the eighteenth century. Despite the proliferation of orangeries, oranges continue to be identified as fruits of foreign origin, imported for sale rather than produced within the domestic economy. Even when texts refer to the successful cultivation of fruits, and even when these are described as "large," they may not have been large in the modern sense, or suitable for dessert eating. Fruits described as edible may have been more like kumquats than navel oranges, or small bitter Seville oranges rather than sweet dessert ones. The caché of the aristocratic orangery with its winter color and fragrant blossoming trees is juxtaposed with the continuing cultural resonance of the itinerant orange vendor and her sexually suggestive wares with their foreign origin.[92]

The status of the orange began to be eclipsed in the early decades of the eighteenth century, as gardeners such as Bradley, Cowell, and Fairchild appropriated methods developed for cultivating orange trees in their attempts to raise the pineapple, or ananas. Gardening books are full of eulogies on the virtues of this horticultural Holy Grail. Miller suggests in 1724 that the pineapple "is justly esteem'd for the Richness of its Flavour, as it surpasses all the known Fruits in the World" and names it "this King of Fruits."[93] John Cowell comments in his *Curious and Profitable Gardener* (1730) that it is "one of the high Favourites of the Curious in Fruits," while John Giles's *Ananas: Or, A Treatise on the Pine-Apple* (1767) refers to "this polite article of gardening."[94] The pineapple is now thought to have originated in Brazil and Paraguay and spread through South and Central America and the Caribbean as it was domesticated and traded.[95] It was brought to Europe by Christopher Columbus, having been discovered in Guadeloupe on his second expedition of 1493 to 1496.[96]

John Evelyn's diary contains two separate encounters with the fruit in the court of Charles II. The entry for August 9, 1661, records that he "first saw the famous Queen Pine brought from Barbadoes, and presented to his Majesty; but the first that were ever seen in England were those sent to Cromwell four years since."[97] Despite speculation, the source of Cromwell's fruit has not been established.[98] Evelyn's second pineapple experience, in 1668, occurs during a ceremonial visit from the French ambassador:

> Standing by his Majesty at dinner in the presence, there was of that rare fruit called the king-pine, growing in Barbadoes and the West Indies; the first of them I had ever seen. His Majesty having cut it up, was pleased to give me a piece off his own plate to taste of; but, in my opinion, it falls short of those ravishing varieties of deliciousness described in Captain Ligon's history, and others; but possibly it might, or certainly was, much impaired in coming so far; it has yet a grateful acidity, but tastes more like the quince and melon than of any other fruit he mentions.[99]

Richard Ligon enthused over the pineapple in his *True and Exact History of Barbados* (1657) as "all that is excellent in a superlative degree."[100] He compares its color to "an Abricot not full ripe, and eates crispe and short as that does," although he suggests that its smell "is as far beyond the smell of our choisest fruits of *Europe*, as the taste is beyond *theirs*" (84). Evelyn juxtaposes the grandeur surrounding the consumption of the pineapple as part of a state banquet with his own disappointment at the taste.

Ligon laments the difficulty of transporting pineapples to Europe from Barbados, noting that of the seventeen fruits "of severall grouths" that he tried to bring home, "all rotten before we came halfe the way"; he suggests, however, that if there was an unusually quick passage, fruits could be brought from Bermuda "in their full ripenesse and perfection." Evelyn's first account indicates that the Queen Pine offered to Charles was from Barbados, although it is unclear whether the fruit was edible; it may have been presented as a curiosity rather than as a food. The source of the second fruit is more equivocal, but Fran Beauman argues that it was also probably from Barbados, functioning as a symbol of British power for the consumption of the French Ambassador.[101]

One reason for the identification of the pineapple as a royal fruit was the resemblance between its leaves and a crown, but it is particularly associated with Charles II from the well-known painting, attributed to Hendrick Danckerts, titled *John Rose Presents Charles II with a Pineapple*, (c. 1675–80) (Figure 11). The painting depicts the king being ceremonially presented with a fruit and it encouraged the idea that, in the words of the nineteenth-century horticulturalist Henry Phillips, "Mr. [John] Rose, the king's gardener, raised the first pineapples that fruited in England, if not Europe."[102] It is now generally recognized that pineapples could not be grown successfully in Britain in the seventeenth century,

Figure 11. Hendrick Danckerts (attributed), *John Rose Presents Charles II with a Pineapple*, c. 1675–80. Royal Collection Trust / © Her Majesty Queen Elizabeth II 2018.

so Philips's statement is only accurate if "raised" is interpreted as meaning "ripened." Pineapples were brought to Europe from the Caribbean as green fruit and then kept warm until they were edible. They can therefore be associated with the development of colonialism, as the colonial project moved from the phase of acquisition or conquest toward the phase of legitimation. As shown in the poetry of the seventeenth and eighteenth centuries discussed in Chapter 3, the exotic fruits flourishing in the tropics can be represented as signs of the providential ordering of a benevolent deity who distributes the flora to suit the climate and needs of every part of the world. The importation of these fruits to the colonial center has very different symbolic resonances, however, exposing the alteration of this divine distribution that can be effected as a consequence of colonialism. The pineapple in the hand of an English king is not the same as a pineapple growing in Brazil or Barbados, and its fetishization as a material object can be interpreted as a manifestation of colonial difference, power, and control that resonates through literary texts.

The celebration of the pineapple as an exotic import was soon followed by attempts to cultivate the fruits within Britain, which Tigner has identified with a desire to re-create Eden by assembling the fruits dispersed by the fall.[103] Johann Beckmann, looking back at the late seventeenth century from the perspective of the late eighteenth, notes that "as in the beginning of the seventeenth century it was reckoned among the marks of royal magnificence to have orange-trees in expensive hot-houses, it was hoped that this fruit [the pineapple] could be brought to maturity also in the artificial climate of these buildings."[104] These hopes were unfulfilled, however, until the beginning of the eighteenth century, when several European gardeners had the satisfaction "of seeing ananas ripen."[105] Bradley's *General Treatise* contains several chapters devoted to the pineapple, including the account, reproduced in various subsequent publications by the entrepreneurial Bradley, describing the cultivation techniques developed by "Mr *Le Cour* of *Leyden*" [Pieter de la Court] who "resolv'd to spare no Pains or Expence to bring this delicious Fruit to Perfection" (Figure 12). After considerable efforts, he "had the Happiness of producing and ripening several hundred Fruit in a Year, and increasing the Plants to that Degree, that his Gardiner told me, he often bury'd or flung away some hundreds of them. By this Gentleman's Curiosity and generous Disposition, the excellent Flavour and rich Qualities of this Fruit became known to most of the great Personages in and about this Nation."[106]

Central to the process was the construction of hot beds, or "pits" filled with manure covered in tanner's bark, to provide a gentle warmth for the plants during the summer months. Tanner's bark, or tan, was chosen because it "will maintain a constant Degree of Heat, sufficient to give these Plants the utmost Vigour they require, from about the end of *February* to the end of *October* following; and then the Plants must be again remov'd into the Stove or Conservatory" (2: 282). Hot beds had previously been used to encourage germination rather than as a source of additional summer warmth, and employed manure, which decomposed more rapidly than tan and generated an extreme but transitory heat, as well as an uninviting odor. The innovation of the pit was combined with the pineapple thermometer, to ensure that the "Bed breathes

Figure 12. Theodorus Netscher, *Pineapple grown in Sir Matthew Decker's garden at Richmond, Surrey* (1720). © Fitzwilliam Museum, Cambridge.

a right Heat" (2: 282). Bradley suggests that this "Method of Culture" could be extended to other plants, including the guava, banana, plantain, and mango (2: 283). In 1740 George Martine boasted, "With the help of Thermometers, we can so adjust our stoves, green-houses and hot-beds, as to imitate the temperature of any clime we please; and to support and keep in strong life and vigour the plants, which nature has given only to the warmer countries" (298).

Yet as with accounts of seventeenth-century orange harvests, some caution may be necessary in interpreting these descriptions of pineapple production. Bradley exclaims that he has "seen some Fruit . . . which were about Four Inches long," in Leiden, although he subsequently suggests that the fruits produced in England are larger, with one fruit at Sir Matthew Decker's at Richmond that was "near seven Inches long" (2: 276–77). Cowell suggests that there are two sorts of pineapple. The first sort "brings its Fruit of a good Flavour, though so small as seldom to be above three or four Inches in length" and Cowell notes that "this Kind is the most subject to bear Fruit" (28). The other sort has fruit that is "pyramidal, and often measures ten or twelve Inches in length, and is accounted to be the best sort for eating; and therefore is called the King or Queen-Pine" (28–29). John Giles points out the distinction between "the oval fruited pine, which was the first raised here" and the "sugar-loaf, or Montserrat-pine." Giles suggests that the former is easier to grow, but the latter is "reckoned to be superior in flavour" (3). This suggests that the early successes in pineapple production involved varieties which were more productive but less suitable for eating. As with the accounts of oranges, which focus on numbers of fruits rather than their size, it may be that many of the fruits were too small for consumption and therefore had a primarily decorative function, at least in the early decades of the century. This might explain why Pieter de la Court was prepared to throw so many away. Bradley emphasizes appearance in suggesting that the fruit is "commonly cut from the plant with a long stalk, so that it may be set upright in a Tube of Glass, to crown the Top of a Pyramid of Fruit" (2: 280). The illustration for October in Furber's *Twelve Months of Fruit* (1732) includes apples, cherries, grapes, medlars, peaches, pears, a plum, service, an almond, and barberries, with a pineapple that is about the size of the pears and peaches (Figure 13).

Through the eighteenth century, techniques for the cultivation of pineapples and other tropical fruits were progressively refined and disseminated. Cowell claims that "Stoves and Glass-Cases for the Culture of the Pine-Apple" are now to be found "in almost every curious Garden" (27–28). An article in *The World* in 1755 uses the spread of pineapples to exemplify the dissemination of knowledge, claiming that "every gardener, that used to pride himself in an early cucumber, can now raise a pine-apple; and one need not despair of seeing them sold at six a penny in Covent-garden, and become the common treat of taylors and hackney coachmen."[107] Yet while the expansion of pineapple cultivation is frequently noted in horticultural texts, pineapples were regarded as rare, expensive, and exotic into the nineteenth and even the twentieth century. They did not feature regularly in the diets of tailors or hackney coachmen. Some novels describe gardeners who sell off pineapples from their masters' hothouses as a profitable sideline, but this tends to reinforce the elite status of

a fruit which can only be purchased in expensive fruiterers' or confectioners' shops or through a semi-illicit trade.[108]

The construction of a pinery involved an enormous initial outlay and substantial running costs. An article in the *Gentleman's Magazine and Historical Chronicle* for 1764 on "Improvements in Agriculture" calculated the cost of constructing a stove for 150 pines at £80, plus £50 for the plants, and annual running costs of £21. Although the article concludes that "you will have 150 pines of one pound and a half weight each, one with another, for less than 3s. a piece," this simply includes the annual expense, ignoring the initial outlay of £130. This was a considerable investment around the time when it has been estimated that an artisan or "humble curate" could expect to maintain his family on around £40 a year and a gentleman could exist on the margins of gentility on somewhere between £100 and £200.[109] The complex and time-consuming nature of the cultivation process also required the services of a professional specialist rather than a gentleman amateur.[110] Nonetheless, the development of improved cultivation techniques ensured that pineapples gradually became more widely available. Ruth Levitt comments: "Although pineapple growing in Britain had started as an extravagant hobby for a few of the wealthy, it stimulated broader interest and demand, which in turn created opportunities for humbler nurserymen and market gardeners to invest in pineries and frames to grow the plants and supply plants and fruit direct to the gentry."[111]

The production of pineapples and other exotic fruits is celebrated as a triumph of technical ingenuity, as shown by the article on "Ananas" in Johann Beckmann's 1797 *History of Inventions and Discoveries*. The achievement is represented in horticultural literature in terms of overcoming the challenges posed by nature through the application of scientific reasoning and practical skill to develop systems for providing artificial heat. Yet even within the horticultural treatises which are dedicated to celebrating the human ability to control the natural world, there are some suggestions of anxiety. Martine eulogizes the technological knowledge that has made it possible to raise tropical plants within a temperate climate, but he nonetheless recognizes that hothouse cultivation is unnatural. In the wild, plants "have a freer and opener air; where consequently they can bear greater heats than in our smothered and pent up stoves and greenhouses" (299). Cowell describes how to raise tropical plants, including bananas, pineapples, mangoes, papa-trees [papaya], and guavas. Although encouraging the cultivation of these fruits, Cowell regularly reiterates the warning that he gives in relation to bananas, "that when we propose to keep these like Plants in the Winter, to be strong and vigorous, so as to bear good Fruit the Year following, we must not stifle them by too much heat, or too little room" (25, compare 30). Giles uses similar language in suggesting that "it is . . . detrimental to pine plants to stifle them up too close, and not give them proper air" and when they receive too much heat "they are apt to grow weak therein . . . and are made very tender thereby, and consequently very much prejudiced" (16). Tropical fruit is exotic and enticing, but when it is produced in heated greenhouses it can be associated with unnatural heat and images of confinement. As will be shown in Chapter 6, these associations are developed in the radical novels of the Romantic period, drawing on the Caribbean origins of the fruit to provide language and metaphors for the discussions of slavery and the treatment of women.

The development of cultivation techniques in the early modern period therefore complicates and diversifies the inherited iconography of fruit. While echoes of the forbidden fruit and the apple of discord continue to resonate, different meanings accrue to different fruits and different kinds of production and distribution. The orchard sustains a rhetoric of naturalness that can be invoked within nationalistic discourse, either through a trope of pastoral abundance or through the georgic concept of virtuous labor inherited from classical tradition. Orchard fruits are hardy and good for the constitution of laborers and the state, and as the fruits that are best adapted to the landscape and climate of the British Isles, their cultivation manifests an acceptance of divine providence. The delicate fruits of the walled garden, by contrast, are a testament to human skill and ingenuity in conquering nature and subverting the postlapsarian dispersal of fruits across the world, and this emphasis on power and control becomes increasingly explicit with the introduction of tropical fruits from colonized territories. The mercantilist focus on the production of large quantities of apples and pears for the sustenance of the laboring population is countered by a preoccupation with recreational gardening and raising delicate peaches, apricots, and then pineapples for the tables of the elite. This distinction is perhaps more significant than the difference between works addressed to cabbage planters and those to the best refined in determining the attitude toward fruit in horticultural writing. The salient factor is about whom the tracts are written, rather than to whom they are addressed. But even within recreational texts there is evidence of ambivalence toward the cultivation of delicate fruits. Wall fruits and hothouse fruits can symbolize not only refined taste and elite culture but also the inegalitarian distribution of wealth. The manipulation of nature manifested in the trained and grafted peach tree, reared in the hot bed and shaped against a wall, culminates in the stifling artificial heat of the pineapple house, which can be celebrated as technological triumph or condemned as hubristic, reifying the unnaturalness of colonialism. The remaining chapters will explore how this iconographic repertoire is deployed in a range of literary texts and genres from the early modern period and the extent to which the representation of fruits responds to the changes in horticultural technique and horticultural discourse that have been discussed here.

Chapter 3

"Stumbling on Melons"

Negotiating the Garden in Seventeenth-Century Verse

In his famous poetic eulogy, Ben Jonson guides the reader around the gardens of the eponymous Penshurst, where

> The early cherry, with the later plum,
> Fig, grape, and quince, each in his time doth come;
> The blushing apricot and woolly peach
> Hang on thy walls, that every child may reach.[1]

Fruit clearly has an important role in both the landscape and the text of Penshurst. Robert Sidney's letters home during his lengthy periods of absence from the estate are full of detailed instructions and solicitous inquiries about the care of his fruit trees, while Jonson's litany of fruit has loomed large in discussions of how the country house is represented in seventeenth-century verse.[2] In a recent work of ecohistory and ecocriticism, Amy Tigner explores the poem "in relation to its various ecosystemic networks," arguing that it has a crucial role in shaping attitudes toward food, nature, and landscape; it has been elsewhere hailed as a founding text of the genre of country house poetry; and both pastoral and georgic have been cited in disputes over its parentage.[3] Its images of fruitfulness have been associated with the Garden of Eden, the Golden Age celebration of rural life, and the Cockaigne myth of a land of plenty.[4] Don Wayne has devoted an entire book to analysis of Penshurst as poetic and architectural space, identifying the poem with "emergent middle class values," while Andrew McRae has connected it with an "emerging tradition of pastoral celebration" and nostalgia for the old manorial model, in response to the increasing dominance of the language of improvement within the discourse of husbandry.[5] As a text in which fruit is abundant, contentious, and ideologically freighted, Jonson's poem, probably written in 1611 or 1612, seems an excellent starting point for analysis of the iconography of fruit in early modern verse.[6] This chapter will draw on a range of seventeenth-century texts to consider the implications of the language of fruit in representations of country estates and tropical islands that are identified as earthly paradise, as well as in evocations of paradise itself. But it will begin among the fruit-decked walls of the gardens of Penshurst.

Alastair Fowler, as part of a wider argument emphasizing the typological structure of the poem, has highlighted the importance of time in the passage quoted above and suggested that the fruits are arranged in three sections, constituting a formation of two–three–two. There is an opposition of an early fruit (cherry) and a late fruit (plum); then three fruits that come "each in his time"; then the apricot and peach, which Fowler identifies as another early/late opposition.[7] The reading presented here is only slightly different from Fowler's account, but the distinction has a crucial bearing on the horticultural and ideological implications of the lines. It hinges on the clause "each in his time," which Fowler interprets as referring to the fig, grape, and quince in line 42, but which I would argue should be read as applying to all the fruits. Instead of a pattern of two–three–two, contrasting two pairs of fruits that are out of time and three fruits that are in their time, this reading suggests that each of the seven fruits arrives at the time that is natural for it, even though they ripen in different seasons. Cherries and plums are orchard stone fruits and both are members of the genus *Prunus*. Cherries are the earliest fruits to ripen, described by Gervase Markham as "one of the oldest children of the summer" (73), while *The Husband Mans Fruitfull Orchard*, appended to the 1623 edition of Lawson's *New Orchard and Garden*, suggests that cherries introduced from France are available from May, even though "our owne natural Cherry . . . is not ripe before June" (1). Plums, by contrast, usually ripen between August and October. In the seventeenth century, May, June, and July were the summer months and August was the first month of autumn, so cherries would be summer fruits and plums autumn fruits.[8] Figs are available from July, grapes from August, and quinces from Michaelmas (September), so again, although these fruits ripen in their own time, they manifest temporal range.[9] Apricots and peaches are both wall fruits, and, while apricots can be harvested from July, peaches are not ready until August.

The passage therefore demonstrates that fresh produce is available for an extended period in the gardens of Penshurst, but, as in Homer's Garden of Alcinous, this is portrayed as having been achieved naturally, through the planting of different varieties, rather than through artificial forcing in hot beds or hothouses. This is particularly significant given the contemporary preoccupation with horticultural techniques for extending the fruit season and the association of out-of-season fruit with magic, modernity, and innovation noted in Chapter 2. While Markham and Lawson stress the foreign origins of early fruiting varieties, within the gardens of Penshurst these have been naturalized. Despite the effort involved in growing orchard fruits and, particularly, wall fruits, the emphasis in the poem is on the skill and knowledge of the landowner collector in accumulating appropriate varieties that can extend the season, rather than the physical effort of the gardener in subjugating nature. The range of produce can therefore be accommodated within the rhetoric of pastoral abundance rather than georgic labor and concepts of wholesome domestic produce rather than foreign luxury.

In analyzing the tension between rhythmic forms and political institutions, Caroline Levine emphasizes the "surprising layering of temporal registers" in Elizabeth Barrett Browning's 1837 poem "The Young Queen."[10] The rhythms of Jonson's poem similarly play with temporal schemes, exploring the timing of the fruits in relation to each other and the patterns of nature. The regularity of the elegiac verse identified by Joshua Scodel exemplifies the harmony between the fruits so that they comprise an orderly procession.[11] The verse as well as the fruit is in time, and this reinforces the image of the estate as fundamentally natural and the source of a continuous sequence of fresh produce. Jonson plays down the idea of showing power through control of nature manifested in the prodigy houses with which Penshurst is compared and instead constructs an alternative rhetoric based on technical knowledge and sympathy with the patterns of the year and metrical form. Yet although the passage is centrally concerned with fruiting times, its organization is not, contrary to Fowler's argument, purely temporal; it is also spatial and, by implication, social. The first line describes cherries and plums, which, as the Norfolk orchard survey has shown, were the most common orchard fruits after apples and pears and fall into Austen's category of "courser, and harder kindes of fruits," with hard here referring to resilience rather than firmness.[12] The figs and grapes of the next line were less hardy and less common, rarely appearing in orchard lists. Chapter 2 indicated some disagreement over whether quinces could be considered hardy in Britain, but they seem to have been relatively unusual, comprising only three of the 664 trees identified in Norfolk.[13] Quinces are only fit for human consumption when cooked for a considerable period, usually into a jam or jelly, and Parkinson suggests that these preserves were used at banquets and that "Ladies and Gentlewomen" liked to give them to one another.[14] The previous chapter has suggested that figs and grapes produced in Britain were also primarily consumed in preserved form, with Parkinson explaining that "Figges are served to the table with Raysins of the Sunne, and blanched Almonds, for a Lenten dish."[15] These half-hardy fruits occupy an intermediate status between the common orchard fruits of the first line of the quatrain and the more delicate and exclusive wall fruits represented by the apricots and peaches in the third line.[16] Within each line, therefore, the fruits are arranged in their fruiting sequence, but the lines are distinguished by degrees of hardiness, location within the orchard or garden, and class connotations. The different types of fruit symbolize different economic interests, which are united within the Penshurst estate. The ordering is simultaneously chronological and social, with the fruit disposed in an ascending hierarchy of status, while the harmony with nature is manifested in the natural timing of the harvesting of each fruit. The fruits are not "forced" through techniques to make them ripen early but are allowed to appear in their own time, and, as in the Garden of Alcinous, sustained productivity is ensured by the skillful choice of varieties.

The emphasis on harmony is extended to the human labor force, since the passage ends with an assurance that "though thy walls be of the country stone, / They're reared with no man's ruin, no man's groan" (45–46). Tigner has suggested that these lines mark a "transition from the outside world to inside the house" and Don Wayne argues that "Jonson had in mind the main entrance to the house."[17] Yet the reference is surely to the garden walls that protect the blushing apricots and woolly peaches and were a crucial part of contemporary fruticulture. As the previous chapter has shown, these constituted one of the major costs of production of tender stone fruits, but we are assured that their construction caused no suffering to the laborers who built them. The amicable relationships among laborers, tenants, and landowner are embodied in fruit as the poem describes the tributes brought to the "lord and lady" by "the farmer and the clown" (48–50). Wayne suggests that this represents a longing for a mythical past in which social relations are not exploitative rather than for a mythical abundance, yet the two are surely interdependent.[18]

The traditional Tory image of benevolent aristocratic paternalism is reversed
with the portrayal of the elite as recipients rather than providers of bounty:

> Some bring a capon, some a rural cake,
> Some nuts, some apples; some that think they make
> The better cheeses bring them, or else send
> By their ripe daughters, whom they would commend
> This way to husbands, and whose baskets bear
> An emblem of themselves in plum or pear. (51–56)

The local community is emblematized as common and hardy orchard fruits
(apples, pears, plums, and nuts) so that Sidney's knowledge of fruit varieties
manifests his understanding of the interests of tenants and farmers. The harmony with nature that characterizes fruit cultivation at Penshurst is social as
well as horticultural.

But the symbolism has additional connotations of gender and sexuality,
drawing on the mythic heritage of fruit. Despite the phallic associations of
pears in earlier literature, and the popular use of plums as a euphemism for
testes, the transferred epithet connects both pears and plums with female
fecundity, anticipating the subsequent praise of the fruits of Sidney's own
family tree (90–98). The implication is that the tenants' daughters, like the
plums and pears, have ripened in their own time and are ready to show their
fruitfulness in marriage. Similar iconography is evident in the art of the early
modern period, in the vogue for portraits depicting nubile women holding
fruits (Figure 14).[19] As will be seen in the next chapter, the use of ripe fruit
as a metaphor for female sexual maturity (and availability) becomes a recurrent feature of Restoration comedy, where ripe women are contrasted with
women who are green fruits or with those who are identified as overripe.
Here the emphasis on the natural ripening of both fruits and women contributes to the image of the estate as harmonious but also fertile and therefore
dynastically secure.

The positive connotations of the imagery are in line with the iconography
of the Song of Solomon rather than with the story of the fall, and they demonstrate a rejection not only of horticultural discourse directed at the gentleman,
with its emphasis on control over nature through forcing plants to make them
ripen earlier, but also of the commodification associated with imported fruit.
This suggests that the poem should be seen in the ideological context of a

Figure 14. Abraham van den Tempel (1622–72), *Portrait of a Lady Holding Fruit* (1622), Louvre Museum. Notes on the Louvre website from Don Jules Maciet in 1894 suggest that this might be a betrothal picture and that the apple is a symbol of love. The fruit, however, resembles a ripe peach rather than an apple, and may indicate that the girl has reached maturity. © RMN-Grand Palais (musée du Louvre) / Franck Raux.

rhetoric of plenty and productivity which invokes the nationalism of mercantilist writers, rather than as a celebration of emergent capitalism or a reaction against the language of improvement. The sustained productivity of Penshurst is portrayed as a consequence of the knowledge of its proprietor, whose connoisseurship ensures an appropriate choice of varieties, rather than the labor of the gardeners, who have planted and maintained the trees. The idea of improvement, which McRae identifies, is thus elided with a pastoral trope of abundance to construct an image of social relationships that are perceived as harmonious from the perspective of a landlord whose knowledge has ensured continuity of supply. The feminizing of fruit evokes positive images of fecundity and dynastic stability rather than the negative ideas of female temptation and destructive sexuality discernible within Genesis. It draws on the image of Britain as a place of plenty, exemplified in the frontispiece to Michael Drayton's *Poly-Olbion* (1612), which Fowler has translated as "Profusion Britain."[20] Lady Albion is shown in a robe resembling a map of Britain, bearing a cornucopia of fruits (Figure 15).

A similar denial of labor is evident in Andrew Marvell's "The Garden," which describes fruits that, as Robert Watson notes, would not grow in Britain without "considerable human intervention."[21] Nigel Smith proposes that Marvell's status as a poet has long been linked with "indecipherability, with irresolvable ambiguities, with seeing things all ways at once and yet never really revealing what the hidden author thinks."[22] These ambiguities have helped to sustain divergent critical interpretations and the identification of a range of sources. John Dixon Hunt has shown how the poem draws on contemporary developments in garden design and the emergence of the Italianate hortulan style, while intertexts ancient and modern have been claimed, from Genesis, the Song of Solomon, and Horace, to Jonson and Mildmay Fane.[23] The suggestion that the date of composition should be moved forward to around 1668, rather than the early 1650s as proposed by Elizabeth Donno, means it can also be read as a response to garden poems by Royalist writers Abraham Cowley and Katherine Philips.[24]

In recent years, "The Garden" has provided an arena for the exercise of critics drawing on ecocritical approaches. Watson highlights epistemological uncertainties which he connects to the anxieties generated by the changing economic relationships of emergent capitalism and to the development from a "feudal-agrarian society toward an urban-industrial one."[25] McColley also stresses nominal instability, suggesting that Marvell "literalizes the allegorical

Figure 15. Michael Drayton, *Poly-Olbion* (1612). William Hole's frontispiece shows Lady Albion in a robe resembling a map of Britain and bearing a range of fruits in a horn of plenty. Used by permission of the Folger Shakespeare Library under a Creative Commons Attribution-ShareAlike 4.0 International License.

passages from the Song of Solomon . . . and makes an enclosed garden his love."
A. D. Cousins focuses instead on Marvell's use of Calvinist allusions, connect-
ing "The Garden" to the literature of mystical experience and suggesting that
"the hortulan and the paradisal merge" within the verse.[26] Yet although, as
Smith argues, the poem provides "a hint of the paradisal garden from which
Adam and Eve were expelled after their Fall,"[27] the fruit iconography implies
a more complex relationship between humanity and nature than the harmonious interdependence of lord, tenant, and fruit tree found in Penshurst.
Marvell draws on the imagery of Horace's second epode, perhaps inflected by
the terms of Jonson's appropriation, to evoke prelapsarian bounty, but the
active verbs present the abundance as almost menacing to the hapless poet,
suggesting a postlapsarian world in which:

> Ripe apples drop about my head;
> The luscious clusters of the vine
> Upon my mouth do crush their wine;
> The nectarene, and curious peach,
> Into my hands themselves do reach;
> Stumbling on melons, as I pass,
> Insnared with flow'rs, I fall on grass.[28]

The fruit is arranged in a clear social hierarchy, starting with the humble and
hardy apple, and then moving through grapes, to the tender nectarines, peaches,
and melons, which connote the gardens of the aristocratic elite. These fruits
are not only available but are actively offering themselves; Timothy Raylor
describes how "the alarmingly (if benignly) animated apples, grapes and melons
. . . bombard or press upon the speaker."[29] Moreover, the biblical connotations
of the apple suggest sexual temptation, reinforcing the threatening aspect of
the increasingly sensuous imagery and anticipating the final flower-induced
fall. This rejection of the physical pleasures of fruit is reinforced in the subsequent stanza, where the poet portrays a retreat from the desires of the body as
"the mind, from pleasures less / Withdraws into its happiness," before finally
"Annihilating all that's made / To a green thought in a green shade" (41–48).
But even prior to the fall, the tone of pastoral celebration is subverted.

The poem's representation of the melons, nectarines, and peaches ostensibly
denies the effort required to enable them to thrive in the British climate, but
the language is colored by implications of unnaturalness as the curious fruits

obtrude themselves inappropriately upon the poet. Inherited connotations of temptation and sexuality enhance the impression that fruit constitutes not only a physical trap by which the poet is threatened and ultimately prostrated but also a metaphorical trap for readers who associate the garden with ideas of nature. The assertive behavior of the fruits reinforces their ambivalent role as simultaneously natural products and manifestations of technological development so that their representation collapses the opposition of nature and culture. Marvell presents fruit cultivation as a consequence of art as much as nature, and this perspective is developed in the four mower poems, and particularly "The Mower Against Gardens," which uses dramatic monologue to explore horticultural innovation from a perspective that is socially and physically beyond the garden wall. Robert Watson argues that by replacing the shepherd of pastoral with the "less sentimental" mower, Marvell questions the economic system "by showing that what gets called radicalism may really be a return to some time-honored roots."[30]

The mower is a mower to the same extent that the thresher of Stephen Duck's "The Thresher's Labour" is a thresher. Mowing and threshing were both agricultural tasks that were carried out at specific times of year and were performed by laborers. Nobody can be just a mower, so in choosing to denominate his laborer as a mower, Marvell is inviting the reader to identify the critique of the garden with the working landscape of the hay meadow. The Mower laments how

> Luxurious man, to bring his vice in use,
>   Did after him the world seduce:
> And from the fields the flowers and plants allure,
>   Where Nature was most plain and pure.
> He first enclosed within the gardens square
>   A dead and standing pool of air.[31]

Critics from Christopher Hill to McColley have emphasized the significance of the assimilation of gardening with enclosure, with McColley commenting that the use of "enclosed" in the fifth line is "politically charged," while the sense of confinement is reinforced by the poem's closed couplets.[32] But the opening adjective, characterizing man as "luxurious," was similarly "charged" and ideological in the early modern period. Cousins connects the term with Calvinist condemnation of concupiscence, identifying luxury with "urban humankind's inclination to material self-indulgence in general and to sexual self-indulgence in particular."[33] But, as noted in Chapter 2, the spread of mercantilist rhetoric in the seventeenth century emphasized the connection of luxury with the consumption of imported foreign goods, rather than simply excessive or unnecessary consumption or personal decadence. The reference to the perverting influence of "luxurious man" within the garden suggests the introduction of alien plants and designs into a supposedly natural space and this theme is developed throughout the poem, as the mower satirizes modern trends in terms which acknowledge the role of sexuality in the garden but signals its condemnation through the identification of foreign origins or associations.

While "The Garden" represents the dangers of sensual overload inherent in fashionable wall fruits, the mower's criticism is directed toward fashionable flowers such as the tulip, with origins in the Iberian Peninsula, North Africa, and the Levant, and the "Marvel of Peru," from the West Indies and South America. The pursuit of highly patterned tulips famously culminated in the financial bubble of the 1630s known as tulipomania and the mower invokes the perhaps apocryphal incident at the height of the crisis when a single tulip bulb sold for twelve acres of land. The description of the tulip's "onion root" may also reference the story that when the bulbs first arrived in England, people tried to eat them.[34] The mower mocks the preoccupation with exotic varieties, yet suggests that this might have been acceptable had "man" not intervened in the sexual reproduction of plants and "dealt between the bark and tree / Forbidden mixtures there to see" (21–22). Although grafting and inoculation are ancient processes, detailed in classical georgic as well as horticultural literature, they involve at once asexual reproduction and the intersection of different plants, with shoots from one variety growing on the roots and trunk of another. They therefore represent the "forbidden mixtures" prohibited in Leviticus (19:19) and Deuteronomy (22:9) and are constructed as a form of sexual exploitation, resulting in illegitimacy and miscegenation. The association of such "uncertain and adult'rate fruit" (25) with foreign despotism is reinforced by the invocation of the Oriental stereotype in the mower's lament that

> His green *seraglio* has its eunuchs too;
> Lest any tyrant him outdo.
> And in the cherry he does Nature vex,
> To procreate without a sex. (27–30)

Donno has identified these lines as a further reference to grafting, and Smith's annotations draw on the use of stone as a slang term for testicle to suggest a stoneless cherry, which Markham claims can be achieved through grafting.[35] Yet the opening of the passage seems to introduce a change of subject, and it is possible that the horticultural eunuchs refer to the development of self-fertilizing fruit varieties that are associated with hermaphroditism. Deidre Lynch has emphasized the repression of any suggestion of hermaphroditic auto fertilization in Erasmus Darwin's account of *Loves of the Plants* (1789), indicating eighteenth-century anxieties over vegetable challenges to heter-onormativity, and these may also inform the concern about cherries in Marvell's verse.[36] Either way, despite their ancient heritage, human interventions in the sex lives of fruit trees are identified with unnatural practices and this association is reinforced by the reference to the Oriental stereotype. The garden is con-structed as a locus of artificiality, despotism, and perversion, which contrasts with the "sweet fields" (32) that are the province of the mower.

Some critics have identified cabalistic or numerological meanings in the poem and McColley argues that "the alternation of ten-syllable and eight-syllable lines might remind us that ten is the number of law, the decalogue, regulation, rules, and the eight of the octave, the symbol of heaven and earth and their joining by grace."[37] Yet this verse form may have a simpler function, reinforcing the class dynamic of the poem by juxtaposing the ten-syllable lines, derived from the pentameter-based poetic genres of the garden-owning elite, with the eight-syllable lines of the vernacular tradition of tetrameter songs and ballads associated with the voice of the mower. Anxieties about miscegenation and human intervention in the processes of procreation are reinforced by social tensions that relate the grafted fruits of the garden with the artificiality, foreign luxury, and perhaps impotence of the aristocracy, while the laborer is associated with the natural fecundity of the world beyond the garden and a simpler cultural heritage.

The idea of fruit as a natural commodity is similarly problematized in poems representing tropical islands. Richard Grove has emphasized the importance of islands in the history of colonialism, as "the first landfalls and navigational points of reference, and ... later ... the first colonies." They therefore "became the subject of economic and literary interest as well as myth," providing "a powerful cultural metaphor in Western European thought."[38] Grove's account of the early history of ecological awareness demonstrates this metaphorical potency across a range of texts and discourses, including poems of Waller,

Cowley, and Marvell. The archipelago of Bermuda came into the news in the early seventeenth century, after 150 passengers and crew from the *Sea Venture*, a ship bound for the Virginia Company's settlement in Jamestown, were shipwrecked there in 1609. They survived for ten months, living on a healthy and varied diet of fruits, fish, and feral pigs, and established a settlement (sometimes known as the Summer Islands in a punning reference to the ship's commander Sir George Somers) before continuing their journey. They reached Jamestown in time to assist the few remaining inhabitants after famine had wiped out most of the settlers and this privation provided a stark contrast to the bounty of Bermuda, reinforcing its mythical status. William Strachey's report of the experience was incorporated into *Purchas his Pilgrimage* (1625) and drew heavily on images of Cockaigne and the Garden of Eden, with abundance manifested in fruit; Lewis Hughes's *Letter Sent into England from the Summer Islands* (1615) represented the Bermudas as a gift from God to which the English had been providentially led.[39] The islands were initially administered by the Virginia Company and then in 1614 by the Somers Isles Company, although they had previously been claimed by Spain and settled by shipwrecked Portuguese sailors. The latter were probably responsible for the pigs.

The establishment of the colony is celebrated in Edmund Waller's "The Battle of the Summer Islands" (1645), a mock epic which draws on Strachey, Hughes, and John Smith's *Generall Historie of Virginia, New England and the Summer Isles* (1624) to construct an image of a tropical paradise in which plenty is manifested in fruit. Bermuda is

> That happy island where huge lemons grow,
> And orange trees, which golden fruit do bear,
> The Hesperian garden boasts of none so fair.[40]

The comparison between the citrus fruits of Bermuda and the golden apples of the Hesperides reinforces the island's quasi-mythical status and sanative properties, since Hesperian fruits convey eternal life. The poem goes on to explain that while tenants pay their English landlords in tobacco, denoted by the pejorative term "weeds," they themselves feed on "precious fruits," such as "candied plantains, and the juicy pine / . . . choicest melons, and sweet grapes" (32–34).

The description of the island connects its natural profusion with the Garden of Eden and emphasizes the contrast between this abundance and English orchards and gardens. In Bermuda,

Ripe fruits and blossoms on the same trees live;
At once they promise what at once they give.
So sweet the air, so moderate the clime,
None sickly lives, or dies before his time.
Heaven sure has kept this spot of earth uncursed,
To show how all things were created first.
The tardy plants in our cold orchards placed,
Reserve their fruit for the next age's taste. (42–49)

The orange tree, bearing simultaneous blossom and fruit, provides permanent harvests, without seasons of plenty and dearth. The passage exemplifies what Tobin has identified as the "trope of bounty" in her account of later depictions of the tropics, in that the fruits of the island are freely available, without the curse of labor.[41] As this study has shown, this trope was far from unique to the tropics, informing many depictions of domestic orchards and gardens, exemplified in Drayton's image of *Poly-Olbion*: in Waller's poem, however, the evocation of abundance is in line with Tobin's argument, juxtaposed with a British landscape conveyed through postlapsarian imagery. In Britain, oranges die prematurely, and even hardy orchard trees take a generation to reach maturity. In Bermuda, by contrast,

a small grain in some few months will be
A firm, a lofty and a spacious tree.
The palma-christi [castor oil plant] and the fair papa [pawpaw],
Now but a seed, (preventing nature's law)
In half the circle of the hasty year
Project a shade, and lovely fruit do wear.
And as their trees, in our dull region set,
But faintly grow, and no perfection get;
So, in this northern tract, our hoarser throats,
Utter unripe and ill-constrained notes. (50–59)

The description draws on the tradition of magical lands with multiple harvests and trees growing from seed to maturity in months. But just as it is vain to attempt to raise tropical fruits in Britain, so, Waller suggests, it is not possible to celebrate this paradise using the poetic conventions and forms of English literary tradition. He invokes Phoebus Apollo as god of both the sun and poetry to suggest that sunshine encourages the growth of poetic invention as well as fruit trees in the Summer Islands, whereas poets in the cold and uncongenial climate of Britain can only produce "ill-constrained notes" that are, like exotic fruits in British gardens, "unripe" (58–65).

Waller's representation of the mystical fruits of the tropical paradise manifests the development of the colonial project and the fetishization of material objects to reinforce the differences between the colonized countries and the colonial center. The sensuous fruits of the tropics are distinguished from the plants grown in the "dull region" of the "northern tract," and the latter can be censured as weak and retarded precisely because British power is manifested not in its domestic fruitfulness but in its colonial control of the islands on which the luxurious produce can be found. The abundance of the islands can be invoked as a sign of the providential underpinning of the colonial project and this symbolism is not necessarily weakened by the difficulties of transporting fruit noted in Chapter 2. Fruit functions as a reification of imperial control, a point ultimately reinforced by the irony that most of the fruits described in the poem were not native to the Caribbean—as Waller may or may not have been aware. The oranges, melons, and pineapples were probably, like the wild pigs, introduced by the Spanish or Portuguese and were themselves colonists. The slow growth of fruits in the cold climate of Britain necessitates a culture that plans and plants for the future and cannot rely on the almost instant gratification that characterizes the tropics. This intemperance is presented as seductive, but the parenthetical comment (53) identifies it as unnatural, through comparison with the normative standards of maturation established in the colonial center.

Waller's identification of tropical fruits as evidence that the colonies have been provided for the benefit of Britain is more explicitly articulated in his poetic celebration of the Restoration, "To the King upon his Majesties Happy Return" (1660). This draws a comparison between the King and the sun, describing how

> the lost Sun, while least by us enjoy'd,
> Is the whole night, for our concern imploy'd:
> He ripens spices, fruit, and precious Gums,
> Which from remotest Regions hither comes.[42]

Like the sun, Charles II is now rising in Britain, having previously been employed overseas. Readers are assured that when not engaged in providing

British people with light and warmth, the sun is "imploy'd" for their benefit, ripening fruits and other exotic luxuries on the other side of the world, with the implication that the principal purpose of the rest of the world is to supply to Britain goods that cannot be produced at home. This ethnocentric imperialist outlook is directly opposed to the economic philosophy of mercantilism, which stresses the superiority of domestically produced goods and identifies imports as a threat to the wealth and strength of the nation.

David Armitage and Bridget Orr have emphasized the complexity of attitudes to colonialism in the early modern period and have warned against the danger of projecting later imperialist assumptions back into the seventeenth century. Armitage highlights the anti-imperialism within the classical sources that were at the heart of British culture, while Orr draws on the representation of colonial settlers within drama to suggest that "the creation of a mercantile *imperium* driven by material interest rather than a civilizing or conversion mission . . . aroused antipathy."[43] The ambivalence toward the colonies is manifested in the representation of tropical fruit by writers such as Marvell, for whom the exoticism and fecundity are simultaneously seductive and threatening. Marvell's "Bermudas" appropriates elements of Waller's description, but it invokes some of the suspicion of vegetative abundance expressed by the mower to present a more complex vision of the fruitfulness of the islands and their relationship to the colonial center. This is in line with the ambiguities discernible in the descriptions of English gardens by the poet and mower, and which Smith has suggested characterizes Marvell's poetic voice in general.

In Marvell's poem, the portrayal of the island paradise is reoriented by being put into the mouths of sailors in an "English boat" who have been identified as Puritan exiles from Laudian persecution.[44] Cousins and Smith draw on C. B. Hardman's argument that the poem adopts the form of the metrical psalms in the translations of George Sandys to suggest that the incorporation of works of the Royalists Waller and Sandys into a Puritan reenactment of the biblical exodus can be read as an act of political appropriation.[45] Cousins contends that the poem manifests "Calvin's form of *contemptus mundi*,"[46] yet this spiritual reading does not entirely accord with the tone of the poem. As Timothy Raylor argues, it contains "too many traces of the sybaritic and morally questionable classical and romance tradition of the Fortunate Isles."[47] These traces are most conspicuous in the representation of fruit, which shows a marked absence of contempt for things of the *mundus*. In the Bermudas,

He [God] hangs in shades the orange bright,
Like golden lamps in a green night.
And does in the pom'granates close,
Jewels more rich than Ormus shows.
He makes the figs our mouths to meet,
And throws the melons at our feet;
But apples plants of such a price,
No trees could ever bear them twice. (lines 17–24)

The description echoes the active abundance of Marvell's "The Garden,"
but while the subtropical climate should facilitate the natural production of
exotic fruit that is eulogized by Waller, the imagery subverts the association
of fruitfulness with nature. The oranges have been hung on the trees like lamps
and the pomegranate seeds are like jewels. They are presented as the work of
a divine artificer, but the similes suggest the artificial luxuries of commodified
society rather than natural products for the satisfaction of basic human needs.
The apples in line 23 were interpreted by Donno as pineapples, but this reading
has been rejected by more recent editors, not least because pineapples do not
grow on trees, although it is possible that Marvell was not aware of this.[48] The
apples have been planted by God, but even these humble fruits are evaluated
using monetary lexis to subvert the idea of the double harvest. The materialism
manifested in these images is reinforced by the reference to ambergris (28),
the oxidized whale excretion used in the manufacture of perfume. The celebration of this expensive commodity is with difficulty accommodated either
in a reading of the poem as a "devout and polemical myth" that seeks to "over-
write the satirically secular verse" of Waller, or in Grove's assimilation of the
poem with the works of Waller and Cowley, and his argument that for Marvell
"the tropical island clearly constituted a mental refuge from political turmoil."[49]
The fruit is constructed in the language of artificial luxury that subverts the
trope of natural bounty embodied in Waller's verse and, as in "The Garden,"
does not wait to be harvested but violently obtrudes itself on visitors. The
colonial paradise is identified with the language of materialism and commerce
that renders it alien to the values associated with nature and poetry.

The disconcerting imagery gives credence to ironic readings of the poem.
Eric Song challenges Annabel Patterson's argument that the poem is a successful exercise in Protestant poetics and instead suggests that it is not clear whether
the poem "celebrates a Puritan paradise or gently derides the quest for a colonial

Eden as misguided."[50] In contrast to Waller's poem, the poetic voice does not explicitly endorse the pastoral vision by describing the island but only recounts the views of the proselytizing sailors. There is no indication whether the "small boat" (3) is approaching the island for the first time and thus whether the description represents experience or expectation.[51] While the mower's fruit imagery subverts the eulogistic tone of country house poetry by highlighting the unnatural horticultural practices on which their fruitfulness depends, "Bermudas" can be read as a satire on, rather than an example of, the trope of foreign bounty epitomized by Waller. The celebration of plenty is put into the mouths of sailors. It is thus distanced from the perspective of the narrator and located in the realm of popular myth informed by customary concepts of the Golden Age and the Land of Cockaigne, undermining the evocation of a spiritual paradise. While the poem may not be attacking Puritan providentialism as such, its wit is directed to the terms of its portrayal of exotic fruits. The lexis of artificiality challenges the legitimation of colonial subjection within providentialist writing, as the fruits are described in terms which suggest a seditious sybaritism and the discourse of luxury.

But while tropical and subtropical fruits only grow naturally in certain geographical locations, this was not true in the prelapsarian world of Milton's *Paradise Lost*, which Tigner reads in the context of "the popular seventeenth-century notion that all plants originated in the Garden of Eden, but exploded out into the world after the fall."[52] Adam and Eve can dine on hardy orchard fruits, the peaches and nectarines of the walled garden, and oranges and melons of the tropics, all of which grow naturally, abundantly, and incessantly, without the interruption of changing seasons, and Milton's evocative fruit-centric narrative establishes many of the iconographic codes that were deployed and adapted in texts over the following century. Robert Appelbaum and other literary critics have written extensively and eruditely on Milton's portrayal of the forbidden fruit,[53] so this account will focus primarily on the unforbidden fruits, to show how the poem incorporates classical and biblical traditions to create a landscape that would have been familiar to readers of horticultural literature. Adam and Eve face many of the challenges that beset early modern fruit producers, and even within the prelapsarian garden the trope of pastoral abundance is juxtaposed with the georgic trope of labor within the epic narrative structure.

At the start of Book 4, Satan arrives on earth and looks on paradise, which is described as surrounded by a "verdurous wall."[54] This has been the subject of extensive critical scrutiny, with Barbara Lewalski seemingly interpreting it as an actual wall, while Jeffrey Theis refers to a "forested wall" of trees and a "wood ringing paradise," which he links to the legal discourse of forest law.[55] In her fascinating account of *Milton and the Natural World*, Edwards has marshaled extensive evidence to challenge previous assumptions that Milton draws on "old science" rather than on the new experimental methodology in his account of paradise and emphasizes "the brevity and unadorned nature" of the "catalog of trees" which she associates with the verdurous wall.[56] Like Tigner and McColley, Edwards relates the fragrant plants within Eden to John Evelyn's plans in *Fumifugium* (1661) to create a "plantation" of "most fragrant and odoriferous *Flowers*" around the city of London in order to counteract the impact of air pollution.[57] Yet the "verdurous wall" which surrounds paradise is clearly distinguished in Milton's Edenic geography from the "sylvan scene" of cedar, pine, fir, and palm (4: 139–40) which comprise a belt of trees that is located within its bounds. The "wall" is described as

> so thick entwined,
> As one continued brake, the undergrowth
> Of shrubs and tangling bushes had perplexed
> All path of man or beast that passed that way (4: 174–77)

Rather than a wall, a belt of trees, or a plantation, fragrant or otherwise, this would have been interpreted by seventeenth-century readers as a hedge, like the "quickset hedge" around the Garden of Alcinous in Chapman's translation of Homer, or the hedges surrounding seventeenth-century orchards.

The entrance to Heaven, in contrast, is fitted with automatic gates on golden hinges, "as by work / Divine the sovereign architect had framed" (5: 255–56). The Kingdom of Heaven is walled and gated like the gardens of the aristocracy; Eden is hedged, like an orchard, with one gate to the East. There is thus a clear distinction between the landscape of Heaven and the landscape of paradise. The Garden of Eden is the work of a divine architect, but it is modeled on the English orchard and the meadows celebrated by Marvell's mower. The flowers are not disposed by "nice art / In beds and curious knots" but rather are "Poured forth profuse on hill and dale and plain" (4: 241–43). Despite containing flowers and fruits from across the globe, this is a landscape of agricultural production associated with the "honest plaine English Husbandman" addressed in contemporary husbandry and horticulture manuals, rather than the formal walled gardens associated with the aristocratic elite.[58]

The boundaries of Eden invoke the quotidian, but the fruit trees are described in superlatives. They are

> a circling row
> Of goodliest trees loaden with fairest fruit,
> Blossoms and fruits at once of golden hue (4: 146–48)

The ability to blossom and fruit simultaneously is a definitive characteristic of the citrus, but Milton may be suggesting that all fruits have this capacity in Eden, where constant fruitfulness is not disrupted by postlapsarian seasons. References to Hesperian fruits (4: 249–51) and the fate of Proserpine (4: 268–71) invoke fruit myths which, as Lewalski notes, "underscore the fragility of all paradisal places."[59] But these classical allusions also signal a connection between fruit and ideas of female vulnerability and sexuality and this association is reinforced by the description of "the mantling vine," which, in line with the classical concept of "nupta vitis," is gendered female. She "Lays forth her purple grape, and gently creeps / Luxuriant" (4: 258–60). The verb "creep" has sinister overtones, having previously been used twice in Milton's poem, once in relation to the hounds of Hell, who would creep back into the womb of their mother Sin (2: 656), and once in the dramatic account of "the Fiend," who "swims or sinks, or wades, or creeps, or flies" (2: 950) through Chaos. Satan is subsequently compared to "a black mist low creeping" (9: 180) when he searches for the serpent. The femininity, and perhaps nascent sexuality, of the vine are highlighted in the "mantling" or blushing of her ripening grapes. The adverb "Luxuriant" invokes the emergent discourse of mercantilism, and, as the writings of Taverner, Hartlib, and Austen emphasize, is identified in the postlapsarian world with the consumption of imported wines, which are contrasted with the hardy masculine domestic produce of cider and perry. So, although the vine is a source of food and provides the "nectareous draughts" enjoyed by Adam and Eve (5: 306), it is associated both physically and lexically with Satan, the fallen condition, femininity, and deleterious trade.

The gendering of the vine as feminine is anticipated in the first description of Eve, where she is distinguished from Adam. While Adam, like a good Puritan, wears his hair manageably short:

> She as a veil down to the slender waist
> Her unadorned golden tresses wore
> Dishevelled, but in wanton ringlets waved
> As the vine curls her tendrils, which implied
> Subjection, but required with gentle sway,
> And by her yielded. (4: 304–9)

I Corinthians condemns long hair in men but suggests that "if a woman have long haire, it is a glory to her: for her haire is given her for a covering" (2: 14–15). Eve's hair covers her as a veil, but it is also like the vine, which needs support from the male elm and is "wanton." John Knott argues that when describing the growth in the garden of Eden, this adjective "carries the older meaning of profuse or rank,"[60] but I would argue that here it also has resonances of the *OED*'s second definition, of "given to amorous dalliance," although not of "Lascivious, unchaste, lewd," since the text goes on to explain that "Then was not guiltie shame" (4: 313). Eve epitomizes modest reluctance rather than shame, and "Yielded with coy submission, modest pride / And sweet reluctant amorous delay" (4: 310–11). Recent criticism has tended to challenge readings of *Paradise Lost* that have identified the portrayal of Eve as misogynistic, stressing her intellectual independence, her role as the poet of Eden, and her understanding of the ecosystem of the garden,[61] yet in this passage it is made clear that she, like the vine and her own unruly hair, needs to be trained and tended. When she leaves Adam so that she can work alone, she may have justified her decision by arguments which critics have identified as fundamentally rational,[62] but she is compared to

> Pomona when she fled
> Vertumnus, or to Ceres in her prime,
> Yet Virgin of Proserpina from Jove. (9: 394–96)

The references to Pomona and Ceres suggest fruitfulness, but also vulnerability. Vertumnus would have raped Pomona had she not consented to marry him, and Ceres was raped by Jove, leading to the birth of Proserpine. By implying that Eve's innocent state is transitory, these allusions, like those to the fruit of the Hesperides, anticipate the approaching fall, reinforcing the connections between classical fruit imagery and ideas of sexual violence.

The association of Eve with fruit is compounded by her responsibility for the culinary arrangements in Eden. For their first supper, Adam and Eve pluck "Nectarine [juicy] fruits which the compliant boughs / Yielded them" (4: 332–33). But while eating fruit from the tree may be acceptable when they have just moved in and Adam and Eve are alone, a much more elaborate meal is required when the angel Raphael comes to visit. As soon as Eve hears that a guest is due, she becomes preoccupied with her "hospitable thoughts" (5: 332). This involves not only identifying the best delicacies but also arranging them in the right order, for although the dinner is comprised entirely of fruit, it follows the early modern fashion of having a range of different courses in ordered sequence, with a variety of tastes and textures, rather than the simultaneous spread of different dishes that characterized medieval feasts. The banquet is

> So contrived as not to mix
> Tastes, not well joined, inelegant, but bring
> Taste after taste upheld with kindliest change (5: 334–36)

It contains

> Whatever earth all-bearing mother yields
> In India east or west, or middle shore
> In Pontus or the Punic coast, or where
> Alcinous reigned, fruits of all kinds, in coat,
> Rough, or smooth rined, or bearded husk, or shell (5: 338–42)

As Tigner notes, the meal combines fruits that are now dispersed around the world, including citrus from the Black Sea and figs from the Mediterranean.[63] As in the Garden of Alcinous, this variety is available from one place and in prime condition. Yet Eve's role comprises more than simply choosing and assembling available resources:

> for drink the grape
> She crushes, inoffensive must, and meaths
> From many a berry, and from sweet kernels pressed
> She tempers dulcet creams (5: 344–47)

Nature has provided the raw materials, but human labor and culinary art are necessary to make them palatable—at least when the couple are entertaining their first guest. The focus on fruit drinks and semi-liquid desserts may indicate the refined appetites of angels, who can be more easily conceived tasting perry or almond pudding than munching through pears or almonds, but it also echoes the significance of orchard fruits as the raw material for beverages.[64]

A similar fruit banquet is prepared by Porphyro in John Keats's "The Eve of St. Agnes" (1820), with exotic "spiced dainties" from Fez, Samarcan, and Lebanon, including "candied apple, quince, and plum, and gourd / With jellies soother than the creamy curd, / And lucent syrops" (30, 264–70). The insubstantiality of the dishes prepared by Eve for Raphael may be explained by the angelic guest's lack of corporeality, but in Keats's poem the meal is designed for the human figure of Madeleine. The cloying excess of a meal comprised of fruits, jams, jellies, and syrups provides a sickly parody of the literary trope of the meal as metaphor for seduction, most famously epitomized in the scene between Fielding's Tom Jones and Mrs. Waters in the Inn at Upton.[65] Porphyro's feast signals the liminal status of the narrative between dream and reality and perhaps the unreality of the relationship between the lovers. In *Paradise Lost*, however, the account of the meal emphasizes Eve's role in the preparation of the food, converting it into a product of human industry rather than a natural commodity. The worth of the goods is related to the transformative effect of labor rather than simply the use value of the unrefined form, challenging the identification of fruit as a natural product, independent of systems of exchange.

The work in the Garden of Eden is not confined to female culinary endeavor; the trees and flowers also require maintenance. Eve laments that

> The work under our labour grows
> Luxurious by restraint; what we by day
> Lop overgrown, or prune, or prop, or bind,
> One night or two with wanton growth derides
> Tending to wild. (9: 208–12)

The wanton plants, like Eve's wanton tresses, must be restrained, and Lewalski suggests that the requirement to lop and prune the garden symbolizes the need for Adam and Eve to restrict the growth of their own natures.[66] Yet the primary consequence of pruning fruit trees, as Eve points out in this passage, is enhanced rather than restrained growth. Anthony Low highlights the extent to which the pastoral images of nature's bounty are juxtaposed with georgic references to the importance of husbandry, and this argument could be extended to include culinary as well as horticultural labor.[67] Focus on the representation of fruit within the text highlights the tensions between the trope of abundance and the trope of labor, indicating that Milton's original audience would have read the poem in the context of the competing generic visions of landscape. It is the pastoral abundance of Eden that necessitates the georgic labors of Adam and Eve. They lop and prune excessive growth to maintain control over an environment that derides their efforts and contains some of the menace of Marvell's obtrusive fruit, while the adjectives "wanton" and "luxurious" invite comparison with Eve and her unruly locks. At the same time, the framing of the garden in terms reminiscent of the orchard of the husbandman, in contrast to Heaven which is presented as the walled garden of the landowner, connects these images of inevitable labor with ideas of humble social status, even in the prelapsarian landscape.

The work of Adam and Eve is required

> where any row
> Of Fruit-trees over-woody reached too far
> Their pampered boughs, and needed hands to check
> Fruitless embraces: (5: 212–15)

The abundance of the pampered boughs needs to be pruned back, to ensure that the plants produce fruit rather than excess vegetation and thus encourage procreation rather than "fruitless embraces." To this end, they

> led the vine
> To wed her elm; she spoused about him twines
> Her marriageable arms, and with her brings
> Her dower the adopted clusters, to adorn
> His barren leaves. (5: 215–19)

Milton draws on the viticultural practices of classical Rome to develop the marital metaphor and suggest that Adam and Eve must help the feeble vine to find support from the male elm so that she can fruit successfully. The lexis challenges Marvell's presentation of human intervention in fruit propagation as a form of pimping, manifesting aberrant postlapsarian sexuality and instead

indicates that horticultural labor is desirable in facilitating vegetative reproduction, but it also reinforces the identification of fruit with femininity. While
the Song of Solomon uses fruit imagery to represent both male and female
sensuality, and Chaucer's pears are clearly identified as male, the fruits in
Paradise Lost are almost exclusively female. The grapes are the dowry paid by
the vine to the elm for his adornment, rather than the fruits of the marriage
between the two. The vines and other exotic fruits are feminized because of
their delicacy and their reliance on male strength, and this paves the way for
the portrayal of the forbidden fruit as a symbol of explicitly female moral
weakness.

This is emphasized in Book 9 of *Paradise Lost*, much of which is devoted to
the account of how Eve persuades Adam to allow her to work alone to prove
her strength and independence (9: 205–25), how she is tempted by the serpent
to eat the apple (9: 532–732), and then how she convinces Adam to share the
consequences of her action, even though he knows that to do so will be fatal
(9: 961–89). Recent criticism has followed Dennis Danielson in challenging
the idea that *Paradise Lost* draws on the concept of the fortunate fall in the
construction of its theodicy,[68] highlighting the legitimacy of the arguments
proposed by Eve in her debate with Adam.[69] But while Milton may be cleared
of some accusations of misogyny, the story dictates that Eve is responsible for
initiating the fall, and in Milton's account the eating of the fruit is much more
explicitly associated with female frailty than in the Genesis version.

Satan, in the guise of a serpent, tells Eve how he has found

A goodly tree . . .
Loaden with fruit of fairest colours mixed,
Ruddy and gold (9: 576–78)

and "To satisfy the sharp desire . . . / Of tasting those fair apples" (9: 584–85),
he climbed the tree and ate his fill. The description of the fruit as red and gold
suggests the English russet but also the apple of discord from the Garden of
the Hesperides, especially when Satan claims that it will give life rather than
death (9: 679–732). Edwards has related the uncertainty over the identity of
the fruit to Satan's lying and trickery, comparing him to the figure of the
mountebank.[70] Appelbaum has also discussed how the forbidden fruit changes
from being an apple when Eve eats it to something more like a peach when

she carries it to Adam. It has become "A bough of fairest fruit that downy smiled, / New gathered, and ambrosial smell diffused" (9: 851–52).[71] Appelbaum describes the superior sensual qualities of the peach, but as the previous chapters have emphasized, the distinction also has a class dimension. While clearly consumed across the social spectrum, apples are associated in both literary and horticultural writing with the humble husbandman. The peach, by comparison, is a delicate wall fruit, identified with the gardens of the gentleman or aristocrat. Eve is tempted by an ordinary apple, whereas Adam is offered a much higher status fruit, yet still resists its sensual attractions (9: 906–16). He only finally succumbs in a heroic gesture of self-sacrifice, motivated by his love for Eve, and eats "Against his better knowledge, not deceived / But fondly overcome with female charm" (9: 998–99).

The other occasion when the fruit is identified as an apple is when Satan reports back to the assembled hordes in Pandemonium, gleefully recounting the success of his mission and how he seduced "man," "From his creator, and the more to increase / Your wonder, with an apple" (10: 486–87). The words echo the disbelief expressed in "Adam Lay Ybounden" at the disproportion between the benefit and cost of the fall, revealing the gullibility of humankind. But in *Paradise Lost* it also reinforces Eve's specifically female weakness, as we are told that when she finally eats the apple, "Greedily she engorged without restraint" (9: 791). She is an unrestrained as well as an undiscerning consumer, displaying excessive appetite, which evokes the symbolic association of fruit with sexuality and anticipates the consequences of the fall. The poem thus reinforces the negative connotations of the portrayal of women as active consumers of fruit, rather than as fruits that are awaiting consumption by men. McColley has suggested that Italian Renaissance paintings of the story of the fall "give many viewers an impression that Eve herself—for better or worse—was the forbidden fruit" and her *Gust for Paradise* provides a convincing demonstration of the influence of these images on Milton's representation of the prelapsarian world.[72] The poetic condemnation of female fruit consumption is perpetuated into the nineteenth century in Christina Rossetti's *Goblin Market*, when the fall of Laura is manifested in her unrestrained greed as she

sucked and sucked and sucked the more
Fruits which that unknown orchard bore;
She sucked until her lips were sore.[73]

Paradise Lost therefore depicts a landscape of fruit as a backdrop to a story in which fruit plays a pivotal role. The fruits within paradise are luxurious and exotic and grow naturally and abundantly. Adam and Eve tame and train their rampant growth, providing support for vines and boughs in a metaphor for female weakness that is reinforced by allusions to classical fruit myths of female temptation and sexual assault, which culminate in the portrayal of the destructive consequences of female appetite. The identification of Adam as a husband-man, engaged in physical work within the prelapsarian orchard, emphasizes the labor required to produce fruit, but it also reinforces the growing identification of horticulture as an appropriate gentleman's hobby. The fruit trees need to be pruned to encourage rather than restrain their growth and fecundity. The condemnation of Eve's greedy feeding, and her association with wanton fruits, identifies women as fruits for male consumption, or preparers of fruits for men, rather than as themselves legitimate consumers of fruit. The fruit narrative therefore provides a mechanism for the discussion of female sexuality before the development of the Linnaean system of classification, which has been identified as enabling such discussions in the nineteenth-century novel.[74] As Chapter 4 shows, this is fully exploited in the drama of the Restoration.

The fruits in the poetry considered here are growing in an aristocratic garden or an idealized paradise, and are constructed as desirable, available, and seductive. Jonson's apricots and peaches flourish alongside native cherries and plums, constituting a harmonious sequence that models idealized social relationships within the landed estate, while the orchard fruits are symbols of fecundity. Marvell develops the idea of abundance, but his active fruits are waiting to fell the poet within the garden or the sailors approaching the islands of Bermuda. They invoke the mythic associations of the forbidden fruit and the snares of sensuality, but they also represent the human intervention in the natural world through artificial techniques of husbandry and colonial conquest. This emphasis on the artificiality of fruit cultivation renders the produce of the garden menacing, collapsing the distinction between nature and culture, and drawing on negative associations with the foreign and exotic inherent in the concept of luxury. Even when growing in tropical locations, Marvell's tropical fruits are described in terms that suggest commodification and challenge the trope of bounty to provide an implicit critique of the colonial appropriation manifested in the writings of Waller.

Marvell's garden is a place of potentially dangerous artifice with fruits that are comically tyrannous. Milton's representation of paradise is based on the hedged orchard, in contrast to the walled gardens of heaven, with their golden gates and angelic attendants. Adam and Eve are humble husbandpeople, deployed to maintain and control the abundant growth of the trees. Even in Eden the fruits require human intervention, through techniques which Marvell has presented as unnatural, subverting the ecocritical preoccupation with the binary opposition of nature and art. The emphasis on the labor that is required in the orchard paradise is very different from the gardens in Jonson, where the activities of the gardener and the farmer are invisible to poet and proprietor, for whom fruit appears as a manifestation of natural abundance and the activities of an enlightened connoisseur. While recent criticism has heralded Milton as an early modern ecowarrior and emphasized the scientific approaches to nature and the interest in environmental improvement discernible in early modern verse, this chapter has argued that representations of fruit, and, by extension, the natural world, involve a negotiation of horticultural practices within a framework of mythic references and genre conventions. The hardy fruits of the orchard are associated with the honest simplicity of rural laborers, whereas wall fruits connote the refinement of the elite, but the biblical and classical resonances ensure a pervasive identification of fruits of all kinds with female appetite and weakness. Whether growing within the orchard, the garden, or a tropical paradise, fruit can be portrayed as a manifestation of natural prelapsarian abundance, invoked through pastoral imagery, or the product of horticultural expertise and human labor, through the georgic tradition. Chapter 4 will explore how these themes are developed in Restoration drama, but the kinds of fruits represented within plays are clearly distinct from those depicted in poetry. The disjunction between the fruits of poetry and those of the plays of the seventeenth century will be related to differences in the way the texts were consumed by their respective audiences, showing how the commodified nature of the theater in the Restoration is manifested in the commodification of fruit.

Chapter 4

"You Have Only Squeezed My Orange"

The Fungibility of Fruit in Restoration Drama

In 1663, Mary Meggs, a widow from Covent Garden, familiarly known as "Orange Moll" or "Orange Mall," paid the very substantial sum of one hundred pounds to the Kings Company, for which she was granted "Full, free, & sole liberty, licence, power, & authority to vend, utter, & sell oranges, Lemons, fruit, sweetmeats, & all manner of fruiterers & Confectioners wares & commodities" within the King's House in Drury Lane.[1] A further daily fee of six shillings and eight pence purchased the right to sell fruit everywhere in the New Bridge Street playhouse except the upper gallery. The concession ran for thirty-nine years and on her death in 1691, Meggs bequeathed it to the actor Philip Griffin, by which time it had doubled in value. She also left a considerable estate, including three houses and extensive portable property. The reference to "fruit" as distinct from oranges and lemons indicates that the trade included both imported citrus and home-grown orchard and wall fruits, an interpretation that is substantiated by records of a court case in 1670, when Meggs was sued by Reverend William Grant, of Isleworth, to the west of London, "for money she owed him for the previous three years for eight acres of fruit trees." This suggests that Meggs was renting an orchard, and presumably subcontracting its cultivation to a tenant who could supply her directly with produce to sell in the theatrical market. This would produce much higher profits than the "regrating" or reselling of purchased goods conventionally associated with fruit hucksters. The story of Mary Meggs therefore supports the identification of fruit-selling as a female occupation, but it also shows that fruit-selling encompassed a wider range of social and economic groups than the humble "orange wench," including successful female entrepreneurs as well as itinerant vendors. While the theaters that opened after the Restoration in 1660 were significantly different from those of the Renaissance, with female actors, elaborate stage machinery, purpose-built playhouses, and a more exclusive clientele, the consumption of fruit remained central to the ritual of playhouse attendance and its sale was a potentially lucrative business.[2]

In her study of playhouse refreshment during the Renaissance, Hillary Nunn highlights the connections between on-stage food references and the snacks available to the audience, with the popularity of apples in Renaissance playhouses matched by apple references in the plays. She argues that representations of apple eating and apple buying entice playgoers "to indulge in the purchase of fruit near their own reach," but she also argues that the onstage trade in apples "makes the exchange familiar and desirable by acting out the interplay between vendor and customer while highlighting the allure of the forbidden fruit."[3] Thus the audiences are encouraged not only to consume apples but also to reflect on "profound questions about the nature of hunger, temptation, and human desire."[4] This chapter will consider depictions of, and references to, fruit on the Restoration stage as part of the continuing discussion of the development of fruit iconography through the early modern period, but it will also illuminate some of the central critical controversies over these texts, particularly over the portrayal of gender and sexuality. The libertine plays of the period have been identified as liberating for women through their acknowledgment of female sexuality, but they have also been seen as permeated with "misogyny and fear and dislike of women's sexuality."[5] Jeremy Webster has highlighted the inherently performative nature of the libertine culture of the Restoration, arguing that the theater provides "a special arena in which to subvert the dominant discourses of the day," whereas other critics have suggested that plays largely endorse the dominant ideology.[6] This analysis will show how fruit is deployed in the negotiation of these social and political debates, focusing on the comedy of the period, since fruit references are significantly less abundant in tragedy. This may be because fruit is inherently comic, making it inappropriate for serious drama, but it may also reflect the preoccupation in comedy with the themes of commodification and exchange that are raised by the representation of fruit consumption.

Compared to the apple-rich drama of the Renaissance, the Restoration sees a significant shift in fruit symbolism. As imported oranges replace domestic orchard fruits as the playhouse snack of choice, the apple is displaced by the orange and the apple woman by the orange wench in theatrical representations. While apples were still available for sale, and presumably continued to be popular with certain sections of the audience, the orange emerges as the symbol of the Restoration stage, epitomized in the figure of Nell Gwyn, who famously rose from orange wench in Drury Lane to actress and ultimately mistress of King Charles II.[7] The oranges consumed within the Restoration playhouse were, however, very different from the products of the orangeries of Britain, which, as Chapter 2 has indicated, were very small and bitter. Playgoers enjoyed large sweet fruits imported into London, not from tropical paradises on the other side of the world that were subject to British control but from Portugal and Spain. Portugal became an ally of Britain following the marriage of Charles II and Catherine of Braganza in 1662, and, in the eighteenth century, Portugal supported Britain and the Netherlands against France and Spain in the War of the Spanish Succession. Yet Spain and Portugal were both colonial powers in the seventeenth century, representing Britain's main rivals in the expansion of its overseas territories. This meant that these fruits had very different associations from the exotic fruits growing in the colonized territory of Bermuda, which were depicted in Waller's nationalistic verse.

The poetry explored in Chapter 3 is preoccupied with a diverse range of fruits that were available from bush or tree, whether growing along English garden walls made of "country stone" or in the paradises of Bermuda and Eden. Jonson's fruits can be plucked by "every child"; Marvell's fruits hurl themselves at passing poets and sailors; Milton's Eve helps herself from "compliant boughs." In drama, by contrast, the fruit is not part of a natural landscape but is a commodity in an economic system, the profitability of which is epitomized in the career of Mary Meggs. Fungibility has displaced fecundity as fruit's defining feature, and anxieties over unnatural methods of propagation have been supplanted by debates over the merits of international trade. In the poems of Waller discussed in Chapter 3, the consumption of foreign goods is celebrated as a sign of national power and the providential ordering of a world that has been created to supply the needs of Britain. Yet in the mercantilist rhetoric of the horticultural treatises discussed in Chapter 2, imports are identified with luxury and seen as a threat to the strength and prosperity of the country. This chapter will explore these competing visions through analysis of the representation of fruit—in particular, the orange—within the drama of the late seventeenth and early eighteenth centuries, as the associations with sex and violence derived from biblical and classical myth come into conflict with the economics of fruit production and distribution.

Evidence of the significance of fruit within the theatrical space comes from references in the plays. The Prologue to Aphra Behn's *The Young King, or, The Mistake* (1679) contains the line "Half Crown my Play, Sixpence my Orange cost" implying an integral connection between these items of expenditure, while a character in Charles Sedley's *The Mulberry-Garden* (1668) suggests that courting a fashionable woman involves "kissing the cards at ombre, or presenting oranges at the playhouse."[8] Robert Hume, in an analysis of the financial cost of different kinds of cultural consumption in the period 1660 to 1740, explains that the price of a seat in the second gallery of the playhouse was one shilling, while it was four shillings for a box.[9] At sixpence, an orange cost half as much as the cheapest seats, and more than twice as much as the meal of shin of beef, bread, and beer purchased in a cookhouse by Tobias Smollett's eponymous hero Roderick Random.[10] The persistent identification of oranges with playgoing reinforces the cultural resonance of the fruits, even though oranges would have been prohibitively expensive for many theatergoers. Buying an orange was what you did, or what you aspired to do, when you went to the theater and was a recognized part of the ritual of courtship.

Although oranges were luxury commodities in the sense that they were imported and relatively costly, the conventional discussion of imported goods within the discourse of luxury is compromised by the mechanism of distribution. Notwithstanding the financial resources of entrepreneurs like Orange Mall and the rags-to-riches story of Nell Gwyn, the vending of oranges was still commonly associated with the "hucksters" whom Marion Wynne-Davies has identified, in her study of itinerant vendors, as largely poor and female (Figure 16).[11] She suggests that the "vocalization of economic independence" symbolized in the cries of the orange women "was linked in popular perception with sexual availability" and the crying of wares was identified as a form of self-advertisement.[12] Natasha Korda has similarly argued that female criers of all kinds were "vulnerable to charges of sexual wantonness" and that the particular denigration of orange women discernible in early modern drama represents an attempt by the professional males working within the theater to discriminate between their own legitimate activities and the marginalized figures who function as a reminder of the illegitimate origins of their industry. She concludes that "the figure of the female crier represented a convenient scapegoat or foil against which the professional players sought to distinguish themselves."[13] The arguments of Wynne-Davies and Korda are directly

Figure 16. "Buy a bill of the play" from William Marshall Craig and Richard
Phillips, *The Itinerant Traders of London in their Ordinary Costume, from Modern
London; being the history and present state of the British Metropolis* (1804).
Illustrated with numerous copper plates. © The British Library Board. Each plate
was accompanied by a detailed description, explaining the nature of the trade
depicted. The account of the playbill seller explains: "The doors of the London
theatres are surrounded each night, as soon as they open, with the criers of
playbills. These are mostly women, who also carry baskets of fruit. The titles of
the play and entertainment, and the name and character of every performer for
the night, are found in the bills, which are printed at the expense of the theatre,
and are sold by the hundred to the criers, who retail them at one penny a bill,
unless fruit is bought, when with the sale of half a dozen oranges, they will present
their customer a bill of the play gratis."

concerned with the period before the Commonwealth, but they also make sense in relation to the Restoration, even after women were permitted to appear on the stage, since the distinction between legitimate and illegitimate performance was perpetuated in dramatic representations of the conduct and composition of audiences.

The Epilogue to Susanna Centlivre's *The Platonick Lady* (1707) provides an account of the different types of men who attend the Haymarket and who are described as having vanities and moral failings at least equal to those for which women are conventionally censured. Susan Owen has argued that, in the period after the Exclusion Crisis, "the playwrights seem to be writing for an audience which at least aspired to identify itself, in class terms, with the aristocracy, or as part of an aristocracy of taste."[14] Yet Centlivre describes an audience that includes "Cheapside-Bobbs" and "cits," that is, characters who are unashamedly members of the mercantile class. They, "Like Cock-Sparrows, hop about the Benches, / And court, with Six-pences, fat Orange-Wenches."[15] As with Behn's prologue to *The Young King*, the epilogue draws attention to the performance taking place within the auditorium. The house lights were kept on in the Restoration playhouse, so the division between audience and stage was less marked than in the modern theater and, as William Hogarth's illustration of *The Laughing Audience* shows (Figure 17), the vending of fruit and other activities continued throughout the drama. Centlivre's epilogue also reinforces the stereotype of the sexually available fruit vendor, through the implication that sixpence can buy you the favor of an orange wench, as well as an orange. The texts make clear an emblematic association between the hawking of fruit and the sale of sex, cemented by the identification of the vendors with the "forbidden fruits" they sell. Orange sellers were frequently the victims of sexual violence and impropriety, as shown in a scene set within a theater in Thomas Shadwell's *A True Widow* (1678), where the stage directions suggest "*Several young Coxcombs fool with the Orange-Women*" and later one of the men "*sits down, and lolls in the Orange-wench's lap.*"[16]

While the orange is the quintessential metonym for the experience of Restoration theater, the list of commodities in the license granted to Mary Meggs shows that audiences could purchase "fruit . . . & all manner of fruiterers . . . wares & commodities." Many of the wall and orchard fruits were produced in market gardens, which expanded rapidly on the outskirts of London between 1660 and 1721,[17] and were transported by boat to London markets. In an article in the *Spectator* from 1712, Joseph Addison describes sailing from Richmond

Figure 17. William Hogarth, *The Laughing Audience* (1733), originally produced as a subscription ticket for *Southwark Fair* (1733) and *A Rake's Progress* (1735). The orange sellers are attempting to tempt the audience in the box with their wares but are subjected to sexual attentions. © Trustees of the British Museum. All rights reserved.

to the Strand at four o'clock in the morning, accompanied by "a fleet of gardeners, bound for the several market-ports of London," stopping at Nine-Elms in Battersea to pick up a cargo of melons "consigned by Mr. Cuffe, of that place, to Sarah Sewell and Company, at their stall in Covent-garden."[18] Dried fruit and nuts were also available, providing support for the argument that much of the fruit produced in Britain was consumed in this form. The prologue to John Dryden's adaptation of the story of Antony and Cleopatra, *All for Love* (1677), suggests:

> since that plenteous Autumn now is past,
> Whose Grapes and Peaches have Indulg'd your taste,
> Take in good part from our poor Poets boord,
> Such rivell'd Fruits as Winter can afford.[19]

Laura Rosenthal and Paulina Kewes have both discussed Dryden's use of the metaphor of the "Bowe of *Ulysses*" in his preface to *All for Love*, in the context of their accounts of literary originality and imitation in the Restoration. Everyone is free to try the bow, and Rosenthal suggests that Dryden "locates himself as Shakespeare's heir," while Kewes argues that he "affirms his ambition to build and improve on Shakespeare."[20] But the poet's relationship with his source text also generates the metaphor in the prologue, as the contrast between the fruitful summer of the Elizabethan era and the winter of the present day is evoked through an image that draws on the audience's theatrical experience. Dryden's adaptation is, in the self-deprecating language characteristic of the prologue form, "rivell'd" or dried fruit. The *OED* defines rivelled as "shrivelled or wrinkled, esp. as a result of some drying process," suggesting that the play does not represent fresh produce but rather is a preserved form of a familiar story previously retailed by Shakespeare. The implication is that the work is old, dry, and durable rather than new and perishable, but the terms of the invitation to the audience to dine at the metaphorical table of the poet also signals the fruits that were available during the performance. The first recorded production was at the Theatre Royal in Drury Lane on December 12, 1677, when there would have been no ready supply of fresh wall fruits, such as peaches and grapes, to sell in the theaters, even given the extension of the season provided by the introduction of new varieties.[21] Assuming these fruits were produced in Britain rather than imported,[22] they would have been harvested in August and September and horticultural writers note the poor keeping qualities of peaches in particular. Many writers in the late seventeenth and eighteenth centuries follow Nicholas Venette's distinction between "those Fruits which are easily corrupted, as *Figgs, Nectarins, Peaches, Plums, Apricocks, Mulberries,* and *Cherries*" and "those which are not easily corrupted, . . . as *Pears, Apples, Portugal Quinces, Medlars* and *Services*."[23] The prologue indicates that while the audience may have been eating fresh grapes and peaches earlier in the year, these would have been replaced by dried forms, such as raisins and preserved peaches, in the winter months.

In contrast to wall fruits, apples were harvested throughout the autumn and winter. A well-planted orchard contains different varieties which ripen at different times, with later varieties, such as beefings and russets, particularly suitable for storage. These "keepers" can last for a considerable period, becoming gradually sweeter and more flavorsome. *The Fruiterers Secrets* (1604) is specifically concerned with "how to gather all kindes [of orchard fruit] in their prime and season, and afterwards to carry or conveigh them, either by land or by water, and then how to reserve or keep them, to endure longest." The section on apples records: "There are divers sorts, which will naturally last, some but til Alhollantide, some till Christmas, some till Candlemas, & other some till Shrovetide, &c. But especially, Pippins, John apples, or as some call them Dewzins, Pear-maynes, winter-russettings, and such other lasting serviceable fruite, with good usage, will last till new fruite come in."[24] Apples would thus have been in plentiful supply in December, so the prologue may indicate that apples are not considered sufficiently fashionable to indulge the taste of the theater audience, or at least to be explicitly referenced in the texts, hence the relative paucity of apple references in Restoration drama. While there were presumably playgoers who were eating apples, they were not the section of the audience to whom the prologue was directed.

An alternative explanation, however, is that apples are encompassed within the term "rivell'd fruits," suggesting that the stored fruits were not regarded as fresh wares. Indeed, apples are a stock metaphor for a wrinkled appearance, from Falstaff's reference to himself as "withered like an old apple-john" in *Henry IV, Part 1* to the 1757 novel *The Sedan*, when a portrait painter disdainfully denominates one of his sitters "that old wither'd John-apple."[25] The pippins, pearmains, russets, and john apples that were identified as keepers in *The Fruiterers Secrets* were the less juicy apple varieties and would have been considerably drier and starchier than the modern apple and thus susceptible to withering rather than rotting. The advice on storage and transportation provided within the tract shows a recurrent concern with the prevention of withering. The secret is in waiting until the fruit is fully ripe, for if apples are gathered before they "have . . . their ful grouth . . . they will shrinke, wither, and eate tough, and doe no service."[26] Even modern varieties of beefing are unpleasant when eaten raw, but in the seventeenth and eighteenth centuries they were slowly dried in a warming oven. I have tried this and it produces fruits that are unprepossessing in appearance, but are soft, sweet, and palatable, and can be stored for over a year. Shriveled apples of this kind may have been available to Dryden's December audience as they watched the "rivell'd Fruits" of his attempt to preserve the Antony and Cleopatra story.

Theatergoers did not always eat the fruits they bought; they also used them to throw at actors if they disapproved of the performance, whether on aesthetic, moral, or political grounds, thus reinforcing their role as participants in, rather than simply observers of, the spectacle. A character comments at the end of Dryden's *The Wild Gallant* (1663) that "'tis like the last Act of a Play when People must marry; and if fathers will not consent then, they should throw Oranges at u'm from the Galleries."[27] Peter Holland cites Richard Legh's letter to his wife in 1667 complaining that the play showing at the King's House, *The Custome o' th' Country*, "is so damn'd bawdy that the Ladyes flung theire peares and fruites att the Actors."[28] Pear references are rare within drama, so mention of pears within a letter supports the theory that orchard fruits continued to be available even though the focus of dramatic allusions shifted toward oranges and wall fruits. The ladies may have been more willing to throw pears than expensive oranges and their phallic associations perhaps added point to the protest against bawdry.

Pepys recounts how Katherine Corey performed the part of Sempronia in Jonson's *Catiline* as an overt impersonation of the courtier Lady Harvey. Harvey persuaded the Lord Chamberlain to imprison the actress, but this decision was overturned by the king at the instigation of his mistress, the Countess of Castlemaine. The next time the play was performed, with Corey reprising her role and with the imitation "worse than ever," Pepys records that "Lady Harvy provided people to hiss [Corey] and fling oranges at her."[29] The throwing of fruit seems to have been a recognized element of the ritual of playhouse attendance and in Thomas Shadwell's 1676 satire on the Royal Society, *The Virtuoso*, it is incorporated within the drama as part of the enactment of dissent beyond the theatrical space. The play depicts a group of ribbon weavers who are protesting against the virtuoso, Sir Nicholas Gimcrack, in the belief that he has invented an "engine loom" that will put them out of business. In fact, they have been misinformed, for as Sir Nicholas exclaims, "I never invented anything of use in my life" and the central object of the satire is to demonstrate precisely this.[30] Nonetheless, the weavers set upon his friend and "*beat him, kick him, and fling oranges at him*" (5, 3, 62). The dramatic representation of public protest replicates the conventions associated with the expression of popular opinion within the theater, even though in practice it is probably unlikely that economically vulnerable weavers would have had access to oranges, or would have used them as missiles if they did.

The propulsion of fruit is frequently described using the verb "to fling" rather than the more common synonym "to throw," even when used in relation to specific types of fruits like oranges and pears for which there is no alliterative justification for the lexical preference. The *OED* has a fruit-related example as the first recorded usage of "fling" as a noun, citing Richard Harvey's 1590 text, *Plaine Percevall the Peace-maker of England*, which contains the lines, "Why may not we have one cast in his Orchard, and a fling at his Medlar tree?" Fling perhaps suggests a way of throwing that is particularly suited to fruit missiles or the technique required to detach fruit from a tree, but the verb may also connote a lack of careful aim that conveys additional derision. Fruit and oranges may be pleasant to eat and are frequently identified with luxury and elite taste, but the association of fruit with ideas of rottenness and a sexual fall means that it can provide an appropriate symbol of public scorn. It is flung rather than thrown within the performance, drawing on the audience's recognition that this is an acknowledged gesture of protest.

More often, however, oranges and other fruits are used as symbols of love, affection, or sexual desire. In George Etherege's *She Would If She Could* (1668), Sir Oliver Cockwood drops a China orange which rolls under the dining table where the rake Courtall has been concealed by Lady Cockwood.[31] Sir Oliver is very anxious to find the fruit since it was intended as a gift for his wife, in reparation for earlier misconduct. Its foreign origins are stressed in the description of it as "recommended . . . for one of the best that came over this year" (5, 1, 220–21). Lady Cockwood acknowledges, "'Tis a lovely orange indeed" (5, 1, 278), although this line may be delivered with irony in performance, given that Sir Oliver has just retrieved the orange from under the table. It is given and accepted as a token of love and repentance, but the use of the fruit in this capacity, replete with associations with theatrical performance, sexual laxity, and commodification, in addition to the more general overtones of female frailty, suggests to the audience the hypocritical nature of the union between Sir Oliver and Lady Cockwood, of which the wandering orange is an appropriate emblem.

Fruit is used to explore female sexuality in William Wycherley's city comedy *The Country Wife* (1675). The rakish protagonist Horner identifies "the orange wenches at the playhouses," as well as "city husbands" (cuckolds) and "fumbling keepers" (of mistresses), as suitable conduits for spreading the fake news of his sexual impotence.[32] As an impotent libertine, Horner appears to provide an oxymoronic embodiment of the conflicts of male identity in the Restoration, but the audience is aware that his supposed emasculation is a device to facilitate schemes of seduction. His attention is particularly focused on cuckolding his old acquaintance, Jack Pinchwife, a former rake who has recently married the "country wife" of the title and manifests the jealous and controlling spirit that customarily legitimates adultery within the comic drama of the period.[33] After Horner disappears offstage accompanied by Margery Pinchwife, his success is signaled when she returns bearing a hat full of oranges, as well as some equally suggestive "dried fruit" (3, 2, 484–87). Horner subsequently responds to Lady Fidget's equation of gastronomic and sexual appetite with the observation that "ceremony in love and eating is as ridiculous as in fighting. Falling on briskly is all should be done on those occasions" (5, 4, 80–82).

The play was first performed in January 1675 and thus at a time of year when there were unlikely to be supplies of fresh wall fruits such as peaches, apricots, or grapes. Like Margery, and like the audience of Dryden's *All for Love*, the playgoers would probably have been falling on imported oranges, but also "rivell'd" and scrotal fruits such as dried apricots, raisins, and prunes. Margery is disguised as a boy and when Horner tells her husband, "I have only given your little brother an orange, sir," Pinchwife's aside in response makes the innuendo explicit: "You have only squeezed my orange, I suppose, and given it me again" (3, 2, 489–90). John Crowne's *The Country Wit* of the following year uses the same fruit metaphor to represent being cuckolded, indicating that this was either a recognized euphemism before Wycherley's work, or that it became so afterward.[34]

Horner later complains that he is required to attend the ironically titled "virtuous gang" of ladies, whom Sir Jasper Fidget has entrusted to him. Maintaining the pretense of his physical incapacity, Horner grumbles, "I'd have you to know, since I cannot be your journeyman by night, I will not be your drudge by day, to squire your wife about and be your man of straw, or scarecrow, only to pies and jays that would be nibbling at your forbidden fruit" (4, 3, 82–87).

Sir Jasper interprets this as Horner's reluctance to chaperone women whose sexual favors he cannot enjoy, yet the biblical reference reinforces the intimations of female desire of the orange imagery. The audience is aware that far from being fruits that need to be protected from the magpies and jays, the virtuous gang are the predatory birds. They are all interested in nibbling Horner's fruits, even though these are forbidden, because they are proscribed by traditional moral codes, as well as through the myth of Horner's impotency. The play evokes the Genesis story, satirizing female sexuality not only through bestial imagery but also through the representation of fruit consumption.

Like the orange that Sir Oliver Cockwood drops under the table in *She Would If She Could* (5, 1, 219), the fruits that Horner gives to Margery are China oranges (4, 2, 11). This provides a linguistic anticipation of the scene in which Horner's successful seduction of the "virtuous gang" is signified by presents of china, including a suggestively shaped "roll-wagon," which is usually the source of visual comedy in performance (4, 3, 80–200, 186). Robert Markley has emphasized the irony that all the participants believe they are tricking the others, while all are ultimately "victims of the language that they finally cannot control," while Harold Weber suggests that the success of the scene resides in "the joy that Horner takes in revealing the hypocrisy of Lady Fidget and the stupidity of her husband."[35] China shops were regarded as sites of sexual assignation, which may perhaps explain the origins of the innuendo, but the shift in meaning, or "dialogic undermining of social discourse," that Markley notes seems to have inspired a continuing semiotic association of china, oranges, and sexual desire.[36] Susanna Centlivre's *The Busybody* (1709) combines a range of sexual references in portraying the attempts of the aging roué, Sir Francis Gripe, to unite himself in marriage with the body and, more important, the thirty thousand pound fortune, of his beautiful eighteen-year-old ward, Miranda. His intentions are signaled when he enters her room peeling an orange. Miranda protests that he cannot throw the peel in the chimney breast because she has concealed a monkey in there, which is "so wild 'twill break all my china" if it is released. The double entendre is extended by Miranda's suggestion that she is waiting for the man "that is to tame it."[37] The audience is aware that the chimney conceals Miranda's lover, who can tame a passion that has been rendered "wild" by confinement. The smashing of china and the monkey provide images of female sexual appetite to counter the orange eating that represents male desire.

But the denomination of the fruits given to Margery Pinchwife as China oranges also reinforces the foreign status of the oranges—first, through reference to the idea that oranges originated in China and, second, because, in this period, they were known to be imported from the Iberian Peninsula. They connote the world of commerce and trade so that illicit sexuality is connected to the rhetoric of exchange, luxury, and metropolitan commodification, and the sophisticated urban recreational setting of pleasure gardens and theatrical entertainment, which Margery is so anxious to enjoy (2, 1, 71–76). The rhetoric of fruit therefore reinforces the juxtaposition of country and city that is evident throughout *The Country Wife*, with the orange symbolizing urbanity rather than the rusticity of hardy orchard fruit. The continuing resonance of the metaphors is in line with the lack of resolution of the ending, with Horner unmarried and uncontained, and his deception undiscovered.[38] Margery is sent back to the country with a husband for whom she has no affection, having exposed herself through her unashamed acknowledgment of her fondness for Horner's fruit.

The opening of George Etherege's *The Man of Mode* (1676) follows the tradition identified by Nunn within Renaissance drama, with the representation of the onstage buying and consumption of fruit replicating the activities of the audience. Webster argues that the play is a response to the decline in the social, economic, and political status of libertinism in the mid-1670s, but critics are divided over the extent to which it depicts the reformation of the rake hero Dorimant, whom Webster identifies as a portrait of the Earl of Rochester.[39] Susan Staves locates the play as part of the movement in middle and late Restoration drama in which "marriage is increasingly represented as a problematic institution."[40] The opening scene shows Dorimant in his dressing room bargaining for fruit with "Foggy Nan, the orange-woman."[41] Dorimant acknowledges that "fruit is refreshing in the morning," but Nan is treated with disrespect, described as "that overgrown jade with the flasket of guts before her" (1, 1, 23). A "flasket" is a basket that could be hung around the neck, in which a huckster's goods would be displayed. Here, the fruit is obscured by Nan's ample flesh, which spills over into the basket. Dorimant addresses her familiarly as "double-tripe" (1, 1, 27), while both he and his friend Medley refer to her as a bawd (1, 1, 45; 1, 1, 79). Robert Markley has identified these exchanges as evidence of "a not-too-subtle class antagonism" between the libertine aristocrats and the prosperous capitalists, Nan and Tom the shoemaker, who challenge their discourse and authority.[42] Medley's name implies a miscellany but also perhaps a medlar, a fruit which is only suitable for consumption when it has started to rot. His opening words, "Dorimant, my life, my joy, my darling sin!" and Nan's response, "Lord, what a filthy trick these men have got of kissing one another!" (1, 1, 73–76), have been cited in arguments to support associations between libertinism and sodomy.[43] The suggestions of libertine effeminacy may be reinforced in performance by Dorimant's protracted preoccupation with choosing fruit, but the polymorphous nature of libertine sexuality is signaled by the questioning of Nan that accompanies this activity. "Fruit woman" was a synonym for a bawd, but Nan functions more as a genteel matchmaker, informing the rakes of attractive young women and wealthy heiresses. This fits the stereotype of the loquacious orange woman, as shown in Pepys's portrayal of Mary Meggs as a source of theatrical gossip as well as a conveyer of messages and assignations,[44] but the assimilation of the role of matchmaker with the sale of fruit also invites the identification of the two commodities.

Nan's conversation with Dorimant switches between an account of "a young gentlewoman lately come to town with her mother" (1, 1, 48–49) and praise of her merchandise as "the best fruit has come to town t'year" (1, 1, 33–34). Her boast that her fruit is "all culled ware" (1, 1, 38) may relate to the circumstances of its initial harvesting, but since this comment is in response to Dorimant's reference to "the nasty refuse of your shop," it probably means that the fruit has been selected by hand, instead of being the leftover, damaged, or dropped fruit, which itinerant traders were often accused of vending.[45] The implication is that the young woman has been similarly carefully "culled." When Nan urges Dorimant to eat a peach since "it comes from the stone; 'tis better than any Newington you have tasted" (1, 1, 54–55), it immediately follows her description of Harriet Woodvill, and the suggestion that "there are few finer women . . . and a hugeous fortune" (1, 1, 52–53). The Old Newington or Royal Newington peach was an early ripening variety, originating in the glasshouses in Walworth in south London, and available around the time of Bartholomew Fair in August. The suggestion that the flesh comes easily from the stone indicates that the peach is a freestone rather than a clingstone variety, but it also conveys that it is at a perfect point of ripeness, a comment that can be related to Harriet as well as the peach. The elision of the two is reinforced when Dorimant insists that Nan will only be paid for the fruit when she brings "the gentlewoman hither" (1, 1, 100–101).

The unacknowledged and marginalized performances of the itinerant vendors that Korda has identified are thus parodically incorporated into the staged production. Through representing acts of exchange, the audience is invited to scrutinize the etiquette of the commodified relationships within the playhouse. The respectable figure of Harriet Woodvill is, however, symbolized by a peach rather than an apple or orange. She is associated with fruit which, although in practice probably raised by a commercial grower, carries literary echoes of the walled gardens of the gentleman or aristocrat, rather than of the husbandman's orchard or imports from abroad. The peach is both tender and wholesome and the reference to the Newington indicates that Harriet is at a point of perfect ripeness and ready for consumption in the form of consummation.

This opening scene is referenced throughout the play, as the purchase and consumption of fruit are used as a source of comic sexual innuendo. After Bellinda has spent the night with Dorimant, she attempts to deceive his previous mistress, Mrs. Loveit, with the suggestion that she has been to the fruit market, motivated by "a strange desire . . . to eat some fresh nectarines." The double entendre is reinforced when she replies to Mrs. Loveit's question, "And had you any?" with the smug response, "The best I ever tasted" (5, 1, 49–51). When she later turns faint at the news that Dorimant is approaching, the waiting woman Pert responds, "She has eaten too much fruit, I warrant you," later adding, "I was a strange devourer of fruit when I was young—so ravenous" (5, 1, 85–91). Bellinda's supposedly unrestrained taste for fruit exposes her sexual appetite and her choice of nectarines shows that she aspires to consume the delicate wall fruits of the nobility rather than the playhouse oranges or orchard fruits that might be more fitting to her social status. Like that other fruit enthusiast, Margery Pinchwife, Bellinda is denied a happy ending and is left to repent her folly as the company celebrates the marriages of Young Bellair and Emilia and the prospective union of Dorimant and Harriet.

Much of the critical debate over the play has focused on whether Dorimant's conduct toward his mistresses constitutes a critique of libertinism, whether there is any reason to believe that he has reformed by the end, and who wins in the battle of wits between Harriet and Dorimant.[46] These questions can be illuminated by attention to fruit, since Bellinda's explicit acknowledgment of her inappropriate desire can be interpreted as a legitimation of Dorimant's desertion and his union with the virtuous Harriet. Whereas Bellinda has shown her weakness by constructing herself as a voracious consumer of fruit, Harriet is figured as a freestone peach and therefore ripe for consumption by Dorimant. Bellinda frames fruit metaphors both to conceal and to represent her sexual transgression, whereas Harriet is objectified in metaphors constructed by others. Bellinda eats while Harriet is eaten. Critical readings have highlighted the independence of Harriet and her success in the battle of wits between herself and Dorimant, arguing that "she is able to play Dorimant's game better than either he or his mistresses."[47] Yet the resonance of the fruit imagery undermines the linguistic play to complicate the gender politics. Harriet's wit functions to provide piquancy but does not necessarily subvert the representation of women as objects of consumption, fixed by images imposed on them.

The equation of fruit consumption with sexuality and female frailty invokes forbidden fruits from both biblical and classical traditions, and the cultural condemnation of women as illegitimate consumers rather than the consumed is reinforced by the fate of Dorimant's cast off mistresses. The fruit imagery therefore provides a misogynistic undercurrent within the scene, challenging the idea that Harriet is entirely "triumphant" and providing a reification in fruit of Robert Markley's argument that "the ending of the play . . . pits our expectations of a happy ending against our knowledge of the characters and the world they inhabit."[48] The suggestion that Dorimant's commodification of women survives the romantic denouement helps to explain his secret assurances to Mrs. Loveit that he is only marrying for money (5, 2, 327–28), assurances which have proved problematic in those readings that have emphasized his reformation. A more general cultural ambivalence toward the happy-ending convention may be discerned in the tradition of creating sequels to popular dramas, presenting the disintegration of the romantic unions established at the end of the original play.[49]

Fruit also provides a subversive ideological undercurrent, but of a different kind, in Aphra Behn's *The City Heiress* (1682), which Susan Owen, in an argument that seeks to "reinstate gender in the language of 'high' politics," has identified as a Tory response to the proposed revival of Shadwell's *The Libertine*.[50] Behn's "old Tory Knight," Sir Anthony Meriwill, uses an image of ripe apples to celebrate the beauty and simplicity of country girls, in contrast to the artificial and proud women of the city. He tells his nephew Sir Charles that in the country "every Grove affords us Rustick Beauties, that know no Pride nor Painting . . . Fine wholsome Girls that fall like ruddy Fruit, fit for the gathering."[51] The girls are ripe and thus sexually available, but they are also shown as having ripened naturally, coming to maturity in the appropriate season, instead of being forced to develop early through artificial husbandry techniques. They are hardy orchard fruits rather than the wall fruits or hothouse fruits that require special care to flourish; they are associated with domestic production rather than the complex exchange system on which imported fruits depend. Yet these connotations of wholesomeness, naturalness, and sexual availability do not appeal to Sir Charles, who has been introduced at the start of the play as one of the "young imitating Fops in Town" (1, 1, 29). He rejects his uncle's suggestion with a brief and dismissive, "Oh, Sir, I cannot relish the coarse Fare"

(1, 1, 421) and his search for a partner is exclusively concentrated among the more carefully cultivated women of the city. Even for the Tory Sir Charles, women who are associated with natural and domestic orchard produce are homely and unappealing, unable to compete with imported goods or the artificial products of the hothouse and hot bed that signify urban sophistication and expensive delicacy.

Behn's hero is named Tom Wilding, a surname shared with the protagonists of Thomas D'Urfey's *Sir Barnaby Whigg* and, later, Henry Fielding's *The Temple Beau* (1730).[52] As with Wildair in George Farquhar's *The Constant Couple* (1699) and *Sir Harry Wildair* (1701), as well as Richard Wilkinson's *Vice Reclaim'd* (1703), and Wildish in Sedley's *The Mulberry-Garden*, this was primarily a type name to suggest wild and rakish behavior. But *wilding* is a term for a wild or crab apple, used to describe a tree grown from seed rather than a graft, and so a product of sexual rather than asexual reproduction. Wildings were therefore identified with hybrid vigor in fruticultural writings and they were seen as a source of new varieties.[53] In Behn's play, this fruit reference reinforces the recurrent allusions to uncertainties over the parentage of various characters and the preoccupation with personal and political illegitimacy that displays Behn's Tory ideology, but it also contributes to the identification of the rake character with positive qualities. This is in line with Owen's argument that both Behn and D'Urfey present Tory libertinism as "something jolly, wild, and cavalier, and preferable to whey-faced Whiggery and puritan sexual hypoc-risy."[54] While naturalness and hardihood are rejected by the rakes when associated with women, they acquire more positive connotations as aspects of male behavior.

But although Sir Charles Meriwill is reluctant to accept the country women who are characterized as natural and humble orchard fruits, the commercial-ization of fruit production associated with the emerging capitalist economy generates images that are equally susceptible to negative and misogynistic inflection. Increasing commodification and the need to keep fruits for longer periods and transport them to market meant a movement toward harvesting fruits—particularly delicate wall fruits—while still green. *The Fruiterers Secrets* recommends that stone fruits such as "Apricocks, Peaches, Peare-plums, Damsons, bullase, &c." should be picked while green and then packed into a sieve or basket lined with nettles "which will hasten the ripening of them, make them keepe their colour, and cause them to eate as kindly as if they had been fully ripened upon the tree. But if you let them hang upon the tree until they be full ripe, they will drop off, for the most part: and the rest that hang, will quickly rot after that they be gathered, and doe little service, except they bee presently used."[55] The movement toward picking fruits before they were properly ripened reinforces long-standing anxieties derived from Galenic medicine about the dangers of consuming green fruit.[56] There were equivalent concerns that the protracted supply chain would result in overripe or rotten fruits, which were regarded as equally threatening, and these preoccupations are manifested in a medicalization of fruit imagery in drama, which is very different from the association with healthy and natural abundance in the poetry of the period. Fears of the green and rotten fruit that were identified with an increasingly commercial market provide metaphors for the expression of anxieties about a general commodification of sexuality.

In *She Would If She Could* (1668), Courtall assures Lady Cockwood that he "may more safely swear that Sir Oliver has been constant to your ladyship, than that a girl of twelve-years has her maiden-head this warm and ripening age" (3, 3, 418–21). Just as fruits are being ripened before their natural time, so young girls are being forced to premature experience in the overheated sexual economy. Shadwell's *Virtuoso* opens with a discussion between two "gentlemen of wit and sense" on the conduct of modern youth, with rueful condemnation of a young man boasting of his third attack of venereal disease, "when you would think he was not old enough to be able to get one." This elicits the response that "these youths, like untimely fruit, are like to be rotten before they are ripe" (1, 1, 49–57). Young men, like fruit, are plucked green and taken to market too soon so that they go straight from being underripe to decaying from venereal disease, without ever reaching the point of perfect maturity. This contrasts with the fruits in the country estate of Penshurst, which ripen "each in his own time," the ripe "Rustick Beauties" celebrated by Behn's Sir Anthony Meriwill, or Harriet in *The Man of Mode* who has come to town from the country like a ripe peach. Metropolitan society is a hothouse or a hot bed, fostering precocious development, which is portrayed through images of physical corruption, and the sense of unnaturalness is reinforced when fruit imagery is applied to boys rather than to girls.

The denomination of young women as green fruit also incorporates allusions to green sickness. This has been identified with the condition that is now called chlorosis, or hypochromic anemia, which is particularly common in young women, but in writings of the Renaissance and early modern period it was regarded as resulting from repressed female sexuality.[57] The name is normally assumed to derive from the green tinge observable in the skin of some anemic patients, but it could equally come from the identification of the condition with adolescent or unripe girls. References to green fruit, green sickness, or the "green pip" (a depression of spirits related to the female condition) reinforce the association of adolescent sexuality with unhealthiness, unnaturalness, and commodification.[58] Ken Albala suggests that the "usual cure" for green sickness, marriage and sex, ensured that "medical theory was used as an instrument for male dominance."[59]

The sexually freighted discussion among Dorimant, Medley, and the orange woman that follows the men's embrace in *The Man of Mode* draws on the dangers of green fruit. Medley accuses the orange woman of being "in fee with the doctors to sell green fruit to the gentry that the crudities may breed diseases" (1, 1, 82–83). The term "crudities" refers to imperfectly digested material in the stomach that was associated with the consumption of green fruit and was identified in contemporary medical works as a source of disease.[60] But the explicit meaning of Medley's claims, that the fruit sellers conspire with the doctors to generate business by causing stomach ailments, is inflected by the persistent sexual resonances of the fruit references within the play to carry an alternative meaning relating to venereal disease. Young girls were valued as sexual partners in part because they were thought less likely to be infected than "riper" women, but, as *The Virtuoso* indicates, even green fruits can be subject to decay.

Green fruit can also be used to connote greenness in the sense of naïveté and ignorance as well as sexual immaturity. Etherege's *She Would If She Could* and Sedley's *The Mulberry-Garden* both suggest that, compared to other places of fashionable resort, the Mulberry-Garden was associated with the more unsophisticated, "green" visitors to the town. In Etherege's play, it is the site of a meeting between the city rakes Courtall and Freeman and the country girls Ariana and Gatty (2, 1). In *The Mulberry-Garden*, two foppish characters, Modish and Estridge, falsely boast to Wildish of their success in seducing "two young juicy girls that stick as close as the bark to the tree, and part as unwillingly from us as green fruit does from the stone" (4, 1, 85–86). The oxymoronic image suggests that the girls are simultaneously ripe (juicy) and therefore sexually available, but also that they are green fruit. This suggests physical unripeness, as well as the idea that they are inexperienced and credulous, supposedly manifested in their unfashionable fondness for their suitors. But the duplicity of the gallants is signaled by the inconsistency of the imagery, and the girls prove themselves to be neither as green nor as juicy as the men would like to make out.

In John Dryden's *All for Love* (1677), Marc Antony complains that he first fell in love with Cleopatra when she was "too young to know it" (2, 1, 265). He "left th'acknowledgement for time to ripen" (2, 1, 266), but before he could reap the harvest:

> *Caesar* stept in, and with a greedy hand
> Pluck'd the green fruit, ere the first blush of red,
> Yet cleaving to the bough. (2, 1, 267–69)

This willingness to wait for Cleopatra to "ripen" and fall from the bough is juxtaposed with Caesar's precipitance, which is presented as greedy, unhealthy, and unnatural. Like a selfish child, he plucks the fruit before it is ripe to engross it to himself. In contrast, Antony and Cleopatra's mature love is like an orange tree on which blossom and fruit constantly succeed each other. As Antony exclaims,

> There's no satiety of Love, in thee;
> Enjoy'd, thou still art new; perpetual Spring
> Is in thy armes; the ripen'd fruit but falls,
> And blossoms rise to fill its empty place. (3, 1, 24–27)

Just as the orange eschews the natural order by producing fruit and blossom at the same time, so the love between Antony and Cleopatra defies the normal pattern of ripening, maturation, and rotting that was associated with both fruit and passion. It flowers and fruits simultaneously and is both attractive and productive. Moreover, the existence of blossoms alongside the fruit ensures that it will continue to yield.

Cleopatra's ripe love is relished by the enamored Antony, but in other texts the dominance of rakish philosophy ensures that female sexual desire generates disgust, even when it is associated with the ripeness of a woman who has just reached maturity. In Congreve's *The Old Bachelor* (1693), the fickle rake Vain-love receives a passionate love letter, supposedly from the beautiful and virtuous Araminta. The letter has been forged by a rival on the (accurate) assumption that Vainlove will be deterred by the idea of reciprocated female affection. His friend Sharper urges him to go "To her, Man," arguing that Araminta is "a delicious Mellon pure and consenting ripe, and only waits thy cutting up—She has been breeding Love to thee all this while, and just now she's deliver'd of it."[61] Ripeness suggests sexual availability and consummation is portrayed in terms of consumption, which is preceded by violent dissection. Araminta's melon is ready for the penetration of Vainlove's knife, but the significance of fruit as a symbol of both sexual congress and sexual reproduction is manifested in the development of the image into a reference to Araminta becoming pregnant and giving birth. This may draw on the association of pregnancy with fruit consumption seen in Chaucer's "Merchant's Tale" and the identification of the pregnant female form with the melon. Araminta is simultaneously the fruit that awaits male consumption in an image of passive sexuality and the fruiting body within which love gestates, ready to burst forth as an autonomous entity.

These images of pregnancy and birth do nothing to assuage the anxieties about female sexuality manifested by Vainlove, who responds that Araminta's love is "an untimely Fruit, and she has miscarried." Vainlove believes that it is not appropriate for a woman to express her feelings before the man has declared himself, so, in the birth metaphor, Araminta's love is premature and will not survive, and, in the fruit metaphor, it is an untimely fruit, rather than the perfectly ripened melon described by Sharper. Melons were usually produced in this period within hothouses or hot beds and therefore signify artificial methods of cultivation to encourage fruit to ripen out of season. The ripeness of Araminta is regarded as unappetizing by Vainlove because it appears to manifest autonomous female desire as well as images of pregnancy, but Vainlove's distaste is identified by Sharper as symptomatic of "a sickly peevish Appetite." He can "only chew Love and cannot digest it." Vainlove responds to this accusation by arguing that he can digest love when he feeds himself, but he hates to be "cramm'd" (4, 5, 14–19, 76). While Sharper relates his friend's reluctance to consume the fruit to images of sickness and disease, Vainlove draws on the language of force feeding. He is characterized in the dramatis personae as "Capricious in his love" and associates female desire and reciprocated passion with lack of control and the nausea of overfeeding.

Araminta and her friend Belinda are figured as hothouse fruits, in contrast to the "plump, cherry-cheeked country girls" (4, 8, 26) encountered by Araminta when she goes shopping. In gratitude for Araminta's assistance in acquiring a more fashionable appearance, one of the girls produces "two apples, piping hot, out of her under-petticoat pocket" (4, 8, 41–42). Cooked apples are here used as a snack but one that connotes rusticity. These anonymous daughters of "A Country Squire" (4, 8, 22), like the unnamed girls in *The City Heiress*, are associated with the produce of the orchard, and their sexual availability is signaled by where they keep their hot apples. But even the sophisticated Araminta is unappetizing to Vainlove because of her apparent willingness to offer the fruits of her love, so he is reluctant to put his knife into her melon. Weber has interpreted the "sickly peevish Appetite" as a reference to Vainlove's impotence, which he associates with the transformation of the rake stereotype that takes place after 1685.[62] Yet the fruit imagery in the dialogue with Sharper invokes a more general cultural association between male disgust and the explicit display of female fruit/sexual desire. I would argue that Sharper's imagery invites the Restoration audience to share Vainlove's squeamishness at the idea of being crammed, and it is only when the letter is shown to be a forgery that he can accept the love and pluck the fruit that he did not want to have forced on him. His appetite only functions if he is in control of consumption.

The extension of the fruit season that was at the heart of the horticultural innovations of the Restoration involved the production of very early fruit, but it also encouraged the development of methods to ensure that harvesting could continue well into the winter months. Vainlove rejects the metonymic melon that is Araminta in her prime, but where ripeness is associated with women in the autumn and winter of life, it is a source of more generally shared disgust. This provides scope for misogynistic comedy, manifesting ideas of female monstrosity, which Susan Owen has associated with the political rhetoric of both Whigs and Tories.[63] In *The Man of Mode*, the "antiquated beauty," Lady Woodvill condemns "the depraved appetite of this vicious age," which "tastes nothing but green fruit and loathes it when 'tis kindly ripened" (4, 1, 41–42). Lady Wishfort, the fifty-five-year-old widow in William Congreve's *The Way of the World* (1700), is described as "panting ripe,"[64] and in George Farquhar's *Love and a Bottle* (1698), the matronly servant Mrs. Pindress makes sexual overtures to a young page who is a woman in disguise. Her sexual appetite is shown in her declaration "O my little Green-Gooseberry, my Teeth waters at ye" (5, 60). The dessert gooseberries which were suitable for consumption as raw fruits were reddish in color, so a green gooseberry is either a cooking variety, which would be sharp to the taste, or, as seems most likely here, an unripe specimen.[65] Either way, it would be unlikely to make good eating and Mrs. Pindress may be exposing her social position, and referencing the presumed status of the page, in expressing her desire for the humble gooseberry rather than for a more refined fruit. The lexis of consumption reinforces the association with unnatural appetites as the older women seek to indulge in fruits that are unsuitable either because they are young, green, and sexually immature or because they are of the same sex, or both. Young girls ripen too early and old women stay ripe for too long. Even women in their prime can cause nausea if they are perceived to be cramming their prematurely ripened fruits down the throats of men instead of passively waiting to be consumed. The period in which the fruits of femininity are desirable is shown to be limited and, above all, it is defined by men.

Yet the preference for young lovers over old ones is not uniquely male and numerous plots revolve around heroines who scheme to ensure that they are united with the youthful hero rather than an older, wealthier suitor, who may be the father or uncle of the favored lover, and/or the guardian of the potential bride. Women, one of the characters in Centlivre's *The Gamester* (1705) argues, "generally love green Fruit best" and will favor a young man over "a Lover ripe with Discretion."[66] In Congreve's *Love for Love* (1695), the romantic heroine, Angelica, engages in a flirtatious exchange with the aging and mercenary beau Sir Sampson Legend, whom Markley identifies as "a Restoration wit grown old and tyrannical" and Weber sees as an "unnatural monster."[67] Like Old Bellair in *The Man of Mode*, Sir Sampson is attempting to seduce the heroine, even though he is fully aware that in doing so he is in competition with his own son. Sir Sampson boasts of his virility in a way that, Markley argues, "prepares the audience for his gulling."[68] Angelica plays on this vanity by declaring that she has known "very considerable Beaus that set a good Face upon fifty" and has seen "fifty in a side Box, by Candle-Light, out-blossom five and twenty."[69] The side boxes were usually located immediately to the right and left of the stage in the Restoration theater, in front of the pit, so that although they had a much more restricted view of the play than the front boxes, they provided an excellent view of other members of the audience (Figure 18). Mark Dawson suggests that these boxes tend to be identified with fops and beaux and the references within the plays confirm the association with those who were more interested in the social element of theatrical attendance than the play itself.[70] Each box accommodated up to twenty people, so they would have been rather cramped.[71] Angelica claims that within the transformative and artificially illuminated space of the theater, a man of fifty can rival one of half his age, thereby not only feeding the aspirations of Sir Sampson to displace his son in

A Side Box.

Figure 18. "A Side Box," printed for R. Sayer & J. Bennett, London 1781. A gentleman offers a peach to a lady in a side box at the theater, indicating the association of fruit with theatrical attendance and courtship. © Trustees of the British Museum. All rights reserved.

her affections but also emphasizing the connection between the theater and ideas of transformation and thus immorality and deceit.

Sir Sampson rejects Angelica's idea that men of fifty should be seen in the flattering light of the theater and distances himself from the effeminacy of attendance in the side box. Instead he adapts Angelica's histrionic metaphor to provide a horticultural image which associates his age with ideas of strength, vigor, and naturalness that are contrasted with the tenderness, affectation, and preoccupation with external appearance (outsides) of contemporary youth: "Outsides, Outsides; a pize take 'em, meer Outsides. Hang your Side-Box Beaus; no, I'm none of those, none of your forc'd Trees, that pretend to blossom in the Fall; and Bud when they should bring forth Fruit: I am of a long-liv'd Race, and inherit Vigour, none of my Ancestors marry'd till fifty; yet they begot Sons and Daughters 'till fourscore" (5, 2, 20–25). Sir Sampson's response draws on Angelica's allusion to blossoming, and the idea of the artificiality of candlelight, to reorient the reference to the side box from a theatrical box to one used for the cultivation of fruit trees.[72] The trees would be kept in boxes in the green-house over the winter and then wheeled out into the garden at the end of the spring, thereby disrupting the normal pattern of the seasons (see Figure 10). Sir Sampson uses horticultural lexis to compare himself to a hardy orchard tree that is "long-liv'd" and full of natural "Vigour," in contrast to the artificiality of the box-grown trees that are a metaphor for young men, such as his estranged and disinherited son. These trees "Bud when they should bring forth Fruit," indicating that they are encouraged to blossom out of season in the autumn. They are identified as unnatural, like the cramped side boxes in the theater, but there is also a suggestion that this disruption of the natural pattern renders these trees infertile, producing only blossoms and buds, in line with the argument in Chapter 2 that the trees within British orangeries were not expected to fruit. Hothouse plants are implicitly associated with the artifice, pretension, and disguise of the theater and with precocity and the disruption of the natural pattern of reproduction. In contrast, orchard trees are healthy and produce abundant fruit over a sustained period. Sir Sampson is the apple tree to Valentine's ornamental orange. This anticipates the celebration of orchard fruit that characterized eighteenth-century georgic, and the preoccupation with unnatural hothouse fruit of the Romantic-period novel, yet this image is ultimately undermined in the play by the fact that Angelica, like Emilia in *The Man of Mode* and Angelica in *The Gamester*, ultimately prefers the small green fruit of the young man to the wrinkled john apples of the old one. Sir Sampson invokes the honest strength of orchard fruit but only in order to forward his schemes of duplicity.

Colley Cibber's *Love's Last Shift* (1696) has been identified as one of the earliest of the sentimental comedies that emerged at the end of the seventeenth century when there was considerable agitation for the suppression of the playhouses.[73] It portrays the reformation of the central character, Loveless, who has left his faithful and beautiful wife Amanda, after only a year of marriage, to embark on a career of rakish debauchery. Aparna Gollapudi has argued that the play should be classified as a reform comedy rather than a sentimental comedy, emphasizing its satirical elements and defending it against suggestions that the final reform is implausible. She provides a detailed analysis of the "visual codes" that anticipate the moral transformation of Loveless, suggesting that the key to making this dramatically convincing is to represent him as destitute at the start of the play and therefore with a vested interest in reformation.[74] But one aspect of the play that merits further consideration is the way the trajectory of the drama, and the reformation of Loveless, are framed by, and manifested in, fruit imagery. Loveless employs fruit metaphors in both the opening and closing scenes to express first his rakish philosophy and then his uxorious reformation. In justifying his desertion of Amanda, he explains: "The World to me is a Garden stockt with all sorts of Fruit, where the greatest Pleasure we can take, is in the Variety of Taste: But a Wife is an Eternal Apple-tree; after a pull or two, you are sure to set your Teeth on Edge."[75] The "Eternal Apple-tree" references the Genesis story but also associates apples with the mundane and quotidian. They are the fruit of the laboring classes and for the man about town a diet of apples quickly becomes monotonous. He requires a variety of fruit to stimulate his appetite. Yet the servant, Snap, picks up and develops his master's wife/apple comparison to highlight the egotism at the heart of libertine behavior. Of Loveless's brief married life, Snap comments, "I warrant you grudg'd another Man a Bit of her, tho' you valu'd her no more than you would a half-eaten Pippin, that had lain a Week a sunning in a Parlour Window" (1, 1, 64–67). The most neglectful husband can be roused to jealousy if another man shows interest in his wife. This belief is at the heart of the play's plot by which Loveless is tricked into courting and falling in love with Amanda. Snap's image of rotting and half-eaten fruit creates an unappealing metaphor for married life particularly since the choice of a pippin, an especially homely type of apple, figures the wife as plain and uninviting.

By the end of the play, Loveless has been led to recognize the beauty as well as the virtues of Amanda, while Snap has slept with her woman, whom he has been forced to marry. As he ruefully comments, "Little did my Master and I think last Night we were robbing our own Orchards" (5, 3, 179–81). For Loveless, however, the fruit metaphor has evolved from the orchard reference to an image of the hothouse, signifying his growing recognition of the value of married life. He explains this new philosophy to a friend's bride, in response to her question of whether he can find a recipe to preserve love beyond the honeymoon:

> *Loveless:* The Receipt is easily found, Madam; Love's a tender Plant which can't live out of a warm Bed: You must take care, with undissembled Kindness, to keep him from the Northern Blast of Jealousy.
> *Narcissa:* But I have heard, your experienc'd Lovers make use of Coldness, and that's more agreeable to my Inclination.
> *Loveless:* Coldness, Madam, before Marriage, like throwing a little Water upon a clear Fire, makes it burn the fiercer; but after Marriage, you must still take care to lay on fresh Fuel. (5, 3, 52–63)

The "warm Bed" suggests the importance of sex within marriage, endorsing the uxorious values characteristic of sentimental comedy. But the passage can also be regarded as a rewriting of the fruit metaphor established at the beginning of the play. Rather than seeing his wife as a hardy orchard fruit that is always available from an old apple tree, and always tastes the same, Loveless has come to appreciate Amanda as a sophisticated hothouse commodity that needs to be nurtured and cultivated in a hot bed. While the orchard tree will keep producing fruit even if it is left to itself, married love needs to be reared under cover and not only protected from the wind but provided with artificial heat. The winds of jealousy and coldness are no longer stimulants to love within marriage but are presented as threats to successful cultivation. This image therefore challenges the identification of marital fidelity as lower class and unfashionable, like an orchard apple tree, and instead suggests that married love is newly fashionable, like the tender and exotic fruits being produced within the heated greenhouses or hot beds of the aristocracy. It embodies the change in drama from the end of the seventeenth century, as audiences became more bourgeois, requiring more spectacular and less risqué theater, and the development of more moral characters with a greater emphasis on the virtues of constancy and fidelity and the reform plots that Gollapudi has emphasized.[76]

But along with the decline of libertine comedy came the decline of fruit, references to which are significantly less abundant in the plays of the eighteenth century than in their Restoration antecedents. This may be because the sexual symbolism of fruit was less appropriate in the more morally censorious climate of the turn of the century, but it may also be a consequence of changing patterns of fruit consumption during the performance. While Renaissance drama is replete with references to the apples that the audience members were buying and eating, the drama of the early Restoration most commonly depicts the purchase and consumption of oranges. While theater goers may well have been happy to eat the apples and pears that were on sale in the theaters, they defined themselves as quintessential consumers of citrus, and this self-construction was manifested within the drama on stage. By the end of the century, however, the physical depiction of oranges within the plays had begun to decline and most references to fruit after Etherege's *The Man of Mode* in 1676 tend to be in the form of metaphors or symbols rather than physical depictions. As has been shown, these metaphors fulfill a range of functions, suggesting fecundity or sexual availability, or representing women as green fruit or ripe fruit or forbidden fruit. The early texts have these symbolic resonances, too, but they are combined with the portrayal of acts of fruit consumption.

In a departure from the conventions of Restoration and early eighteenth-century drama, the action of George Farquhar's *The Recruiting Officer* (1706) is based outside London, in Shropshire. When the recruiting party arrives in the county town of Shrewsbury, Sergeant Kite succeeds in tricking two of the locals into joining the army that is being raised to fight in the War of Spanish Succession. The recruits are called Thomas Appletree and Costar Pearmain, the latter combining the name for an itinerant trader associated with the sale of fruit with the generic name for pear-shaped apple varieties such as the Worcester Pearmain. Both are yeomen, hailing from Herefordshire, the county adjoining Shropshire and a center of apple production, whose orchards are celebrated in John Philips's *Cider*. The characters of Appletree and Pearmain reinforce the stereotype of the hardy English apple, for, as Appletree exclaims to Captain Plume, "If you have two honester, simpler Lads in your Company than we twa ben—I'll say no more."[77] Their simplicity is shown in the ease with which they are conned into enlisting, but their decision is also informed by their bravery, nationalism, and independence, which reinforces the positive connotations of the apple as a symbol of Englishness.

A marked decline even in the metaphorical uses of fruit is discernible after Fielding's plays in the 1720s and 1730s, although one notable exception to this trend is Richard Brinsley Sheridan's *The Rivals* (1775), which deploys fruit imagery at strategic points in the plot. The first occasion is during a conversation between Sir Anthony Absolute and Mrs. Malaprop, in which Sir Anthony condemns the female knowledge that is acquired from a circulating library. Such a library is, he declares, "an ever-green tree of diabolical knowledge! It blossoms through the year! And depend on it, Mrs. Malaprop, that they who are so fond of handling the leaves will long for the fruit at last."[78] The passage draws on the equation of tree leaves and book leaves, which informs Ralph Austen's spiritual and horticultural allegory but with a very different moral purpose. The suggestion that the knowledge gained from the leaves of a romantic novel will encourage young women to seek the fruits of sexual experience invites condemnation of female behavior through reference to the Genesis story, but it also suggests a fear that women are aspiring to be active consumers of fruit, novels, and sex, instead of being the fruit consumed by predatory males. The criticism of popular literature provides a clear signal to the audience that Sir Anthony is an unsympathetic character and it identifies the opposition to female fruit consumption as part of a reactionary rhetoric that is antithetical to the ethos of the play.

In a subsequent exchange with young Captain Absolute, Mrs. Malaprop condemns men who are only interested in "the worthless flower of beauty." The Captain responds: "It is but too true indeed, ma'am. Yet I fear our ladies should share the blame. They think our admiration of *beauty* so great, that *knowledge* in *them* would be superfluous. Thus, like garden-trees, they seldom show fruit, till time has robbed them of the more specious blossom. Few, like Mrs. Malaprop and the orange-tree, are rich in both at once!" (3, 3, 16–21). In this speech, the association of knowledge with fruit is given positive connotations despite the inevitable biblical resonance of any reference to fruit and female knowledge. Yet the dramatic irony ensures that the audience is aware that Absolute is flattering and mocking Mrs. Malaprop. The words that he addresses to her face are juxtaposed with the letter that he has written in the assumed character of Ensign Beverley, in which he describes her as an "old weather-beaten she-dragon" whose "ridiculous vanity . . . makes her dress up her coarse features and deck her dull chat with hard words which she don't understand" (3, 3, 58, 63–65). While Absolute appears to be praising the orange tree which produces fruits and flowers at the same time, contrasting it favorably with garden trees which flower and fruit in sequence, his praise is ironic. His true preference is for the "specious blossom" of orchard trees like the apple and pear represented by Lydia Languish, rather than for the exotic citrus fruit of Mrs. Malaprop. Mrs. Malaprop responds with the declaration that Captain Absolute is "the very pineapple of politeness." The pineapple is a symbol of social aspiration which befits Mrs. Malaprop's pretentions to knowledge and fashionable gentility.[79]

The reference to the pineapple shows the increasing familiarity of this fruit by the final quarter of the eighteenth century, but it also reinforces Mrs. Malaprop's inability to read cultural codes and recognize the mockery of Jack Absolute's fruit metaphor and the implicit elevation of orchard over citrus fruit within his ironic praise for the latter. For Absolute, the natural simplicity of the garden tree and its orchard fruit is identified with fashionable taste, in contrast to the artificiality of the orange or the pineapple. This resembles the terms of the celebration of orchard fruit that, as the following chapters will show, is articulated in the georgic poetry of the eighteenth century and the novels of the Romantic period. In seventeenth-century poetry, the celebration of plenty as a manifestation of divine providence and social harmony is subverted by occasional intimations of the dangers of commodification and the need to control abundance, which is constructed as sinister through associations with rampant sexuality. These suggestions are developed and expanded in Restoration drama, where fruit is not presented growing in orchards and gardens but is part of an urban economy of pleasure. For the metropolitan libertines and ladies, domestically produced orchard fruits are a nostalgic ideal against which the corruptions of the present can be measured, and fruit is an object of exchange within a system of commercial relationships. This representation manifests the efflorescence of the consumer economy in the seventeenth century, and Paulina Kewes has traced how play texts themselves are increasingly commodified as part of the emergent publishing industry.[80]

Yet, as this chapter has shown, the objectification of individuals manifested in fruit symbolism, while partly a result of the reification of capitalism, is also complicated and reinforced through intersection with the symbolism derived from biblical and classical associations of literary tradition. This is given a distinct gender dimension through ideas of the forbidden fruit and the apple of discord, which connect fruit with female frailty. The feminization of fruit leads to the identification of women as objects, not just of the male gaze but of male consumption, embodied in the assimilation of the sale of fruit and prostitution, as well as through the portrayal of marriage through images of fruit consumption. The acts on stage are replicated in the auditorium, as the audiences consuming fruits within the playhouses are also, unlike the audiences of the Renaissance, consuming the performances of female actors who are figured in the texts through fruit metaphors. Whether green, ripe, or overripe, women are presented in the Restoration as available for male consumption on the stage and in the text, while the fear of female sexuality is framed through the formulation of the object of consumption becoming the consumer.

This highlights the complex functions of comic drama, drawing on developments in systems for the production and distribution of fruit to provide a critique of a society that is characterized by materialism and commodification, while the terms of the critique are informed by inherited literary tradition and the physical circumstances of dramatic performance. The decline in dramatic representations of the physical consumption of fruit from the middle of the Restoration period may indicate a weakening of the association of theatrical attendance with fruit eating, as well as the emergence of more bourgeois drama, with less explicit sexual reference and a greater reluctance to construct marriage in terms of images of commercial exchange, commodification, and reification. But the changes in fruit iconography are also connected with developments in fruit production. Mrs. Malaprop's reference to the pineapple coincides with the fruit symbolism that was emerging in the novels of the late eighteenth century, as attention turned from the imported citrus fruits sold by itinerant vendors, to the exotic fruits, and particularly pineapples, cultivated in domestic hothouses. But before turning to the hothouse fruits of the novel, the next chapter will return to poetry to consider its development in the eighteenth century and the significance of the genre of georgic in articulating changing attitudes to fruit.

Chapter 5

"The Native Zest and Flavour of the Fruit"

Constructions of the Apple in Eighteenth-Century Georgic

The county of Herefordshire, sometimes known by its Roman name of Ariconium, is the heart of English cider country and still contains extensive areas planted with apple orchards (Figure 19). It is therefore not surprising that when John Philips set out to write a poem in celebration of his "native soil," he should focus on apples and cider as his main subjects.[1] While Jonson, Marvell, and Milton portray fruits of tropical and garden paradises, and drama represents fruits as objects within an exchange economy, Philips's *Cider: A Poem in Two Books* (1708) describes the orchards of the husbandmen who are addressed in the horticultural writings of the seventeenth century. The first book provides a detailed account of the best conditions and methods for planting and maintaining apple trees and the second book describes how those apples can be turned into cider. The emphasis on the physical effort that is required to produce an abundant crop and a potable product is in striking contrast to the poems of Jonson and Marvell, where labor is invisible, or the plays in which fruit is a fungible commodity, divorced from agriculture and rural life, and epitomized not by the humble husbandman but by the bustling and entrepreneurial figure of Foggy Nan the orange woman. For Philips, labor is not only visible but celebrated; it is a manifestation of moral virtue, as well as an end in itself, ensuring the health and happiness of the husbandman.

This prioritization of labor is a definitive feature of the georgic genre and Philips has been recognized as instrumental in establishing its conventions and popularity in the eighteenth century.[2] Yet the generic roots of *Cider* are complex and various. The horticultural advice is couched in blank verse, the form initiated by Milton in *Paradise Lost* and thereafter identified with epic.

Figure 19. Harvesting cider apples, Herefordshire. From *Scenes in England: for the Amusement and Instruction of Little Tarry-at-home Travellers* (1822) by the Rev. Isaac Taylor. Hand-colored engraving. Reproduced courtesy of the Yale Center for British Art.

The significance of the Miltonic connection is made explicit from the start, as the poem opens with a parody, or an appropriation, of the invocation at the start of *Paradise Lost*:

> What soil the Apple loves, what care is due
> To Orchats, timeliest when to press the fruits,
> Thy gift, Pomona, in Miltonian verse
> Adventurous I presume to sing; of verse
> Nor skill'd, nor studious; but my native soil
> Invites me, and the theme as yet unsung. (1: 1–6)

While Milton's "Advent'rous song" tells of "the fruit / Of that forbidden tree" and calls on the divine influence that inspired Moses to help him to "justify the ways of God to men" (1: 1–26), *Cider* is going to be about the cultivation of apples and the manufacture of cider. Milton's poet suggests that his subject is "unattempted yet in prose or rhyme" (1: 16) and Philips's theme is likewise "as yet unsung." But the incorporation of epic convention does not function to satirize the content as trivial, in the manner of early eighteenth-century mock epics such as Jonathan Swift's "Description of a City Shower" (1711) or John Gay's three-book *Trivia: or, the Art of Walking the Streets of London* (1716). As with Stephen Duck's "The Thresher's Labour," the invocation of literary tradition functions to elevate the subject matter. References to *Paradise Lost* and Virgil's *Aeneid*, as well the *Eclogues* and *Georgics*, abound in Philips's poem to celebrate the importance and nobility of the apple and to challenge the preoccupation with more exotic wall fruits, like the peaches, nectarines, and melons that ensnared the poets of the seventeenth century.

The late twentieth century saw a resurgence of critical interest in georgic after Anthony Low's *Georgic Revolution* (1985) emphasized the genre's role in legitimizing representations of labor in the face of Renaissance prejudices against work as demeaning. Low argues that this facilitated the development of the "New Husbandry" and, ultimately, the industrial revolution.[3] Chris Mounsey has claimed, however, that, unlike Christopher Smart's "The Hop-Garden" (1752), the cultivation techniques discussed in *Cider* owe more to Virgil than to New Husbandry.[4] In an article from 1998, Rachel Crawford identifies fundamentally paternalist and antiprogressive impulses in georgic, suggesting it was superseded in the eighteenth century by the growing cultural importance of prose discourses, such as the agricultural treatise, and these arguments are extended in her subsequent book-length study, which provides a detailed exploration of the role of *Cider* in mythologizing the apple as a symbol of English identity.[5] David Fairer has challenged Crawford and Mounsey's accounts of georgic's resistance to scientific progress and economic change, seeing the form as "an appropriate mode for expressing the energies of trade and colonisation" and reconciling conflicting forces of stability and change.[6] For Robert Irvine, the representation of labor in both *Cider* and Pope's *Windsor Forest* (1713) challenges Locke's claim that land is simply another form of property. He contends that early eighteenth-century georgic needs to be understood "in its dialectical relationship with both classical georgic and the assimilation of labor to be found in the *Second Treatise*."[7] Clare Bucknell has developed Crawford's emphasis on the growing cultural importance of prose discourses such as the agricultural treatise, suggesting that these first reference and then supersede Virgilian georgic.[8] Eighteenth-century georgic in general, and *Cider* in particular, have therefore been extensively debated, with various resolutions proposed to the apparent paradox of a genre that is identified with the celebration of labor, trade, and commerce of progressive Whig ideology but that draws on classical literary forms to express a traditional Tory ideal-ization of rural retirement. This chapter will suggest that Philips's poem needs to be located within the context of wider poetic representations of fruit, a continuing negotiation of the conflicting tropes of labor and abundance and a reorientation of its class and gender associations. While analysis of fruit iconography can help in the exegesis of georgic, georgic represents an important chapter in the story of the development of fruit iconography.

Philips engages with classical myth from the start of *Cider.* The opening dedication is followed by a paean to the West Wind, whose breath nurtures "Hesperian fruits." But as in Waller's "Battle of the Summer Islands," these are not apples but "the orange, and the citron groves" and the wind "wafts their odors sweet / Wide thro' the air" to perfume "distant shores" (1: 31–34). This is a very different environment from Britain with its "Hyperborean blasts / Tempestuous" and its "sprinkling showers" (1: 24–25, 36). The farmer must be careful to ensure that his orchards are planted in a sheltered spot, with fertile and free-draining soil. The trees must be propagated through grafting and although Philips refers extensively to Virgil's *Georgics,* he emphasizes that even more effort is required to produce an apple crop in the inhospitable climate and soils of Britain than in Virgil's Italy. The references to *Paradise Lost* are similarly used to distinguish between the Garden of Eden and the orchards of Herefordshire, where productivity is directly dependent on labor. The reader is urged to activity as the narrator rhetorically questions:

> Wilt thou then repine
> To labor for thyself, and rather chuse
> To lie supinely, hoping Heav'n will bless
> Thy slighted Fruits, and give thee bread unearn'd? (1: 371–74)

This is the postlapsarian world where apples require not only pruning and thinning but also protection from a range of pests, including birds, snails, escaped pigs, wasps, and grubs. A profitable orchard demands a state of constant vigilance (Figure 20).

As noted above, the nationalism of georgic as a genre has been widely recognized, but many of the discussions of the ideology of *Cider* have concen-trated on the historical sections, where the poet digresses from his central

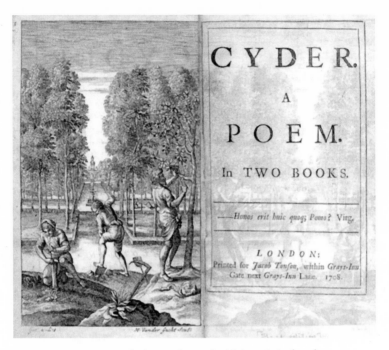

Figure 20. Frontispiece and title page from John Philips, *Cyder* (1708).

apple theme to provide what Dustin Griffin summarizes as "the praise of rural retreat, the praise of English poets who had lived a life of retirement; the survey of heroes and kings of English history from the violent past to the peaceful present; the celebration of England as a commercial and maritime power."[9] This chapter aims to demonstrate that the practical, horticultural sections of the poem are equally ideological, but they also represent a significant reorientation of fruit iconography, developing and extending the emblematic functions of the apple and emphasizing the economic and symbolic importance of hardy native produce.

Jonson and Marvell list the fruits of the aristocratic garden in ascending order of desirability so that apples, grapes, nectarines, peaches, and melons comprise a continuum but also a hierarchy which is designed to replicate the social harmony envisioned within the aristocratic estate. Philips draws a distinction between the apples and pears of British orchards and other, more exotic fruits that are identified with abroad. The poem dwells on the virtues of apples and cider and, in rhetoric reminiscent of the treatises of Taverner,

Markham, and Austen, advocates cider consumption as a nationalistic duty. The manufacture and marketing of cider are framed as competitive and even martial activities in the suggestion that, with the expansion of British power, cider will spread "to the utmost bounds of this / Wide universe," where it will "please all tastes, and triumph o'er the vine" (2: 668–69).

Just as Michael Drayton singles out the "renat" apple for special praise in his description of the orchards of Kent in *Poly-Olbion*,[10] Philips appeals to "every tree in every garden" to acknowledge the superiority of the Red-streak apple

> whose pulpous fruit,
> With gold irradiate and vermilion, shines
> Tempting, not fatal, as the birth of that
> Primaeval interdicted plant that won
> Fond Eve in hapless hour to taste, and die. (1: 513–17)

Philips paraphrases the Miltonic description of the fatal fruit in his account of the Red-streak, but, unlike the destructive fruit that tempted Eve, this apple is constructive because its "nectareous juice" produces the cider which "inspires / Poetic raptures" (1: 522, 518–19). It can be heralded as a muse as both the subject of the poem and the source of the literal stimulus for composition. The poet questions:

> What should we wish for more? or why, in quest
> Of foreign vintage, insincere and mixt,
> Traverse th'extremest world? Why tempt the rage
> Of the rough ocean, when our native glebe
> Imparts, from bounteous womb, annual recruits
> Of wine delectable, that far surmounts
> Gallic or Latin Grapes. (1: 530–36)

The superiority of native cider is framed in moral lexis, with its honesty and purity implicitly contrasted with the adulterated (mixt) condition of foreign wines, which are described in terms of insincerity because of their impurity. The pursuit of such foreign products is presented as both hubristic and unnecessary, rather than as the fulfillment of a providential design. This is very different from the view espoused by the Royal Society in its advocacy of foreign exploration, or the perspective of the Royalist Edmund Waller, in his poetic celebration of the Restoration, "To the King upon his Majesties Happy Return" (1660), and it provides a poetic counterpart to the works of horticultural mercantilism analyzed in Chapter 2. Colonial expansion is not rejected, but it is conceived entirely in terms of the opportunity to export British goods (or, at least, cider) to other parts of the world, rather than as a mechanism to bring foreign goods to Britain.

The second book of *Cider* describes fruits and drinks from different parts of the world, but it explicitly rejects the concept that they are designed by a benevolent providence for the gratification of the inhabitants of the colonial center. Philips argues that foreign fruits are adapted to the soils and climates of their place of origin, and they are likewise appropriate for the constitutions of the inhabitants. This is in line with early modern medicine, which stressed that diet needed to be adapted to environment.[11] The subtle and cooling fruits of the tropics are ideal for constitutions raised in a hot climate, but they are unsuitable for those from cold, tempestuous Britain. The health benefits of consuming domestically produced goods are reinforced by political and economic arguments, rejecting the emphasis on foreign goods, international trade, and colonial expansion. Moreover, the publication of *Cider* at the start of the eighteenth century coincided with a growing interest, within both horticultural works and fruticultural practice, in the development of techniques that would eventually lead to the successful cultivation of pineapples and oranges in Britain. The poem challenges this preoccupation by representing such fruits, whether imported from abroad or produced in domestic hothouses, as fundamentally unsuited to the constitutions of Britons.

Philips's depiction of the virtues of the apple suggests a regendering, or, at least, a complication of the gendering, of conventional fruit iconography. References to Eve and Pomona throughout the poem perpetuate the identification of fruit as feminine and an object of feminine desire that is found in *Paradise Lost*. Moreover, the apple is apotheosized as a muse that has stimulated the poet's creativity by means of his consumption of cider, and muses are always female. Yet, outside these intertextual allusions, the trope of labor consistently connects the apple with masculine virtues of hard work and resilience rather than with feminine sexuality and, as shown in the passage cited above, the apple is consistently characterized as male. Apples and cider are the products of the "bounteous womb" of the feminized soil of the country, but the apples are "annual recruits." This suggests that they are soldiers, but the image is of a citizen militia rather than a standing army; the recruits are raised annually, and their primary duty is to protect affairs at home rather than engage in unnecessary foreign expeditions. They represent independence and integrity, as well as simplicity, like the figures of Thomas Appletree and Costar Pearmain in Farquhar's *The Recruiting Officer*, produced two years before Philips's poem. This personification challenges the association of fruit with femininity, but the metonym of the militiaman also exposes the ideological implications of the rejection of foreign fruit. The cider that is produced each year from British apples is supposedly superior to wines from France and Italy and safeguards the interests of the state, but it does so without having to venture abroad and engage in expansionist wars. In an elision of the language of morality, the military, and fruit, apples and cider are constructed as a fruit yeomanry, associated with masculinity and rural labor and identified in the rhetoric of the country party as the bulwark of the national interest.[12]

This masculinization of the apple is also evident in the advice on techniques of cultivation. In describing how to select the most suitable location for an orchard, the poet warns against soil that is too rich. Even if the trees produce "most ample Fruit / Of beauteous Form," the owner may still find that he "invokes / Pomona's aid in vain" because the fruit, while "pleasing to sight," may be "to the tongue inelegant and flat" (1: 45–49). This leads to the moral reflection that

> so oft we see
> Men passing fair, in outward lineaments
> Elaborate, less inwardly exact. (1: 50–52)

This is a direct reference to *Paradise Lost*, where Adam confides to the angel Raphael his anxieties about Eve and his concern that God may have

> on her bestowed
> Too much of ornament, in outward show
> Elaborate, of inward less exact. (8: 537–39)

Adam fears that the beauty of Eve's external appearance may be disproportionate to her inward worth. *Cider* regenders this image to describe men who, like tasteless apples, have a fine exterior but little real moral substance. As a yeoman militia, apples should be valued for their solid internal qualities rather than for their external appearance. They are not only men but hardworking, masculine men. They are equated with the labor that is required to ensure an abundant harvest of fruit and they symbolize the protection of the state that is identified in mercantilist rhetoric as the consequence of increased consumption of domestically produced goods.

In her analysis of *Cider*, Crawford suggests that while apples symbolize English identity, pears are increasingly used to represent France.[13] Yet the distinction between the fruits has class as well as nationalistic implications. Most pears grown in the seventeenth and eighteenth centuries were starchy warden varieties that were associated with the diet of the poor and grown by farmers as food for living-in servants. While apples were also portrayed in patriotic literature as a good source of food for laborers and husbandmen, they were consumed, both raw and cooked, by all classes. Parkinson suggests that while most apples are only suitable for cooking and cider making, "the best sorts" may be served "at the last course for the table, in most mens houses of account, where, if there grow any rare or excellent fruit, it is then set forth to be seene and tasted."[14] Robert Appelbaum argues that apples were increasingly embraced from Milton's time and represented "simplicity, readiness, hardiness, tastiness, healthfulness and relative incorruptibility."[15] Philips draws on the positive connotations of apples in horticultural works by writers such as Austen and Evelyn but emphasizes that the gustatory and health benefits of apples are relevant to all. They are emblematized not by the waged laborer or servant-in-husbandry but by the independent yeoman or husbandman and the citizen militia.

Critical interpretations of *Cider* focus on the growing cultural significance of georgic at the start of the eighteenth century, but throughout the poem georgic conventions are moderated and subverted by the incorporation of elements of epic tradition, particularly through references to *Paradise Lost*. This is acknowledged by James Thomson who, in his celebration of an English orchard in the "Autumn" section of the 1730 edition of *The Seasons*, eulogizes Philips as a "facetious bard" and also as the poetic heir to Milton. He is the second person "Who nobly durst, in rhyme-unfetter'd verse [i.e., blank verse] / With *British* freedom sing the *British* song." Thomson draws on the account of "The Verse" appended to the opening of *Paradise Lost*, which connects blank verse not only with epic tradition but also with political independence.[16] But, as Thomson recognizes, the utilization of the Miltonic verse form by

Philips represents an appropriation of the concept of freedom, severing it from its Republican associations and adapting it to connote the independence identified with rural life and an explicitly country party concept of nationalism.[17] At the same time, georgic provides a medium for the exploration of economic change and the celebration of physical labor. Both genres function as mechanisms for the elevation of the apple as a metonym for British imperial power and British poetry, as *Cider* clearly and explicitly adapts and combines elements of Virgilian georgic with images, topoi, and traditions from the epics of both Milton and Virgil to provide a response to the political and discursive developments of the early eighteenth century. The ideology of the text is shaped by its generic heritage, but these literary conventions are formulated through fruit.

In the revised version of *The Seasons*, produced in 1744, Thomson changes his epithet to address Philips as "*Pomona's* Bard" rather than the "facetious bard" of 1730, acknowledging the gravitas of the text but also the centrality of the apple, and the appellation is reproduced by James Grainger in his 1764 georgic *Sugar-Cane*.[18] Philips exhorts his reader to "let thy ground / Not lie unlabor'd" (1: 114–15), and the celebration of physical labor throughout the poem explicitly challenges the traditions of pastoral and estate poetry. The trope of abundance, which associates fruit with the fecundity of a feminized nature and an image of pastoral ease, is displaced by a trope of labor, in which fruit production relies on the masculine effort and skill of the yeoman or husbandman. The harvest in *Cider* is the result of the labor of the apple tree, the farmer, and implicitly the reader, who pursues cultivation through the consumption of the apple-based poem.

This celebration of apples, cider, rustic life, and labor did not go unchallenged, however. The blank-verse satire *Wine* (1708) was the first published work of John Gay, then a twenty-two-year-old former apprentice to a London silk mercer. Gay appropriates the "*Miltonic*" form of Philips to celebrate the "sparkling juices, of th' enliv'ning Grape" and his verse includes numerous passages that directly parody both Philips and Milton.[19] Wine is eulogized as "Happiness Terrestrial" and the "Source / Whence human pleasures flow" (1–2):

Whose sov'raign pow'r revives decaying nature,
And thaws the frozen Blood of hoary Age
A kindly warmth diffusing. (5–7)

The Galenic references to the warmth of wine as a remedy for the cold constitution is combined with a description of the *"quickning* tast" which "adds *vigour* to the Soul" (4). The idea of a liquor that has the power to quicken, or bring back to life, invokes the alchemical concept of the elixir of life. Visual evidence of the efficacy of this "cordial restorative" is its ability to "paint with ruddy hue" the "ghastly wan" and "wrizzled Visage" of age and "Gild his dim Eyes" with "Youthful fires" (7–10). It can prevent old people from becoming like wrinkled dried apples. Wine is not only a sanative but also a quasi-magical substance, able to inspire poetic composition and oratory, to cure the dejection of spirits that is an inevitable consequence of married life, disappointed love, or homesickness (12–39, 86–90). But whereas Philips celebrates cider as a domestic product and draws on both medical and mercantilist discourse to associate it with health and wholesomeness, Gay, like Waller, glories in the foreign origins of wine as a sign of Britain's international influence. Britain's supplies need to be obtained from

> those blest *Climes . . .*
> . . . at *Lusitanian* sultry Coasts,
> Or lofty *Teneriff, Palma, Ferro,*
> *Provence,* Or at the *Celtiberian* Shores. (75–78)

These exotic places are compared to *"Paradice,* (Seat of our antient sire,)" (80). Philips displays his nationalism through his prioritization of the consumption of English apples and suggests that foreign travel to obtain exotic fruits is unnecessary and undesirable, since fruits and drinks produced in hotter climates will not be suitable to the diet of British people. But Gay adopts the contrary perspective and elevates the *"British* Marriner" (69) who is prepared to cross the oceans, braving "Tempestuous jarring Winds" and "dangers *Imminent"* (73–74) to obtain the "Fruit Divine" in the form of wine (85). The biblical references reinforce the links to *Cider* and *Paradise Lost,* but Gay challenges both the celebration of the masculine apple of the former and the feminization of fruits of the latter. Wine is portrayed as the product of a prelapsarian landscape, able to dispel memories of the fall as well as reverse the aging process that was its consequence. The grape and its "CELESTIAL Liquor" (91) are thus identified as the antidote to the fall, which was a consequence of the consumption of the apple.

The opening address to wine ends with a reference to Philips, the *"Oxonian Bard"* (120), suggesting that if he had written about wine rather than cider, his Muse would have "retain'd" the "wonted height" at which she "soard *Aerial*" (121–23) in the 1705 poem *Blenheim*, which Philips was commissioned to write as a Tory response to Marlborough's victory. Now, however,

> in *Ariconian* Bogs
> She lies Inglorious floundring, like her *Theme*
> Languid and Faint, and on damp Wing immerg'd
> In *acid juice*, invain attempts to rise. (123–26)

Wine originates in hot countries and is therefore portrayed as having the warming qualities that are required to balance the cold and dry humor associated with the black bile of a melancholy disposition. In contrast, cider is connected to a cold, damp climate and has cooling qualities that are not conducive to poetic inspiration. Ken Albala describes the view of cider expressed by Tobias Venner in his 1620 medical treatise, which suggests that cider drinkers "are pale because the coolness of the drink chills the liver so that good rich blood is never made and thus never colors the face."[20] In highlighting the differences between wine and cider, Gay draws on contemporary medicine, but his lexis also forges a connection between aesthetic failure and sexual dysfunction. David Nokes argues that in the section describing the various causes of melancholy, "Wine is presented not as the prelude to sexual pleasure, but as the antidote to insatiable marital demands."[21] But the tone is very different here. Discussing the example of Roman Republican poet Ennius, Gay suggests that when Ennius drank simply from "*Heliconian* streams" he was unable to stimulate his "*Jaded* Muse" (97–99) and

> oft' with vain attempt
> *Heroic* Acts in Flagging Numbers *dull*
> With pains essay'd, but abject still and low,
> His *Unrecruited* Muse could never reach
> The mighty Theme. (99–103)

It is only when he samples the salutary effects of the "inspiring *Nect'rous* Juice" (105) drawn "from the Purple Font" (103) that he has the power to raise the "drooping Spirits" (106) of a Muse that is presented as an appendage of the poet. In a metaphor that is simultaneously military, poetic, and phallic, the poem celebrates how, under the influence of wine, "aloft she towres / Born on stiff *Pennons*" as the poet "in loftiest Numbers sings" (106–8) and finally triumphs in the heroic epic genre.

Wine inspires activity and courage, since it "check'st Inglorious lolling ease, / And sluggish Minds with gen'rous fires inflam'st" (111–12). Juan Pellicer highlights the "jocular insouciance" of Gay's parodies of Milton, suggesting that lines such as "What is *dark* / Illumin, What is *low* raise and support" (114–15) satirize Philips "by making a mockery of the pains he took in poetic imitation."[22] But these lines can also be read as an extension of the bawdy tone of the account of married life, presenting wine as a stimulant to sexual as well as poetic activity. In striking contrast, cider's muse lies prostrate in the Ariconian Bogs and "invain attempts to rise." Gay satirizes Philips's stated preference for English cider over foreign wine, and his portrayal of the sexual dysfunction of Philips's Muse identifies the apple as a symbol of masculinity, but one that is flaccid and impotent compared to the grape. He reverses the conventional association of the grape with feminized weakness by stressing the superior stiffening qualities of wine.

The second half of the poem draws on mock epic conventions to provide a description of London taverns and clubs. This is very different from the "*Rural Seat*" (128) and "cool Retreat, with few well chosen Friends" (133) enjoyed by "our Pristin sires" (146) and associated with a less sophisticated age, and implicitly with the rusticity of Philips. Instead, *Wine* is set in the world of the metropolitan social elite that is the location for most Restoration drama and it celebrates the pleasures of a carouse with "Boon *Compeers*," served by a waiter who bears "with a grasp secure / A Bottle (*mighty charge*) upstaid" (202–6). The phallic imagery of the upstaid bottle of "Bourdeaux" (201), firmly grasped in the waiter's hand, reinforces the invigorating properties of wine in contrast to the acidic weakness of cider, while the nationalism of the poem is enforced by a series of lengthy toasts to the Queen, her consort Prince George, and her principal ministers, Marlborough, the Duke of Devonshire, Godolphin, Sunderland, and Halifax, and "all the Worthies of the *British* Realm" (212–48). Critical readings of the poem have analyzed these toasts in the context of the political power struggles of 1708 and as part of Gay's pursuit of patronage.[23] Nokes suggests that the poem is "an exercise in literary self-promotion" and Gay "displays a dexterity in political compliment without risking commitment to a clear party line," ultimately endorsing Alan Downie's suggestion that the passage should be read ironically.[24] In contrast, Pellicer argues that the parodic elements of the passage do not undermine its primary function as a panegyric.[25] But despite Pellicer's assertion that "the political element in *Wine* is concentrated in its encomiastic passages," as with Philips's *Cider*, the explicit expressions of political allegiance need to be set against the wider ideological perspective of the representation of fruit.[26] While Gay clearly and explicitly parodies both Philips and Milton, this "adolescent bravado"[27] does not negate the underlying social vision. Gay draws on fruit iconography to construct the ideal polity and a vision of national identity that is very different from that advocated by Philips.

The patriotic tributes are followed by a series of toasts to mistresses such as "*Sylvia* Comely Black" and "Airy *Celia* sprightly Maid" (253–54), emphasizing the aphrodisiac qualities of wine, and the poem ends as the carousers make their way home after hours of "harmless Mirth" and "Joys Unsully'd" (262–63). At the end of the poem, after "*Unnumber'd* Hours" during which "Glass succeeds Glass" (255–56), the "Blithe and Jolly" company finally "Homeward each his Course with *steady* step / *Unerring* steer'd," having discharged the score "with *Lib'ral* Hand" (277–78). The poem associates the consumption of wine with a sophisticated and patriotic urban elite who drink to excess without suffering any loss of control or decline in manners and amiable sociability. This is very different from the simplicity and moderation of the rustic community celebrated in *Cider*. Philips eulogizes a domestically produced fruit militia, questioning why we should "Traverse th' extremest world" and "tempt the rage / Of the rough ocean" (1:532–33). He locates British expansionism in exports of cider, which will "triumph o'er the vine" and spread across the "Wide universe" (2:668–69), while everyone else can remain safely at home. In contrast, Gay celebrates the intrepid "*British* Marriner" who "ventures through the tractless vast Abyss" to acquire supplies of wine (69–70). Gay rejects mercantilist concepts of self-sufficiency, in which the consumption of domestic goods is constructed as a patriotic duty, in favor of a celebration of national power grounded in Britain's international trade that redirects and revitalizes the perspective previously articulated in Waller's Royalist verse. He identifies the ability to import foreign goods as a symbol of economic and political power that has its physical corollary in the ability to drink without betraying signs of drunkenness. Despite the avoidance of party politics that Nokes has identified, Gay presents a distinctly whiggish, colonialist ideology, in contrast to the country

party rhetoric of Philips, exposing the roots of this ideology in the international-
ism of seventeenth-century Royalism.

The evocation of bibulous sociability sits rather uneasily with the celebration of health at the start of the poem and the promotion of the sanative
properties of grapes and wine over apples and cider. Dr. John Armstrong's
The Art of Preserving Health (1744), which David Fairer describes as a "georgic
of the human body," emphasizes the salutary qualities of orchard fruit and
rural life in terms that echo Philips and challenge the perspective of Gay.[28]
The third book is devoted to "Exercise" and eulogizes the "happiest of men"[29]
who can retire to the country surrounded by old friends and, like the addressee
of *Cider*, does not disdain to "To check the lawless riot of the trees, / To plant
the grove, or turn the barren mould" (3: 112–13). The neighbors, "Once fellow-
rakes perhaps, now rural friends" vie with each other to see "who best gives
Pomona's juice / To match the sprightly genius of Champain" (3: 124, 134–35).
The image is of a harmonious community of individuals who have turned
their backs on the urban life of tavern carouses celebrated by Gay and instead
are united in an interest in competitive cider production and convivial consumption. The celebration of cider was perhaps given added impetus by the
embargo on French wines introduced during the War of the Austrian Succession.[30] Social intercourse is characterized by geniality that is both informal
and moderate:

> Sometimes, at eve,
> His neighbours lift the latch, and bless unbid
> His festal roof; while, o'er the light repast,
> And sprightly cups, they mix in social joy. (3: 146–49)

The repast is light and the adjective "sprightly" suggests that the cups circulate
with lively energy as the pleasures of consumption are subordinated to "social
joy." Drinking is portrayed as a healthy stimulant to conversation rather than
a means of deadening consciousness. The visits of these old friends, who are
the "chosen few" (3: 123), are compared to, but also distinguished from, the
visits of other, humbler neighbors, as the passage above is paralleled by the
account of how:

> Sometimes at eve (for I delight to taste
> The native zest and flavour of the fruit,

Where sense grows wild, and takes of no manure)
The decent, honest, chearful husbandman
Should drown his labours in my friendly bowl;
And at my table find himself at home. (3: 152–57)

The juxtaposition implicit in the reiteration of "sometimes at eve" is reinforced
by the parenthetical comment, as the narrator finds it necessary to justify his
enjoyment of characters who, like orchard fruit, have not been artificially
nurtured and cultivated. The natural taste of the apple and cider is equated
with the common sense of the husbandman and both are a source of "delight"
that is directly related to their absence of improvement. Yet the use of brackets
and the shift from the third to the first person denotes this taste for humble,
rustic company as an idiosyncrasy of the poet and a guilty private pleasure to
be confessed and enclosed parenthetically, in contrast to the generalized and
conventional reflections on the more refined pleasures of rural life in the
company of social equals.

For Armstrong, as for Philips, the apple connotes virtue, zest, hardihood,
and naturalness, and is equated with the independent yeoman, combining the
roles of soldier and husbandman. Despite the scorn and incredulity expressed
in *Wine*, both writers claim a preference for cider above champagne, even
though the horticultural writers of the seventeenth century had tempered their
praises for cider with acknowledgment that it was particularly suitable for
laborers and servants rather than landowners. This attitude persists despite
the efforts of Philips and Armstrong. James Thomson's address to Philips is
followed by an account of the content of his poem and its description of

How, from Silurian vats, high-sparkling wines
Foam in transparent floods; some strong, to cheer
The wintry revels of the labouring hind;
And tasteful some, to cool the summer-hours. ("Autumn," 642–45)

Despite the praise of cider as a sparkling wine, Thomson still sees it as the
drink of the laboring hind and identifies it with carnivalesque "wintry revels,"
invoking stereotypes of popular culture. Armstrong reiterates the argument
presented in *Cider* that different fruits are appropriate to the different constitutions in different parts of the world. The account of "Diet" in the second
volume of his poem suggests that "Each rolling month matures / The food

that suits it most; so does each clime" (2: 299–300). Thus, in hot countries, where "the blood / Brews feverish frays," "Kind nature" produces distinct foods from those which tempt the palate in the "frozen world" of "icy Zembla" (2: 309–28):

> Here in livid ripeness melts the grape;
> Here, finish'd by invigorating suns,
> Thro' the green shade the golden Orange glows;
> Spontaneous here the turgid Melon yields
> A generous pulp; the Coco swells on high
> With milky riches; and in horrid mail
> The soft Ananas wraps its tender sweets.
> Earth's vaunted progeny. (2: 329–36)[31]

The reference to the "golden Orange" echoes the lexis of exoticism of Marvell's "Bermudas," while the "green shade" suggests "The Garden," where the encounter with the physical realities of nectarines and peaches precedes a retreat by the poet into the world of the mind.[32] For Armstrong, both fruits and shade are real, but in the postlapsarian world, exotic fruits are natural only for the inhabitants of the tropics, since "What suits the climate best, what suits the men, / Nature profuses most" (2: 343–44). The description of the growth of the melon as "spontaneous" invokes the fruits that threaten to trip Marvell's poet, and inevitably invites comparison with the effort and expense required to raise melons in Britain. The adjective "turgid" suggests the swelling of fecundity and perhaps pregnancy, manifested in the melon metaphor of Congreve's *The Old Bachelor*, culminating in the yield of the "generous pulp." Joined with the "milky riches" and "tender sweets," this connotes abundance, but, as with the description of the banquet in paradise, the abiding impression is of sickly excess and feminized abundance. The identification of the pineapple as "Earth's vaunted progeny" acknowledges the social status of the fruit, but this praise is constructed as fashionable rhetoric through incorporation within an argument emphasizing that this is not a suitable diet for hardy Britons. From an ecocritical perspective, the idea that the produce of each part of the world is adapted to the taste and nutritional needs of its people resonates in a world preoccupied with food miles and the environmental costs of importing goods, and it forms a striking contrast to the perspective informing Waller's poetry, which celebrates the products of foreign countries as evidence of the providential ordering of the world for the convenience of the colonial center.

By 1744, British gardeners were starting to raise pineapples, oranges, and other exotic fruits within heated greenhouses. Armstrong develops the argument that is implicit in Philips's account, that if exotic fruits are adapted to the inhabitants of their native climate, they cannot be appropriate for those who live elsewhere. As foreign goods, they are unsuitable for British constitutions and, furthermore, as the products of an unnatural environment, they are themselves unnatural and therefore unhealthy. They are cosseted within the hothouse environment because they are

> In ruder air
> Too coy to flourish, even too proud to live;
> Or hardly rais'd by artificial fire
> To vapid life. (2: 336–39)

The lexical field of this condemnation, in terms of coyness, pride, artificiality, and vapidity, draws on the stereotype of fashionable feminine behavior, echoing the moral condemnation of the discourse of luxury and gendering hothouse fruit as female. Armstrong's denotation of the apple as masculine, and characterized by the zest, flavor, sense, decency, honesty, and cheerfulness of the husbandman, is juxtaposed with an identification of hothouse fruits as weak, false, proud, and expensive, suggesting a distinction based on both gender and class (3: 151–55). Philips compares man to an attractive but tasteless apple and invokes the idea of a fruit yeomanry and Armstrong uses the apple to represent the uncultivated rustic, the more exotic fruits are associated with femininity or effeminacy and concepts of moral and physical weakness.

In most of the poetry of the eighteenth century, however, exotic fruits continue to be used to signify foreign parts and exotic locations, as in James Grainger's The Sugar-Cane (1766) or Sophia Burrell's "The Enamoured Moor" (1793).[33] Christopher Smart's poetical essay "On the Goodness of the Supreme Being" (1754) cites the suitability of fruits to the climate of their place of origin as evidence of divine providence.[34] The final version of James Thomson's "Summer," published in 1768 "with his last corrections and additions," contains an account of "the wonders of the torrid zone," where the litany of fruits includes lemons, limes, oranges, coconuts, pomegranates, strawberries, and

> thou best Anana, thou the pride
> Of vegetable life, beyond whate'er
> The poets imaged in the golden age:
> Quick let me strip thee of thy tufty coat,
> Spread thy ambrosial stores, and feast with Jove![35]

Tobin has highlighted the absence of any reference in this passage to the labor required to produce these luxuries, which Thomson identifies as "unplanted fruits" in a clear example of the trope of bounty.[36] Yet a similar image of "simple Nature" (650) is invoked in the first edition of "Autumn" in the account of Henry Bubb Doddington's gardens at Eastbury in Dorset:

> And, as I steal along, the sunny wall,
> Where Autumn basks, with fruit empurpled deep,
> My theme still urges in my vagrant thought;
> Presents the downy peach; the purple plumb,
> . . .
>   the ruddy nectarine; and dark,
> Beneath his ample leaf, the luscious fig.
> The vine too here her curling tendrils shoots;
> Hangs out her clusters, swelling to the south;
> And scarcely wishes for a warmer sky. ("Autumn," 666–75)

Despite the effort required to cultivate the wall fruits itemized here in the British climate, as detailed in the gardening handbooks, these tender fruits are incorporated within a discourse of naturalness. Foreign visitors are easily made to feel at home in a British garden and these aristocratic fruits inspire the poet, as Philips has been inspired by the apple. As in Jonson and Marvell, the trope of abundance is directly related to the aristocratic landscape and a perspective from which labor is not seen, just as the labor of the inhabitants of the Tropics is invisible in the texts discussed by Tobin.

In general, there are few references to home-produced exotic fruits in the poetry of the eighteenth century, even after the development of effective hot-houses, and as late as 1783 Richard Graves opens his satirical poem, "The Rural Deities," with the couplet: "When Verse, which once as pine-apple was rare, / Is now grown common as the Cath'rine pear."[37] This has been quoted as evidence that pineapples were still not widely available at this point, yet there may be an element of poetic license in the lines. In lamenting a contemporary mania for versifying, Graves regrets that the "quacks" and "'prentices" who have turned their attention to love poetry are preoccupied with praising the sophisticated maidens of Bath, leaving "no kind Muse" to celebrate "our *country dames*."[38] The pineapple may therefore function not simply as a symbol of rarity but also as a manifestation of the luxury, extravagance, and unnaturalness that are associated with Bath and shown in the malapropism of Mrs. Malaprop of a few years earlier. These moral failings form the primary satiric target of the poem. The implicit comparison of country girls and Catherine pears may invoke the "ripe daughters" of the tenants who present the master of the house with "an emblem of themselves in plum or pear" at Penshurst.

The georgic poetry of the eighteenth century can therefore be read as a response to the fruit iconography of the preceding century and developments in systems of production and distribution. The wall fruit of the country house poem draws on the trope of abundance to suggest an aristocratic elite for whom labor is unseen and unacknowledged, while the exotic fruits growing in the colonies manifest the second phase of the colonial project, with the identification of material objects as a reification of colonial control. In Restoration drama, the opposition is between the domestic produce of orchards and gardens and fruits that have been imported, not from distant colonized territories but from European colonial rivals, symbolizing the commodification of both fruit and sex. In contrast, Philips and Armstrong locate their poetic celebrations in the orchards, which are represented as outside the systems of commercial exchange, with produce constructed as the direct consequence of the labor of the country gentleman or husbandman. The tender fruits of the walled garden or tropical paradise and the commodified citrus retailed by the orange wenches are supplanted by idealizations of the hardy English apple, symbolized by and symbolizing an independent peasantry and yeoman militia. The pastoral abundance of the garden, in which fruit is produced without the appearance of effort, is displaced by the georgic elevation of work that denotes masculinity and national identity and the derogation of other fruits as feminized and foreign. This nostalgic vision is contrasted with Gay's sophisticated metropolitan elite who are defined by exemption from labor and consumption of the products of international trade, but the iconoclasm of this account is a testament to the pervasiveness of the rhetoric it seeks to destabilize. By the nineteenth century, with increased availability of exotic fruits from the hothouses of Britain as well as abroad, there is a clear contrast between the orchard fruits that connote natural simplicity and the exotic fruits that embody ideas of luxury and exploitation. Chapter 6 will explore how this development is represented in the emergent genre of the novel.

Chapter 6

"Unnatural Productions"

Cultivating the Pineapple in the Romantic Period Novel

Sarah Fielding's children's novel, *The Governess* (1749), is set in a school for girls and opens "in a pleasant garden," where the pupils have been allowed "to divert themselves." The governess of the title, Mrs. Teachum, has provided "a little Basket of Apples," and, having been called away, leaves the girls to share the apples among themselves.[1] Unfortunately, "there happened to be one Apple something larger than the rest, on which the whole Company immediately placed their desiring Eyes." The children start by squabbling about who has most right to the apple and end up in a full-scale pitched battle, pulling hair and tearing clothes. The final struggle is not even over who will get the apple, since in the opening stages of the argument Miss Jenny Peace "as a Means to quiet the Disturbance, . . . threw this Apple, the Cause of their Contention, with her utmost Force, over a Hedge, into another Garden, where they could not come at it" (51–52). The conflict nonetheless continues over the question of who would have had most right to the apple if they still had it, and it is only broken up by the return of Mrs. Teachum, who is not pleased to discover that "these wicked Girls . . . had been thus fighting, and pulling one another to Pieces, for a sorry Apple" (53). Her words echo Satan's speech in *Paradise Lost* (10:485–88), emphasizing the triviality of the fruit for which so much has been sacrificed, while the female combat suggests the story of the apple of discord.

Like God, Mrs. Teachum punishes the miscreants, but Jenny Peace helps them to repent, reform, and accept their lot, reprising the role of the Archangel Michael in *Paradise Lost*. She suggests that "it would have shewn much more Spirit to have yielded the Apple to another than to have fought for it," since this "would have shewn that you had too much Understanding to fight about a Trifle" (54–55). The reconciliation of the feuding pupils takes place "in a little Arbour, in that very Garden which had been the Scene of their Strife" (58). In contrast to the incident in the Genesis story, the girls are not expelled from Paradise, since Jenny Peace doubles as a Christ figure, providing immediate redemption for the sinner, and fruit furnishes a further metaphor to underscore the moral: "The poor Girls, who had in them the Seeds of Good-will to each other, altho' those Seeds were choaked and over-run with the Weeds of Envy and Pride; as in a Garden the finest Strawberries will be spoiled by rank Weeds, if Care is not taken to root them out: These poor Girls, I say, now struck with the Force of Truth, and sorry for what they had done, let drop some Tears, which trickled down their Cheeks, and were Signs of Meekness, and Sorrow for their Fault" (59). At the end of *Paradise Lost*, as Adam and Eve make their way out of Eden, we are told that "Some natural tears they dropped, but wiped them soon" (12: 645). Fielding invokes these words, referencing the fall to dramatize the ambivalence of the apple as desirable and inconsequential, tempting and quotidian. At the same time, the links with the apple of discord suggest a wider tradition of representations of female temptation, emphasizing the punishment that will follow the expression of unrestrained female desire. The apple is a potent biblical symbol, but as a humble orchard fruit it also connotes childish appetite and triviality. The hero of Thomas Holcroft's *Anna St. Ives* laments how "children wrangle for and endeavour to purloin, or seize by force, each others apples and cherries," while the inanimate narrator of *The Adventures of a Whipping-Top* ruefully describes one of his owners as a careless boy who, when tired of his play-things, "threw them away, or sold them, for apples, or any trifling thing."[2] Apples represent transitory gratification, and the connection with childhood and infantile desire reinforces their low social status (Figures 21 and 22). They are found in fiction for children, such as in the simple moral fables of Fielding, but they are otherwise relatively scarce in novels of the eighteenth and early nineteenth centuries.[3] While Restoration drama was preoccupied with the fungible orange, and eighteenth-century georgic celebrated the humble apple, the preeminent fruit of the eighteenth-century novel is increasingly the pineapple, which develops a central role in narratives anatomizing luxurious and artificial adult society.

The history of the novel has long been identified with the emergence of consumerism. The work of pioneering theorists such as Arnold Kettle and Ian Watt, locating the origins of the genre in the development of capitalist indi-vidualism, was refined by a subsequent critical tradition analyzing connections

Figure 21. Walter Geikie, *The Fruit Seller* (1824). © National Galleries Scotland.

between the language of economics and the language of narrative to highlight the importance of themes of value, exchange, and luxury within the fiction of the eighteenth century.[4] The preoccupation with circulation and objectification is exemplified in the subgenre identified as the novel of circulation or it-narrative, which uses an object or animal narrator to recount its travels through the world, exposing the fundamentally materialist nature of relationships.[5] The emphasis on economics and fungibility that characterized criticism of the

Figure 22. William Marshall Craig and Richard Phillips, "Baking or boiling apples," *The Itinerant Traders of London* (1804). © The British Library Board. "Baking & boiling apples are cried in the streets of the metropolis from their earliest appearance in summer throughout the whole winter. Prodigious quantities of apples are brought to the London markets, where they are sold by the hundred to the criers, who retail them about the streets in pennyworths, or at so much per dozen, according to their quality. In winter, the barrow woman usually stations herself at the corner of a street, and is supplied with a pan of lighted charcoal, over which, on a plate of tin, she roasts a part of her stock, and disposes of her hot apples to the labouring men and shivering boys who pass her barrow."

twentieth century has been developed in recent years through engagement with the emergent perspectives of postcolonialism and ecocriticism, to show how the reifying tendencies within the novel form inflected representations of relationships between the colonial center and dominions, and between humanity and the natural world. This chapter will draw on these approaches to explore the depiction of fruit within the novel, showing how the commodification portrayed within Restoration drama is modified, through engagement not only with fictional conventions but also in response to horticultural technology and the increasing availability of domestically produced hothouse fruit. The exorbitant costs of producing such fruits ensured that it was implicated in the discourse of luxury, while the preoccupation with tropical fruits can be read as a reorientation of the colonial appropriation and legitimation of seventeenth-century proto-imperialist poetry. The unnatural circumstances of cultivation invite interpretation from the perspective of ecocriticism, while challenging unproblematic distinctions between art and nature.

In the Introduction, I suggest that an approach that might be termed "taxonomic criticism" is discernible in cultural histories of the late eighteenth and nineteenth centuries, with a series of works emphasizing the importance of Linnaean botany in providing a mechanism for the discussion of sexuality at a time when literary works were turning away from the sexual explicitness evident in the writings of the early eighteenth century. Amy King has provided a sustained reading of the courtship plots of novels by Jane Austen, George Eliot, and Henry James to show how the popular understanding of science furnishes a vocabulary, focused on the concept of "bloom," through which it is possible to acknowledge the sexual implications of courtship and marriage. King locates the origins of the language of bloom, and the "botanical vernacular," in the second half of the eighteenth century and argues that this usage replaces earlier deployment of the term to signify physical and largely illicit sexuality. Deidre Lynch has explored the application of Linnaean language and concepts derived from Erasmus Darwin in relation to the greenhouse, to show how Jane Austen represents young girls as delicate hothouse flowers whose education is necessarily associated with artificiality.[6] This chapter draws on the insights of King and Lynch but suggests that while the language of hothouse fruit invokes ideas of unnaturalness that are also evident in the representation of hothouse flowers, there are fundamental differences. Fictional fruit iconography engages with contemporary horticulture, but it combines this with associations from a long-standing tradition of literary representation.

Above all, it involves the concept of consumption that is absent in floral symbolism and significantly changes the function of the metaphor. This will be
shown in the analysis of the representation of an assortment of fruits, but
particularly the pineapple, in the novels of the late eighteenth and early nineteenth centuries, ending around the point at which King and Lynch
commence.

Joseph Spence's *Crito: or, A Dialogue on Beauty* (1752) puts forward the
contention that "a Woman is like a Pine-apple," claiming: "The Similitude
would hold much farther, and in more Particulars, than any one would at first
imagine. She has her Season of growing to her greatest State of Beauty, of
Continuance in it, and of a Decay from it, as well as that; and the highest Season
of their Beauty is just as properly timed in the one Case, as in the other."[7] Both
women and pineapples are valued for their appearance, and the appeal of both
is fundamentally transitory; women, like pineapples, should be eaten at the
point of ripeness. This echoes the symbolism of Restoration drama in which
women are frequently objectified as comestible fruits. Just as drama mocks
sexual desire in women who are identified as overripe, so Spence uses the
pineapple metaphor to suggest that women are expensive luxury goods that
are subject to rapid deterioration. Both women and pineapples are liable to rot.

Spence's essay was published a year after Tobias Smollett's second novel,
The Adventures of Peregrine Pickle (1751), which explores the health implications
of fruit consumption, drawing on Smollett's training as a doctor as well as his
experience editing William Smellie's *Treatise on the Theory and Practice of
Midwifery*. The opening chapters detail the pregnancy of Mrs. Sally Pickle,
during which the expectant mother claims to experience the cravings of pica,
like those which May counterfeits in Chaucer's "Merchant's Tale."[8] The reader
is left in little doubt that Sally's yearnings are entirely spurious, having been
invented to torment her sister-in-law, Grizzle Pickle, who is desperate for a
healthy child to continue the family line. Grizzle prescribes a strict diet, after
studying various medical textbooks, including Nicholas Culpeper's 1651 *Direc-
tory for Midwives* and John Quincy's 1718 *Pharmacopeia Officinalis et Extempo-
ranea: or, A Compleat English Dispensatory*, and prohibits the consumption of
"roots, pot-herbs, fruit, and all sorts of vegetables."[9] John Maubray's *Female
Physician* (1724) recommends that a pregnant woman should not "frequent
Gardens . . . lest she covet some *Fruit* or *Herbs*."[10] Ken Albala suggests that hot
and laxative foods were considered dangerous for pregnant women, with
apricots identified as particularly unsafe.[11] This is illustrated in John Webster's

The Duchess of Malfi, when the pregnant Duchess goes into premature labor as a result of indulging her craving for apricots.[12] Paul-Gabriel Boucé has shown how the concept of maternal imagination functions to put responsibility for birth defects on the mother, while Jennifer Buckley has indicated that belief in the power of maternal imagination to influence the fetus persisted through the eighteenth century and into the nineteenth.[13]

When Sally Pickle plucks a peach from the garden and is "in the very act of putting it between her teeth," Grizzle implores her, "with tears in her eyes, to resist such a pernicious appetite." Yet as she is about to comply, Grizzle recollects that although the consumption of fruit in pregnancy is considered unhealthy, if "her sister's longing was baulked, the child might be affected with some disagreeable mark, or deplorable disease."[14] This is in line with the prevalent medical belief that maternal cravings should be indulged whenever possible to prevent damage to the fetus. Maubray argues that "if the *Woman* doth not indulge her corrupt APPETITE, she *languishes* and *pines* to such a degree, that her *Life* is often endanger'd, together with the FOETUS, by the Disappointment."[15] In Henry Fielding's *Joseph Andrews* (1742), Mr. Wilson's long-lost son "had a Mark on his left Breast, of a Strawberry, which his Mother had given him by longing for that Fruit."[16] Grizzle therefore insists that Sally swallow the fruit to avoid a similar incident, ensuring that she also imbibes "some cordial water of her own composing" as an antidote. This is in line with contemporary medical advice that the dangers associated with eating fruit can be lessened if wine is consumed at the same time.[17]

The next day, a visitor gives an account of a pineapple that he has eaten at a nobleman's house. Smollett's novel was published twenty-six years after Bradley's report of the first successful attempts to produce pineapples in Northern Europe and pineapples were still seen as rare and exotic. The Preface to John Giles's *Ananas: A Treatise on the Pine Apple* of 1767 emphasizes "all the obstacles and difficulties which gardeners have met with in raising these fruits," and although this is a prelude to a description of a method of cultivation that will obviate such obstacles, the publication of the work indicates that pineapples were considered difficult to raise in the 1760s.[18] Grizzle deploys the rhetoric of artificiality of Martine and Armstrong, arguing "that she herself never could eat pine-apples, which were altogether unnatural productions, extorted by force of artificial fire, out of filthy manure."[19] Sally agrees that "for her own part she should never repine, if there was not a pine-apple in the universe, provided she could indulge herself with the fruits of her own country." Native fruits connote health and naturalness and more exotic fruits the opposite, but the ironic narrative voice raises the specter of inappropriate feminine desire, describing the pineapple as "this fatal fruit." It soon becomes clear that Sally's tractability was merely a temporary respite.

Her announcement the following morning that "she had eaten a most delicious pineapple in her sleep" sends Grizzle on "a random search thro' the whole county for this unlucky fruit" to satisfy the craving signaled by the dream. Finding no success closer to home, she eventually arrives at the distant estate of the nobleman cited in the original conversation, who laments "in very polite and pathetic terms, that he was disabled from exerting his humanity, and enjoying the pleasure he should feel in contributing to the happiness of his fellow-creatures" since he has just "sent the two last pine-apples his garden had produced, in a present to a certain lady in the neighbourhood." Shortly afterward, however, Grizzle buys the required fruit from his lordship's gardener and is told by her servant that he had seen "above an hundred pine-apples ripe for cutting in his [Lordship's] garden the evening of that very day on which he had assured her that there was not one left." The incident reinforces the ambivalence of the pineapple not only as a symbol of luxurious consumption but also as something that is unnatural, unhealthy, and associated with deceit. The rhetoric of the nobleman's "pathetic" speech jars uneasily with his avaricious wish to accumulate large numbers of perishable fruits and exposes the extent to which he has departed from the benevolent ideal of the landed proprietor presiding over a harmonious and interdependent community. But alongside the acquisitiveness and hypocrisy of the nobleman, it reveals the corruption of the gardener, who is supplementing his income by selling off fruits on the side. This underscores the extent of the interdependence of domestic cultivation and the commercial market, despite the rhetorical and ideological separation between home production and economic exchange. At least some of the fruit in shops and markets originated in country house gardens and hothouses, particularly from estates situated in the environs of large towns and cities, and it reached the market either legitimately or through illicit trade of the kind practiced by the gardener. Within the novel, however, this commercialization connotes a decline of aristocratic benevolence reinforced by the nobleman's abuse of paternalistic discourse.

George Rousseau analyzes the pineapple incident in his 1971 essay "Pineapples, Pregnancy, Pica and *Peregrine Pickle*," anticipating the critical approach that came to be denominated New Historicism by exploring Smollett's engagement with the emergent discourse of obstetrics.[20] Yet, while the incident clearly hinges on Sally's exploitation of the concept of pica, Rousseau perhaps over-states the extent to which anxieties about pineapple consumption are specific to pregnancy. He cites a passage from Nicholas Culpeper, one of the authorities that Grizzle has been reading, which he claims is entirely devoted to "the benefits and ill effects of the fruit": "It marvellously helpeth all the Diseases of the Mother used inwardly, or applied outwardly, procuring Womens Courses, and expelling the dead Child and After-birth, yea, it is so powerful upon those Feminine parts that it is utterly forbidden for Women with Child . . . for it works violently upon the Feminine Part."[21] Rousseau references the 1684 edition of *The English Physitian*, but pineapples would not have been generally available at this time, let alone in 1652 when the first edition, containing the passage, was published.[22] As described above, the first unreliable report of a pineapple in Britain dates from 1657, and if the fruit was known at all around this time it would have been regarded as an exceptionally rare and expensive imported luxury, fit for the table of a king.[23] The image of a pineapple growing in the Garden of Eden in the frontispiece to John Parkinson's 1629 *Paradisi in Sole* (see Figure 7) is accompanied by a depiction of the "vegetable lamb of Tartary," implying that both plants had semi-mythical status. In fact, the passage, which is repeated in subsequent medical works as well as in the enlarged edition of Culpeper's text, describes the medicinal properties not of the pineapple (*Ananus comosus*) but of *Ajuga chamaepitys*, the ground pine or yellow bugle, a small flower which Culpeper describes as commonly found in Kent.[24] Smollett is clearly satirizing the contemporary concern with maternal cravings, but this scene should perhaps be read in the context of a wider fictional tradition of representations of desire for exotic fruit that is related to female or effeminized appetite, as well as more general medical concerns about the consequences of its consumption.

The focus on hothouse cultivation locates discussion of the exotic within a discourse of luxury, which John Sekora identifies as central to Smollett's political ideology, although more recent criticism has challenged Sekora's characterization of the form and content of the novels as reactionary.[25] Smol-lett's final novel, *The Expedition of Humphry Clinker* (1771) uses the image of the orderly country estate to expose the social disorder of the commercial system. The central correspondent of the multivoiced epistolary text is the irascible country gentleman, Matthew Bramble. In letters to his physician and correspondent, Dr. Lewis, he eulogizes the food grown on his Welsh country estate: "At Brambleton-hall . . . I drink the virgin lymph, pure and crystalline as it gushes from the rock, or the sparkling beveridge, home-brewed from malt of my own making; or I indulge with cyder, which my own orchard affords. . . . My sallads, roots, and pot-herbs, my own garden yields in plenty and perfection; the produce of the natural soil, prepared by moderate cultivation. The same soil affords all the different fruits which England may call her own, so that my desert is every day fresh-gathered from the tree."[26] The fruits are fresh and varied, but they are also native, emphasizing providential abundance. Words like "natural" and "moderate" suggest the Tory rhetoric of Philips and Armstrong and this is reinforced by the allusion to England, even though Brambleton-hall is in Wales. Bramble, whose name invokes the hedgerow harvest, highlights the ease with which fruits that are native to Britain can be cultivated, in implicit contrast to the difficulties involved in raising fruits of foreign origin. At the same time, the heightened language of allusions to the "virgin lymph" and the echo of Horace in accounts of "trout and salmon struggling from the stream" indicate that Bramble's evocation of a Welsh Golden Age may be satirically subverted within the narrative, just as Horace's vision of rural retirement is the transitory dream of an urban usurer. A similar celebration of rural retirement and unpretentious orchard fruit is included in the account of Mr. Wilson's garden in Fielding's *Joseph Andrews*, where "No Parterres, no Fountains, no Statues embellished this little Garden. . . . But tho' Vanity had no Votary in this little Spot, here was variety of Fruit, and every thing useful for the Kitchin."[27] The series of negatives highlights the distinction between this landscape of productivity and the display of contemporary society. Wilson occupies his time in tending the garden to produce fruit that is the staple of the family diet, with an emphasis on utility rather than fashion. Meanwhile, his wife and daughters carry out the housekeeping, producing wine for the family and medicinal cordials for the neighborhood, like those administered by Grizzle Pickle as a prophylactic against peaches (197–98). This leads the classicist Adams to exclaim "that this was the Manner in which the People had lived in the Golden Age" (229).

Smollett's rustic idyll is, however, followed by a description of life in London that is as bitter and jaundiced as the account of country living is romanticized. London is noisy, the water is dirty, the wine is adulterated, and the meat and fish are rotten. By comparison, fruit is presented in relatively positive terms with the acknowledgment that "Covent-garden affords some good fruit."[28] This fruit is, however, part of a commercial system, which means that it "is always

engrossed by a few individuals of over-grown fortune, at an exorbitant price."
The lexis of unnatural growth in the description of the wealth of the customers
means that even the good fruit is not associated with wholesomeness and nature
but rather connotes the artificiality and pretension that characterize Bramble's
critique of metropolitan life and suggests the emergence of a new moneyed
class. This wealthy elite monopolizes the best fruit, perhaps the "culled ware"
of which Foggy Nan boasts in Etheredge's *The Man of Mode* (1, 1, 28–33), while
the rest of the community is left with "the refuse of the market." Bramble is
particularly horrified by what he regards as the contamination of fruit by
itinerant vendors. While the oranges sold in the Restoration theater symbolized
sexual promiscuity, Bramble's concern is with social promiscuity and the
mixing of classes within the urban environment. This is manifested in images
of contagion that reinforce the preoccupation with social pathology in his
correspondence. He recounts that any fruit not sold through Covent Garden

> is distributed by such filthy hands, as I cannot look at without loathing.
> It was but yesterday that I saw a dirty barrow-bunter in the street,
> cleaning her dusty fruit with her own spittle; and, who knows but some
> fine lady of St. James's parish might admit into her delicate mouth those
> very cherries, which had been rolled and moistened between the filthy,
> and, perhaps, ulcerated chops of a St. Giles's huckster—I need not dwell
> upon the pallid, contaminated mash, which they call strawberries;
> soiled and tossed by greasy paws through twenty baskets crusted with
> dirt; and then presented with the worst milk, thickened with the worst
> flour, into a bad likeness of cream.

While the fruit from the Brambleton orchard goes straight from tree to table,
evoking the organic community of country house poetry, the London fruit
circulates through society in a series of commercial transactions. It deteriorates
through excessive indelicate handling and contamination from individuals
who are fundamentally unwholesome. Like the representatives of fashionable
society, the itinerant vendors prize surface appearance over wholesomeness,
leading to the cleaning of cherries in spit. Not only are the fruit sellers deficient
in personal hygiene, but they are also motivated by personal pecuniary interest
at odds with the welfare of the customer. The transitory relationships of metropolitan trade are very different from the long-standing ties of obligation and
dependence within the aristocratic estate. In London, "every person you deal

Figure 23. Pieter Angillis, *Covent Garden* (1726). © Yale Center for British Art, Paul Mellon Collection.

with endeavours to over-reach you by way of business. . . . Your tradesmen are without conscience, your friends without affection, and your dependants without fidelity." In this environment, fruit ceases to be a symbol of naturalness and health and instead acquires connotations of social disorder and physical contagion (Figure 23).

This jaundiced image of the commercial system is, however, balanced in the novel by the perspectives of other correspondents, whose positive and enthusiastic accounts provide a counterpart to Bramble's misanthropy. His young nephew Jery notes with approval that there is no want of "the fruit now in season," in Edinburgh, "such as cherries, gooseberries and currants," adding that "in the gardens of some gentlemen, . . . there is now a very favourable appearance of apricots, peaches, nectarines, and even grapes: nay, I have seen a very fine shew of pine-apples within a few miles of this metropolis" (223). As in so many of the poems explored in previous chapters, this litany begins with the more common and hardy soft fruits, followed by wall fruits, and then exotic fruits. The hardy fruits are described as "now in season," suggesting naturalness; the wall fruits are celebrated in terms of their appearance, which is "favourable"; the pineapples are "a fine shew." This locates the more exotic fruits within a discourse of superficiality and suggests that even in the second half of the century pineapples are still being valued primarily for their decorative value.

Despite the enthusiasm for their cultivation shown in many horticultural tracts, exotic fruits primarily function in the novels of the 1770s to connote corruption and extravagance, developing the condemnation of artifice rather than the praise of ingenuity. This is exemplified in *Musical Travels through England by the late Joel Collier, licentiate in Music* (1774/1775), a satirical travelogue which parodies the "musical tours" of Charles Burney by mocking their self-congratulatory and sycophantic tone.[29] The hero encounters a group of aldermen who offer him melons and pineapples, assuring him that the fruit "cost *them* nothing."[30] In case the satire of this passage escapes the readers' attention, a note was added to the fourth edition (1776), explaining that "this expence, together with sundry other articles of the like nature, were placed to the account of the poor of *Emanuel hospital*, a charity ... to which the Aldermen were then upon a visit, as Trustees."[31] The hero takes a melon and a pineapple while the aldermen devour the rest of the fruit, in a physical manifestation of peculation.

The condemnation of luxury is similarly evident in Frances Burney's *Evelina* (1778), when the eponymous heroine visits Cox's Museum, a private collection of jeweled automata, which proved a popular tourist attraction from 1772 to 1775.[32] On witnessing a jeweled pineapple, "which, suddenly opening, discovered a nest of birds, who immediately began to sing," Evelina demonstrates her taste and discrimination in suggesting that the spectacle afforded "but little pleasure, for it is a mere show, though a wonderful one."[33] The term "show" echoes Jery's words in *Humphry Clinker* and provides a reminder that even real pineapples are primarily considered in terms of their appearance. In contrast, Madame Duval's exclamation that she "never see nothing eleganter" (76) exposes lack of breeding through the double negative but also through inappropriate enthusiasm. The exhibit was clearly something of a cause célèbre since it is also referenced in *Charlotte: Or, One Thousand Seven Hundred and Seventy Three* (1775), a play attributed to Mrs. Cullum. The character Toupee boasts of his master's wealth to the servants of his projected bride, claiming that their mistress "will be finer than the elephant at Cox's museum; she may feed her children with pearls and diamonds as the pretty bird does in the pine-apple."[34] Cox's catalogue explains how the pineapple bursts open to reveal a nest of birds and, as the music plays, the mother feeds her young with pearls. She then flutters her wings and the pineapple closes.[35] Marcia Pointon has emphasized the significance of Cox's Museum as a "seductive metaphor" and a locus for debate over the political and economic issues surrounding luxury in the eighteenth century.[36] The collection and the pineapple were both recognized metonyms of excess, so the combination of the two is doubly resonant.

From the 1790s, there is a marked increase in the significance of fruit within fiction. Since the second half of the twentieth century, works from this period have been discussed within the context of the political debates raised by the French Revolution, with Marilyn Butler and Gary Kelly outlining the characteristics of the Jacobin novel, and Matthew Grenby showing the response of more conservative writers in his account of the anti-Jacobin novel.[37] More recently, feminist critics in particular have moved away from the emphasis on factional debate to explore how the novels contribute to discussion of wider social questions at a time when literature was dominated by professional women writers.[38] Many of the concerns transcend the boundary between radical and conservative, with writers from across the ideological and political spectrum contributing to debates over gender roles and social morality,[39] leading to the replacement of the terminology of the Jacobin and anti-Jacobin novelist with the Romantic period writer. This chapter focuses on fruit iconography in Charlotte Smith's *Desmond* (1792), Mary Robinson's *Angelina* (1796), Jane Austen's *Northanger Abbey* (published 1817, written 1798–99), George Walker's *The Vagabond* (1799), and Amelia Opie's *Adeline Mowbray* (1805). These works encompass diverse ideological perspectives, ranging from the Jacobin radicalism of Smith and Robinson to the conservative anti-Jacobinism of Walker, but they all acknowledge the horticultural changes of the eighteenth century, employing tropical fruits and, particularly, the pineapple, to symbolize British technological ingenuity. The late eighteenth and early nineteenth century was a time when Britain was very active in constructing itself as a commercial and maritime empire and extending its economic interests in the Caribbean and South America, particularly Brazil and Argentina.[40] These were exactly the areas that were most closely associated with the pineapple, since the fruit originated in Brazil and was extensively cultivated in the Caribbean. While the novels concentrate on the fruits raised within British hothouses, drawing on the innovations outlined in the horticultural tracts of the eighteenth century, the representation of these fruits is inevitably informed by attitudes to colonialism and debates over slavery, which received added impetus following the Haitian Revolution of 1791. The tropical produce of the hortulan landscapes of the colonial center that is portrayed within Romantic-period fiction has very different connotations from the fruits flourishing in foreign climes within seventeenth- and eighteenth-century poetry.

Desmond is generally identified as Charlotte Smith's most explicitly radical and polemical novel, not least because the action coincides with the French Revolution.[41] It is based on letters exchanged between the pro-revolutionary English hero, Lionel Desmond, and his more cautious mentor Erasmus Bethel, but the arguments are rehearsed through metaphors that engage with and subvert Edmund Burke's *Reflections on the Revolution in France* (1790). As numerous commentators have noted, Burke maintains a sustained analogy comparing the constitution of a state to the fabric of a building, focusing on the contrast between the edifices of Britain and France. The British constitution is an antique structure which has been progressively altered and extended from the feudal period, ensuring it is fit for purpose in the modern era while maintaining its original style. In contrast, the French constitution has not been adequately maintained and was demolished and rebuilt in the Revolution, rather than repaired and restored.[42] Emma Clery has highlighted similar architectural metaphors in William Blackstone's *Commentaries on the Laws of England*, where the British legal system is identified as a combination of tradition and adaptation.[43]

In Smith's novel, the radical French aristocrat, the Marquis de Montfleuri, shows his rejection of traditional ostentation and inequality through architectural changes that constitute an explicit response to Burke. He has partly demolished and redesigned his ancestral home so that it now resembles the house of an English gentleman (112–14). In contrast, his reactionary uncle, the Comte d'Hauteville, inhabits a vast and moldering chateau, epitomizing the impractical obsolescence of the ancien régime (124–30). Although this binary opposition of revolutionary renovation and counterrevolutionary stasis is unproblematic within the context of France, it is much more complicated in Smith's portrayal of Britain, not least because the English gentleman's residence has been identified by Montfleuri as embodying the social harmony to which he aspires. Tamara S. Wagner notes that "the ideological allegiances of the novel are never clear cut" since "the desirability and extent of change is drawn into debate."[44] Desmond develops the architectural analogy in a letter to Bethel:

> If I had a very good house that had some inconveniencies about it, I should not desire to pull it down, but I certainly should send for an architect and say, alter this room—it is too dark—remove those passages—they are too intricate—make a door here, and a staircase there; make the kitchen more habitable for my servants, and then my house will be extremely good.—But I should be very much startled if my architect were to say, "Sir, I dare not touch your house—if I let in more light, if I take down those partitions, and make other changes you desire, I am very much afraid that the great timbers will give way, and the *party-walls* crush you beneath their ruins." (343)

Desmond argues that the fabric of the constitution is basically sound. Some renovations are required, particularly for the convenience of the working people, symbolized in the domestic metaphor by the servants of the house, and many of the alterations are to promote enlightenment. But while the passage rejects the idea that the constitution needs to be completely rebuilt, it also mocks the argument that any alteration can potentially undermine the whole. The possibly punning reference to party-walls satirizes the claim that factionalism, political divisions, and ideological debate pose a threat to the stability of the state.

Jacqueline Labbe argues that following criticisms of *Desmond* for its explicit engagement with politics, Smith develops a new subgenre of fiction in *The Old Manor House* that Labbe denominates the "property romance."[45] Yet it is possible to trace elements of this subgenre within the earlier novel, since *Desmond* frames its ideological perspective through metaphors of property. The threat to the concord of nature and art is not located in the working people nor in the old aristocracy of Britain but rather in the self-interest and self-indulgence of the new commercial and professional classes who show their unfitness to rule through their lack of respect for the property and landscapes that represent the traditions and constitution of the state. This lack of respect is most conspicuously manifested in the landscape of fruit. In a letter to Desmond enclosing a copy of Thomas Paine's *Rights of Man*, Bethel describes the alterations that have taken place on the country estate at Linwell, following its acquisition by Bethel's erstwhile legal adviser, Sir Robert Stamford: "The beautiful little wood which overshadowed the clear and rapid rivulet . . . has been cut down, or at least a part of it only has been suffered to remain, as what he calls a collateral security against the north-east wind to an immense range of forcing and succession houses, where not only pines are produced, but where different buildings, and different degrees of heat, are adapted to the ripening cherries in March, and peaches in April, with almost every other fruit out of its natural course" (194). Far from celebrating the horticultural skill and technological knowledge that has made possible this triumph of productivity or using the abundance of the hothouse as an image of Edenic fecundity, bringing together the diverse fruits of the earth, Bethel represents the development as a perversion of nature. The ironically economic lexis of the reference to the remnants of the wood as "collateral security" against the wind is followed by an evocation of the size and grandeur of the structures. The contrast between nature and art is emphasized in the account of how the pattern of the seasons has been overturned. In the sixteenth century, the production of grapes in January is used as evidence of the magical powers of Faustus; here, March cherries and April peaches symbolize the disruption of the natural order by new economic forces. This is very far from the harmony with nature and the community of *Humphry Clinker*'s Brambleton Hall and draws on the suspicions of prematurely ripened or unseasonable fruits expressed within medical writings and Restoration drama. The new horticultural technology has overturned the pattern of the seasons enshrined in myth through the story of Proserpine.

Bethel complains that the "hamadryades are driven from the place, which is now occupied by culinary deities" and "every thing is sacrificed to the luxuries of the table" (194). The reference to hamadryads elides regret at the destruction of the trees that supposedly housed these nymphs, with lament for the knowledge of classical culture that perpetuated their stories. Both are presented as threatened by the spread of consumerism. The fruits that are produced within the complex range of hothouses, with their different conditions and temperatures, show not only a disregard for the natural order but also a rejection of a literary inheritance that provides a schema through which nature is to be perceived and appreciated. Like the "rural virtues" that are evicted to make way for a park in Goldsmith's *Deserted Village* (1770), the hamadryads depart, replaced by structures devoted to "forcing" and "succession." The rejection of traditional methods of fruit cultivation is connected to the abandonment of the traditional paternalist labor relations and the classical culture of the aristocracy.

Although Desmond counsels Bethel against his obsession with Sir Robert, warning him, in another image derived from a fruiting body, not to be disconcerted by "the fungus growth of this arrogant upstart," he shares his regret at the displacement of hamadryads by pineapples (202). The terms of his counsel reinforce the association of exotic fruit with distasteful luxury and the perpetuation of injustice and inequality: "Leave him, then, my friend, to waste, in swinish excess, sums which he has earned by doing dirty work, at the expense of those who are now called the 'swinish multitude,' hundreds of whom might be fed by the superfluities of his luxurious table" (202). By drawing on Burke's porcine label for the common people, which was subsequently appropriated by a host of radical writers from Thomas Spence to Percy Shelley,[46] Desmond subverts the image of the harmonious estate to create a vision of fruit cultivation that is grounded in class exploitation and, as a result, is debasing and dehumanizing to the perpetrators rather than the victims. While the walls of Penshurst are claimed to have been "reared with no man's ruin, no man's groan," this is emphatically not the case with the forcing houses of Linwell.

Later, Desmond seeks refuge in a "humble thatched cottage" whose "ancient" occupants make a homely breakfast on "brown bread and cyder" (251, 268). Such simple local fare contrasts with the luxurious and artificial demand for fruits out of season. This reinforces the connection between orchard fruits and the simple husbandman established in horticultural writings, but, at the same time, Desmond equates this rustic diet with health, virtue, and happiness in line with the georgic iconography of Philips and Armstrong. Thus, while ideas of progress, change, and technological advance are represented in positive terms in relation to France, Smith's ideology is more nuanced in the context of England, where a natural landscape and traditional way of life are presented as threatened by corrupt and reactionary forces connected with upward mobility and denoted through the distortion of nature involved in rearing hothouse fruit. The pineapple and fruits raised out of season become metaphors for the ostentation of the nouveaux riches. They are forced to grow in an artificial environment and their unnatural cultivation exposes the disruption of social relations through which they are produced.

This use of exotic fruit to symbolize an inherently exploitative economic system is also a feature of Mary Robinson's *Angelina*. Some recent criticism of Robinson's novel has focused on the final volume, identifying links between the sufferings of the heroine Sophia Clarendon, the interpolated narrative of Eleanor of Brittany, and the biography of Robinson herself.[47] Candice Smith analyzes Robinson's architectural metaphor to suggest that the novel provides a critique of aristocratic values, as South Cliff castle is shown "to be built not only on diseased historical and political foundations, but also upon precepts which endanger and oppress women."[48] Yet biographers and critics of Robinson's nonfiction works present a rather different ideological perspective, emphasizing a tendency to defend aristocratic society, which is identified as a result of her dependence on it. William Brewer has argued that, "instead of calling for the abolition of the aristocracy, Robinson wants the nobility to socialize with and patronize authors so 'women of letters' no longer have to associate with commoners."[49] Diego Saglia has analyzed the representation of commercial society and luxury within Robinson's *Memoirs*, showing the extent to which she herself was constructed as an object of luxurious consumption, particularly through her relationship with the Prince of Wales.[50] To evaluate the social vision presented within *Angelina*, this account will focus on the first two volumes of the novel and the representation of Clarendon Abbey, the home of Sophia and her father, the wealthy trader Sir Edward Clarendon.

Although the Abbey has ancient roots and previously belonged to a distant relation of Angelina's mother, Sir Edward Clarendon is the embodiment of new money, having come from "obscurity" and made his own fortune.[51] His name "is proverbial in the city for every thing low, sordid, illiterate, and unfeeling" (1: 6) and this is signaled in the "confusing and vulgar mix of architectural styles" displayed within the Abbey.[52] His bluestocking sister-in-law has the unusual name of Juliana Pengwynn, which may be a reference to the penguin pineapple rather than the flightless birds.[53] She laments that the "sublime Milton" sold *Paradise Lost* for ten pounds, "a sum which Sir Edward Clarendon gives for a turtle or a few pineapples" (1: 72–73).[54] The Milton reference suggests Clarendon's philistinism, displayed in the account of the library to which he has added only works of political economy, but it also draws attention to the distance between his luxurious consumption and the fruits that were naturally and freely available in the prelapsarian paradise (1: 156). The pinery at Clarendon Abbey is, as Sir Edward is keen to point out, "one of the first in the kingdom," and cost "a world of money" (1: 147–48). As in *Desmond*, the elaborate edifice epitomizes not only the ostentatious extravagance and social pretension of the new moneyed classes but also the unnaturalness and ignorance.

During a visit to the Abbey by the aristocratic Lord Acreland, whom Clarendon intends as a suitor for Sophia, Clarendon proposes a tour of his hothouses, with the assertion that "now the sun is upon them you will see the fruit in the highest perfection." When Lord Acreland protests that "the heat will be insupportable," Clarendon responds that they can follow the tour with a visit to his grotto. Acreland is horrified at this prospect, arguing that "the sudden transition from suffocating heat to intense cold may prove dangerous" (1: 151). Acreland's response displays the foppish effeminacy of the aristocrat, but Clarendon represents the opposite extreme of physical insensibility. His obliviousness to the significance of moderation within contemporary ideas of regimen indicates an absence of refinement. The environment of the hothouse and the pineapples it produces manifest luxurious extravagance, as in *Desmond*, but also extreme and unnatural conditions.

Sir Edward's preoccupation with hothouse cultivation is not simply a random peccadillo. The satire on this obsession forms part of a more general condemnation of his commercial ethics and particularly his attitude toward slavery. Edward Said has shown how novels such as Jane Austen's *Mansfield Park* sublimate "the agonies of Caribbean existence to a mere half-dozen passing references to Antigua";[55] in *Angelina*, however, Robinson's abolitionist agenda ensures not only that the connection between wealth and slavery is made explicit but also that Sir Edward signals his complete absence of moral sense and social propriety by speaking in its defense. Sir Clifford Wilmot describes how "Sir Edward talks of his plantations, and his slaves.... He is all ostentation and ignorance" (2: 24) and Sir Edward responds to his sister's praise of the independence of her niece with the following "vociferation": "Independence is the stalking horse for all sorts of absurdities. I should like to know what would become of my plantations if such doctrines were encouraged: ... Hav'n't I made a fortune by slavery? and I warrant independence had nothing to do with the business" (3: 102). Sir Edward is described by Sir Clifford Wilmot as "a black trader" and Sir Clifford jokingly declines a relationship with Juliana Pengwynn on the grounds that he has "no inclination to promote the slave trade.... I have no idea of selling my freedom for a hogshead of sugar or a bale of cotton" (1: 302–3). Sir Clifford is a fop and facetiously elides the slavery of producing the sugar and cotton on which the Clarendon fortune is based with the slavery of marriage to a rich old maid, in a gender reversal of the comparison between the position of women and slavery, which has been identified within Gothic novels of this period.[56] But his comments indicate how slavery is used to substantiate the aristocratic scorn for the mercantile classes. Even the otherwise immoral Sir Clifford expresses pity for "the sable sons of slavery, who are doomed to toil beneath [the sun's] blaze" to produce the sugar and coffee for his "morning beverage." He claims that while he drinks his coffee, he often thinks "with horror, that it was cultivated under all the agonies of torture and oppression" (2: 29; see also 3: 102–3). Slavery is described through images of incarceration, oppression, and the excessive heat of the sun, and Sir Edward's celebration of his pineapple harvest reinforces the role of the pineapple as a symbol of the slavery and exploitation on which his fortune is based. The fruit has tropical origins but has been taken from its home and produced within the confinement and the extreme and artificial heat of the pinery. It is maintained in unnatural conditions to accommodate the tastes of an elite, just as the slaves are forced to work in unnatural and inhuman conditions to produce the luxury of sugar. The novel therefore develops the association of exotic fruit with new money as well as with the exploitation and commodification inherent within the commercial system to provide an indictment of the values and taste of the nouveaux riches that constitutes a critique of imperialism.

While the pineapple provides a symbol of slavery, one of the primary functions of slavery within the novel is as a metaphor for the position of women in Britain. Clarendon's willingness to offer his daughter for sale in unvarnished commercial lexis is represented as an extension of the immorality of the slave trade (1: 73). Juliana Pengwynn remonstrates: "That though you have acquired wealth, in the barbarous traffic of your fellow creatures; though you have amassed treasures, sullied by the tears, if not the blood of persecuted slaves; you must not hope to sacrifice a daughter, without provoking the indignation and exciting the contempt of those who are friends to the breathing race, and enemies to oppression" (2: 48–49). Sophia's uncle condemns Clarendon's avarice, commenting that if Sophia had been his daughter, "she should not have been put up, like a cargo of sugar, to the highest bidder" (3: 100). The reference to sugar again elides the exploitation of individuals on the grounds of race and sex. Moira Ferguson argues that Robinson is one of the first writers to draw parallels between "female victims of forced marriage, imprisoned debtors, and Caribbean slaves" and Kari Winter has analyzed nineteenth-century gothic novels and slave narratives to demonstrate links between the two forms for the articulation of oppression.[57] The previous tradition of writings invoking classical and oriental concepts of slavery to discuss the position of women, such as Mary Astell's *Reflections Upon Marriage* (1700), was given contemporary relevance through the activities of the abolition movement at the end of the century. Recent cultural commentators such as bell hooks and Gayatri Spivak have challenged the legitimacy of comparisons between marriage and slavery and it is undeniable that the use of slavery as a metaphor for marriage denies the extent of the brutality of enslavement and its implications for the suppression of the slave voice.[58] But this comparison is nonetheless a recurrent topos within fiction from the eighteenth and into the nineteenth century. While critical accounts have tended to identify the metaphor within gothic, it is equally manifest in romantic period novels, often formulated through images of fruit and the horticultural lexis of forcing.[59]

In *Angelina*, slavery and mercenary marriage are both branded unnatural and are equated with the cultivation of the pineapple. The tasteless extravagance of this fruit is contrasted with simpler native produce and particularly with the vines that swathe a rustic hermitage at Clarendon Abbey (1: 127). Candice Smith emphasizes the importance of the hermitage as a "contested site in the novel," as Sophia adopts this space as a refuge from the extravagance of the Abbey, while her father wants to knock it down.[60] The young hero, Charles Belmont, picks "the most delicious offering" for Sophia from the grapes that hang over the door and later similar bounty is found growing around the cottage of a virtuous but impoverished Welsh curate (2: 9). These gifts of grapes, like the brown bread and cider consumed by the peasants in *Desmond*, signify simplicity, taste, and nature. The opposition of domestic and foreign fruits of seventeenth-century and georgic poetry has been displaced by a contrast between domestically raised fruits that are identified as natural and those that are the result of unnatural processes of production. While orchard and wall fruits signify harmonious social relations of traditional agrarian paternalism and the old aristocracy, the pineapple represents confinement and oppression that convey the exploitation of commercial society and find their extreme articulation in slavery.

It could be argued that the subversive implications of Robinson's narrative are contained by a sentimental resolution in which Sophia is reconciled to her newly impoverished father, but I would argue that this conclusion does not undermine the critique of commercial exploitation presented in the body of the novel. Sir Edward is only redeemed when he is separated from the wealth that is the source of corruption. The critique of trade is balanced but not negated by the subsequent condemnation of the landed elite, whose representatives are perhaps even more morally bankrupt than Sir Edward. By the end of the novel, after the destruction of various evil aristocrats, moral virtue is located in Sophia Clarendon, daughter of an alliance between a West India merchant and a member of the minor Welsh nobility, who has been educated in Europe by her bluestocking aunt. She represents the best of commercial and aristocratic values, free from the prejudices and snobbery of the English landowners and the coarseness and materialism of the commercial classes and endowed, through education, with an international perspective that supersedes conventional distinctions of class. Her alliance in marriage to the long-lost son of Lord Acreland and his deserted lover, Angelina, reinforces the role of hardship in building character and moral integrity so that Charles Belmont can represent hope for the hereditary elite.

Pineapple houses also feature in the landscape of Jane Austen's *Northanger Abbey*, which a note from her sister Cassandra suggests was originally written between 1798 and 1799.[61] Amy King has provided a detailed reading of Austen's novels, showing how the popular understanding of Linnaean botany furnishes an acceptable vocabulary for representing courtship and the sexual development of the protagonist, identifying the technique of *"physicalised mimesis,"* which, she argues, "borrows from the taxonomies of sexualized sciences and the representational possibilities of the picturesque garden."[62] Deidre Lynch develops this reading but suggests that Austen employs the specimens of the florist rather than the botanist, portraying female education through images of the hothouse rather than the garden or field, rewriting the "plot of naturalization in an idiom of artifice."[63] Both readings show how the portrayal of Austen's heroines is developed through language and images of bloom and greenhouses but, as in *Desmond* and *Angelina*, the description of the glasshouse landscape at Northanger Abbey principally functions to illuminate the character of its male proprietor, General Tilney, rather than the education of its female visitors. Like Lord Acreland at Clarendon Abbey, Catherine Morland is a rather reluctant participant in an extensive tour of the kitchen garden. The reader is invited to share her awed perception that "the walls seemed countless in number, endless in length; a village of hot-houses seemed to arise among them, and a whole parish to be at work within the inclosure."[64] The hyperbolic references to countless and endless walls highlight the disparity between Northanger Abbey and Catherine's humble parsonage home, and thus the social distance between Catherine and Henry Tilney, but it also satirizes the ostentatious luxury of the general, reinforcing Catherine's sense that it is possible that he is "not perfectly amiable" (206). The lexis describing the hothouses as a village, the gardeners as a parish, and the garden as an "inclosure" invokes the political rhetoric of agricultural protest presented within *Desmond*, particularly at a time of widespread concern about the impact of enclosure and it raises the question of whether it is right that all this effort should go into providing for the table of a single family. Lynch has emphasized the greenhouse as a place where "Nature, miniaturized, was shoehorned into the enclosed feminine sphere of the house,"[65] but General Tilney's hothouses, like those at Linwell in *Desmond* and at Clarendon Abbey in *Angelina*, are vast and the description suggests an area of public industry in which the whole parish is employed. Unlike the greenhouses used for the production of exotic blooms, the succession houses for raising fruit are distinctly masculine and extensive spaces.

The implication of immorality is reinforced by the identification of the project with the vanity and insincerity of the general. Seeing Catherine's surprise at the extent of the gardens, General Tilney "modestly owned that, 'without any ambition of that sort himself—without any solicitude about it,—he did believe them to be unrivalled in the kingdom. If he had a hobby-horse, it was *that*. He loved a garden. Though careless enough in most matters of eating, he loved good fruit—or if he did not, his friends and children did. There were great vexations attending such a garden as his. The utmost care could not always secure the most valuable fruits. The pinery had yielded only one hundred in the last year.'" Austen's use of direct speech to render the indirect speech of the general reinforces the extent of his self-construction and self-deception, as he disingenuously laments the trials of his horticultural activities, culminating in the humblebrag that he has produced "only" a hundred pineapples. When in the ensuing tour of his succession-houses he is informed by Catherine that her wealthy neighbor, Mr. Allen, has only "one small hot-house," we are told that he utters the words "He is a happy man!" with "a look of very happy contempt." General Tilney reverses Horace's apothegm that you should praise a large estate and farm a small one and his praise is entirely insincere. Mr. Allen's rather modest hothouse at Fullerton is like the orangeries of the seventeenth century, which were designed to produce flowers rather than fruit; it only has a fire "now and then" and is used to overwinter Mrs. Allen's plants. In contrast, Northanger Abbey has a series of hothouses which are maintained at different temperatures so that a range of exotic fruits can be cultivated. It represents the fashionable concern with the production of fruit through the buildings and labor-intensive techniques that have been identified in the novels of Smith and Robinson with uncultured extravagance and the distortion of nature (Figure 24). Austen appears to be drawing on these associations to signal the crass materialism of General Tilney. His desire to subju-

Figure 24. Humphry Repton, "Forcing Garden, in Winter," *Fragments on the Theory and Practice of Landscape Gardening* (London: T. Bensley and Son, for J. Taylor, 1816). Reproduced by kind permission of the Lindley Library, Royal Horticultural Society.

gate the natural world is subsequently manifested in domestic tyranny as he rudely expels Catherine from his house, on discovering that she does not have the financial requisites for the perfect daughter-in-law (231–32).

Prior to Catherine's sudden and forced departure, she accompanies the family to Henry Tilney's parsonage at Woodston. The house is a model of comfortable and tasteful simplicity, in contrast to the abbey with its range of hothouses and workforce the size of a parish. In admiring the view from one of the windows, Catherine enthuses, "Oh! What a sweet little cottage there is among the trees—apple trees too! It is the prettiest cottage!"[66] The apple trees locate the parsonage in a natural landscape of healthy rural fecundity, which contrasts with the labor-intensive and industrial fruit production of the general's succession houses. The "ornamental part of the premises" consists of a single "walk" which traverses "two sides of a meadow." This has been improved by "Henry's genius" to form a landscape of recreation. Lynch follows Eric Walker in emphasizing the suggestive imagery of fertility in the fact that none of the shrubs in Henry's "pleasure-ground" is "higher than the green bench in the corner," arguing that they are "newly arrived from some nursery."[67] But the diminutive scale of Henry's landscape intervention may also point to a greater sense of proportion in the younger Tilney than his father possesses. His garden merges with the agricultural landscape instead of dominating it. While the tour of the kitchen gardens and hothouses at Northanger is so protracted that it leaves Catherine "heartily weary of seeing and wondering," the "saunter" through the grounds at Woodston has to be extended by venturing out of the domestic space "into other meadows and through part of the village." The distortion of nature inherent in the general's "succession houses" is associated with dominance of the neighborhood and community, whereas Henry's gardens lead naturally and unobtrusively into, and merge with, the surrounding landscape.

Yet the contrast between Woodston and Northanger is itself subverted. On hearing Catherine's ecstasies over the cottage, the general responds: "You like it—you approve it as an object;—it is enough. Henry, remember that Robinson is spoken to about it. The cottage remains." Catherine is abashed because these words presume that she has an interest in the parsonage, which is not yet warranted by any romantic understanding between herself and Henry Tilney. But the general's orders also show that even the parish of Woodston is under his control. Henry may be the parson, but the general's dominance of the landscape is evident in his use of imperatives in the determination of the fate of the cottage, which is perceived by the general simply as an "object." If Catherine is a plant in the novel's iconographic scheme, she is a hardy apple, in contrast to the general's exotic fruit, but the symbolic opposition of the pineapple, with its connotations of artificiality and confinement, and the apple tree with its associations of natural abundance and freedom, are undermined by the general's assumption of authority over the cottage and its orchard, just as he has assumed unwarranted authority over Catherine.

Northanger Abbey challenges the connection, found in *Angelina* and *Desmond*, between pineapple cultivation and the manners and values of the nouveaux riches. Unlike Stamford and Clarendon who have risen from the professional and trading class, General Tilney is "of a very respectable family in Gloucestershire" (22), which has been in possession of the abbey since the dissolution (144). Yet the identification of narrow-minded materialism with a representative of the landed elite is characteristic of Austen's eschewal of conventional stereotypes and binarisms. The pineapple becomes a metonym for the decay of an aristocracy that is appropriating the commodified values of the emergent financial and commercial classes. Lynch has identified the enclosed space of the hothouse and the greenhouse with precocity and unnaturalness, but it is also associated with tyranny and oppression.[68] These are rather different from the positive images of confinement which Crawford has identified within garden literature and lyric poetry.[69] The hothouse produces exotic fruit which cannot survive outside its confines and symbolizes pampered extravagance, luxury, and weakness. At the same time, the attempt to control nature, combined with the exotic origins of the fruits themselves, provides a metaphor for the tyranny of slavery, patriarchal oppression, and the disruption of traditional patterns of gender and class behavior within the novels of the 1790s. In contrast, native apples (and sometimes grapes) are associated with health and an absence of social pretension symbolized in the figure of the honest and independent farmer or husbandman. In Jane Austen's work, this is extended to encompass the virtuous parson and his unpretentious future wife who, like Sophia Clarendon and Charles Belmont in *Angelina*, become the true inheritors of the mantle of aristocratic paternalism precisely because of their eschewal of the artificiality of pineapple cultivation that connotes patriarchal and unnatural dominance.

George Walker's *The Vagabond* provides a very different perspective on the ethics of pineapple cultivation. The novel is narrated by Frederick Fenton, a devoted follower of the philosopher "Stupeo," a malicious portrait of William Godwin, and satirizes the radical rhetoric of the 1790s. Fenton recounts an argument with Lord B——, in which he questions "What right has one man to eat a pine-apple, for which he gave a guinea, when another is starving for want of a half-penny worth of bread?"[70] Lord B—— responds that "In the state of equality, that is, ignorant barbarism, no pine-apples would be cultivated," but he also goes on to describe some of the people who "depend for their share of the guinea paid for the pine-apple," citing "the fruiterer, the gardener, the glazier, the carpenter, the bricklayer, the smith, the coal-merchant, the mariner, the miner, with all the crowd of others who supply each of these individuals with materials." This is a curious reworking of the account in Adam Smith's *Inquiry into the Nature and Causes of the Wealth of Nations* (1776) of the number of people required to manufacture a pin,[71] and culminates in a reversal of Fenton's initial question, as Lord B—— asks, "Which is the greater good, to aid all those tradesmen and their dependents, by encouraging the luxury, or to give the superfluous guinea to the support of unproductive idleness?" (137).

Walker mocks Godwin's radical critique of consumption and his concern with equality. The choice of the pineapple may be a specific reference to the passage in *Desmond* where the production of exotic fruit is identified as an alternative to feeding the laboring poor, or it may simply represent the fruit's status as the ultimate luxury. Either way, the passage highlights that by the end of the eighteenth century the pineapple was conceived as artificial.[72] This is evident not only in the assertion of Lord B——that there would be no pine-apples in a state of barbarism, but also in the itemization of the range of trades required for its successful cultivation. This is far from the fruits of benevolent nature hanging from "compliant boughs" in Marvell or Milton, or the repre-sentation of tropical abundance in the "trope of bounty."[73] The defense of the pineapple is grounded in a celebration of industry, property, and the interde-pendence of the economic system that is constructed in opposition to radical rhetoric that is satirized as naïve.

Amelia Opie's *Adeline Mowbray* (1804) is loosely based on the life of Mary Wollstonecraft and like *The Vagabond* has been identified with the reaction against the radicalism of the 1790s. Adeline is led by adolescent enthusiasm for the ideas of the Godwin figure Glenmurray to form a union "cemented by no ties but those of love and honour."[74] She constructs this relationship as a principled stand against repressive social constraints, but society regards her as a fallen woman, and Glenmurray is too proud and too weak to acknowledge what he now sees as the folly of his beliefs. His moral and ideological frailty is manifested in physical deterioration, as he succumbs to the ravages of con-sumption, engendering a "capricious appetite" which Adeline struggles to satisfy after the loss of Glenmurray's fortune. One day, having seen "some fine grapes at the window of a fruiterer, she went in to ask the price of them, knowing how welcome fruit was to the feverish palate of Glenmurray. While the shopman was weighing the grapes, she saw a pine-apple on the counter, and felt a strong wish to carry it home as a more welcome present."[75] When she discovers that the pineapple costs two guineas, Adeline realizes that she cannot afford it. The narrator reveals that it would normally be one guinea, which appears to be the standard price in the late eighteenth and early nineteenth centuries, but the shopkeeper asks two on the grounds that "those sort of women never mind what they give." Adeline takes the grapes home to Glenmurray, but incautiously mentions the pineapple as she gives them to him: "'A pine-apple!' said Glenmurray, languidly turning over the grapes, and with a sort of distaste putting one of them in his mouth, 'a pine-apple!—I wish you had brought it with all my heart! I protest that I feel that I could eat a whole one.'" On hearing the price of the pineapple, Glenmurray resolves that "he will not indulge his appetite at such a rate," echoing an incident in the *Memoirs of Mrs. Sophia Baddeley, late of Drury-Lane Theatre* (1787) in which the narrator describes how the notoriously extravagant actress, while out shopping, "asked the price of a pine-apple; and being told a guinea, for the first time since I knew her, ... declined to gratify her inclination at such an expence."[76] But Glenmurray rejects the grapes and "was continually talking of pine-apples, and in that way showed how strongly his diseased appetite wished to enjoy the gratification of eating one." The desire for exotic fruit is symptomatic of a diseased palate and weakened mind. Glenmurray, "who in health was remarkable for self-denial and temperance, scrupled not, overcome by the influence of the fever which consumed him, to gratify his palate at a rate the most extravagant."

Adeline raises the money for the pineapple by selling her veil, symbolically sacrificing her modesty in a gesture that recapitulates her original "fall." But on the way to the fruit shop she encounters a "mulatto" woman who, with her son "the tawny boy," is trying to prevent the bailiffs from arresting her husband for debt. Adeline is torn between her desire to assist and thoughts of Glenmurray "eagerly expecting the promised treat, so gratifying to the feverish taste of sickness." Her charity toward the strangers eventually prevails, not least because Adeline is anxious to dissociate herself from the racial prejudice of the creditor. The narrator comments that the woman's color "made her an object of greater interest to Adeline" and "urged her ... to step forward with an almost irresistible impulse." The money is spent in relieving the exotic victims of oppression and prejudice, rather than in purchasing the exotic object of luxurious desire. When Adeline explains to Glenmurray why she has not brought the pineapple, his initial petulant disappointment is followed by praise for her charity as "the habitual sweetness and generosity of his temper struggled effectually with his malady."

Carol Howard has developed a detailed reading of "the story of the pineapple," showing how the fruit is constructed as an emblem of the mulatto, Savanna, who becomes a devoted attendant in line with the "grateful negro" tradition.[77] The narrative reinforces not only the association of pineapples and slavery found within *Angelina* but also the negative connotations of fruit as the object of irrational and immoderate desire, harking back to the story of the fall and the myth of Proserpine. Ann Hamilton's 1811 it-narrative, *The Adventures of a Seven Shilling Piece*, contains the interpolated narrative of a sailor, Ben Binnacle, who is "confined to his bed with a dangerous illness, and . . . expressed a longing desire for . . . fruit," which represents a luxury he cannot afford. When his wife is taken to court and charged with attempting to steal some grapes, the virtuous Mr. Thornton speaks on her behalf, persuading the Justice to adopt the path of "mercy, rather than strict justice," in a passage echoing Henry Fielding's *Tom Jones* as well as the courtroom scene in *The Merchant of Venice*.[78] In *Adeline Mowbray* and the *Seven Shilling Piece*, the desire for fruit is associated with illness and a diseased appetite that causes uncontrollable cravings. Ben Binnacle pines for the grapes that, at the prices charged in the commercial fruit markets of London, are far beyond his humble social status, while Glenmurray rejects grapes in favor of the costly pineapple that is beyond both his means and his station. Sickness has reduced them to the luxurious desire that is identified by Smith and Robinson with the unnatural and self-indulgent consumerism of the new commercial class.

Opie repeatedly refers to the "feverish palate," the "diseased appetite," and the "feverish taste of sickness" to reinforce the connection between illness and the desire for fruit, and, as with the pica counterfeited by May in Chaucer's "Merchant's Tale" and by Sally Pickle in Smollett's *Peregrine Pickle*, there is an assumption that such cravings should be gratified whenever possible. Shortly before the pineapple incident, Adeline has her fears for Glenmurray's health confirmed when the doctor tells her, "Let him have whatever he likes; nothing can hurt him now" (134–38). Some medical writers believed that acidic fruits and vegetables could be beneficial in cases of fever, echoing the medieval belief in their cooling properties manifested in Sir Gawain's partiality for apples. William Buchan argues in *Domestic Medicine* (1772) that fruits can be used "to quench the patient's thirst and to cool the blood," while Johann Beckmann quotes the sixteenth-century account of the pineapple of Geronimo Benzono to the effect that "no fruit on earth can be more pleasant: sick persons, who loathed all other food, might relish it."[79] Other commentators were more skeptical about the health benefits of tropical fruit in particular, with John Armstrong identifying it as alien to the British constitution and therefore potentially risky, and John Guy referring to the "danger" of eating pineapple.[80] Both Opie and Hamilton connect the cravings for exotic fruit to a departure from the order of the patriarchal state. Ben Binnacle has been reduced by disease to dependence on his wife, and the physical weakness of Glenmurray symbolizes his moral and intellectual decline, as he is increasingly reliant on nineteen-year-old Adeline. The desire for exotic fruit is therefore symptomatic of a diseased appetite, as well as of a disordered social system in which traditional gender roles have been overturned. Glenmurray becomes an Eve or Proserpine figure in a gender reversal of biblical and classical narratives of the temptation offered by fruit, as he is seduced by the object that has become a metonym for the artificial and stratified commercial society which he has rejected in his philosophical writings. This association of fruit with sickness and effeminacy substantiates the readings of the fruit banquet in Keats's "Eve of St. Agnes" that represent the feast as strangely unappealing and disconcertingly insubstantial and cloying, and Byron's Corsair shows his austere manliness in his eschewal of even "the summer luxury of fruits."[81]

The fruit iconography inherited from biblical and classical tradition, with its connotations of a fall that is female and sexual, is reoriented by the turn of the eighteenth century as domestically produced exotic fruit provides a metaphor for a system of production and consumption that is complex and artificial. The cultivation of tropical fruits within temperate climes carries a range of signifiers, beyond the association with sexuality and temptation. It represents various forms of disruption of the natural order, whether social promiscuity and upward mobility, tyranny and slavery, or challenges to traditional gender roles. The development of British hothouses leads to the displacement of the trope of abundance but also the adaptation of the trope of labor. The work required to produce pineapples and oranges in the stifling heat of the forcing house is not the honest labor of the happy, independent husbandman, or even of the contented tenants and laborers of the country estate. Instead, hothouse cultivation is figured in terms of the destruction of traditional tenancies and patterns of labor relations and is associated with distortions of the social compact and natural production methods. The pineapple is thus constructed as a symbol of slavery and a product of slavery both at home and overseas.

Conclusion

In Charlotte Brontë's *Jane Eyre* (1847), Edward Rochester describes how he walked "under the dripping orange-trees of [his] wet garden, and amongst its drenched pomegranates and pineapples . . . while the refulgent dawn of the tropics kindled around [him]."[1] The itemized fruits, soaked with symbolic associations, connote the exotic location and thus the displacement of Rochester. As the younger son of an aristocratic family, he represents himself as having been sold in marriage by his father and brother to the daughter of a West India planter and merchant. This is an ironic reversal of the conventional gender dynamic of the fictional forced marriage, as Rochester sees himself as the subject of a "plot" of the kind usually associated with female heiresses. The gender reversal is reinforced by the reference to pomegranates, since Rochester constructs himself as a Proserpine figure, trapped in the Hades of the West Indies. At the same time, the account of how he was bought for "thirty thousand pounds" invokes the biblical thirty pieces of silver, emphasizing his sense of betrayal. It signals slavery not only through the idea of purchasing humanity but also through its source in the slaving wealth of the Mason family. Critics and readers of the novel have tended to relate the slavery theme to the suffering of Rochester's wife Bertha, in line with the fictional assimilation of slaving and patriarchy discussed in Chapter 6, but in Rochester's own account of events he consistently presents himself as the one who is commodified. He uses the lexis of trade but also of imprisonment as he recounts how "her family wished to secure me" and how he has been "tied" and "bound" and this tone of self-pity is parodied by Jean Rhys in the narrative of the anonymous "Rochester" character in *Wide Sargasso Sea* (1966).[2] The solipsistic narrative culminates in a description of the "fiery West-Indian night" and, although it is Bertha who "had of course been shut up," Rochester identifies himself as the prisoner who must "break away," even while he stresses his proprietorship in the denomination of "my garden." As the storm breaks and the rain descends, "a wind fresh from Europe blew over the ocean." It is when Rochester walks out among the dripping tropical fruit that he forms his resolution to return to a Europe that for him symbolizes "glorious liberty . . . renewal . . . Hope . . . and . . . Regeneration" (305–8). The negative language of subjugation and confinement that is used in literary representations of British hothouse production is here transferred to the fruit growing outdoors in the West Indies and is juxtaposed with images of freedom associated with Europe.

None of the fruits specified in the passage is native to Jamaica, with oranges originating in China, pomegranates in Iran, and pineapples in Brazil, yet by the mid-nineteenth century all three had been naturalized in the Caribbean in a botanical corollary of the movement of peoples associated with slavery and imperialism. The exotic fruits are apparently growing freely, without the continuous human assistance required by British tropical fruit, yet they are still used to symbolize sensory overload and the oppression of which Rochester sees himself as victim. This is in striking contrast to the poetic deployment of tropical fruit as a manifestation of a benevolent deity that has given every climate the fruit that is most suitable to the needs of the people living within it. As with Waller in the seventeenth century, it is not clear whether Brontë was aware of the foreign origins of the fruits described by Rochester, but they are incorporated within a discourse of unnaturalness and excess.

Although Rochester conveys his own version of events, his words are interpolated within the containing narrative of Jane Eyre. Jane is a skeptical auditor, but her reservations largely relate to Rochester's conduct after his return to Europe and the question of whether he is right to regard himself as free to start another relationship or to remarry. She expresses sympathy for his experiences in the West Indies and Rochester accepts her pity as sincere (306–7). Moreover, Rochester's decision to return home follows news of the deaths of his father and elder brother. He can turn his back on the world of commodification and oppression that is built on the profits of slavery and symbolized in the unnatural excess of tropical fruit and return to Europe as a member of a landed aristocracy that seeks to deny the extent of its implication in the system of exploitation on which its wealth is built. Yet despite the refreshing qualities of the "sweet wind" from Europe, and Rochester's position as a member of the landed elite, he is not able to remove the shackles of the West Indian connection symbolized in his marriage to Bertha. The inextricability of the ties binding the British aristocracy to the trading and commercial wealth derived from slavery are manifested in the continuing presence of Bertha in the attic of Thornfield as a metonym for the complicity in slavery of Rochester's class as well as his responsibilities as an individual.

The first betrothal of Jane and Rochester takes place in the orchard at Thornfield and we are told that there was "no nook in the grounds more sheltered and more Eden-like" (248). The prelapsarian English orchard with its humble hardy fruits initially appears to stand in contrast to the tropical fruit garden of the West Indies, but, as so often in Brontë's work, the binary opposition is undermined. Like the Jamaican garden, the orchard is characterized by unnatural fecundity and sensory excess, with gooseberries the size of plums and fragrant ripe cherries. The narrative shifts into the present tense to convey the impact and immediacy of the burgeoning scene: "I see the trees laden with ripening fruit" (248). The "waft of wind" that sweeps through Thornfield invites comparison with the wind that Rochester feels in Jamaica and, like the West Indian wind, is a prelude to a storm which roars through the gardens, culminating in the destruction of the horse-chestnut tree at the end of the orchard (254–57). By the close of the novel, this blasted tree has become a symbol of the disabled Rochester, albeit one that is associated with nurturing shadow and new life, but its initial destruction suggests that the references to Eden initiate a scene of temptation rather than signifying a paradise in which Jane and Rochester can exist in innocence (444). Jane is tempted by the forbidden fruit of Rochester when she is offered the possibility of living with him outside marriage and she can only resist temptation by leaving Thornfield.

The eventual union of Jane and Rochester requires the destruction of Bertha. Gayatri Spivak argues that the "imperialist axiomatics" of the nineteenth-century novel necessitate that Bertha must be "sacrificed as an insane animal for her sister's consolidation."[3] But the ideology of the narrative also demands the destruction of Thornfield as a symbol of the unholy alliance between the English aristocracy and the West Indian plantocracy. Many critics have highlighted the irony that the final romantic resolution is facilitated by the independence that Jane has derived from her uncle in Madeira, which is thus also derived from the profits of slavery (434). Brontë subverts the contrast between the gooseberries and cherries of the English orchard and the oranges, pineapples, and pomegranates of the tropical garden by exposing the extent of the links that bind the two. Neither the English orchard nor the West Indian plantation is untouched by the taint of slavery. Rochester is too hasty in associating the "wind from Europe" with "Regeneration," and his salvation is ultimately only possible through alliance with Jane Eyre. As a governess, she has been identified as a manifestation of the emergent ambiguities of class, challenging the rigid divisions on which British society is built, but the clear indications in the novel that her financial independence derives from slavery negate any reading constructing her as a symbol of a new social order.[4] The tropical fruits consumed by the social elite provide a continuing reminder of their complicity in colonial oppression.

This brief excursion beyond the verdurous wall that constitutes the temporal bounds of this study indicates a continuing role for fruit imagery in the nineteenth century and, while it is tempting to pursue the theme, for example, into the sensual fecundity of Christina Rossetti's fruit-based enactment of fall and redemption in *Goblin Market*, this is outside the scope of this project. What is clear from the range of texts that have been discussed, however, is the flexibility and fluidity of fruit symbolism. The repertoire of images adapts to the conventions and requirements of literary genre; it responds to developments in fruit production, distribution, and consumption; but it also draws on inherited literary and mythic associations. As such, it manifests the interdependence of formalism, historicism, and iconography in the interpretation of literary texts and thus the complexity of any study of representational trends. Nonetheless, some recurrent themes emerge, showing continuing ideological resonances of fruit in general, as well as persistent associations of individual types or varieties.

Tropical and subtropical fruits can be used to evoke images of distant lands, hot climates, and divine or natural benevolence, yet what has been identified as a distinctly tropical "trope of bounty" is also evident in the gardens of the English elite, where fruit is presented falling unbidden and unsought into the hand and mouth. In practice, the propagation and cultivation of delicate wall fruits such as peaches and nectarines clearly depended on extensive horticultural labor, but this is invisible to, or unacknowledged by, the landed proprietors of country house poetry, drama, and the novel in representations of fruit as a simple and natural product. Images of a prelapsarian world, drawing on biblical and classical tradition, present an idealized model of domestic production in which the community of fruit replicates the community of the estate, providing a rejection of systems of capitalist exchange. This is distinct from the georgic vision in which different classes are bound together in acts of labor and communal consumption, but both views share a rejection of the commercial ethos. They celebrate a landscape based on cultivation rather than trade, and they present human activity as consonant with the patterns and rhythms of nature.

Horticultural tracts and treatises of the seventeenth century validate this perspective by locating the celebration of domestic production in the ideology of mercantilism, in which the consumption of indigenous fruits is elevated as an economic as well as a moral virtue, and foreign goods are identified as a threat to the wealth but also the health of the nation, weakening the public and private constitution. The combination of horticultural and medical discourse furnishes a repertoire of fruit rhetoric that can be used to challenge the identification of colonial expansion and the naval Empire as an inevitable source of national good.

While recognizing the increasingly diverse range of fruits portrayed in literary texts and while acknowledging the importance of the supporting cast, this study has given special prominence to the stories of the apple, the orange, and the pineapple, exploring their development across a range of texts and genres. In general, the portrayal of orchard fruits is more stable than that of exotic and wall fruits. Apples, pears, plums, and cherries provide metaphors for honesty, humility, and hardiness from the seventeenth to the nineteenth century, but although their moral and social connotations remain consistent, there is a significant shift in the gendering of the apple in particular. The Genesis story and the apples of the Hesperides suggest the association of apples with female frailty. The nubile tenants' daughters are emblematized as plums and pears at Penshurst, and simple country girls are ripe apples in Restoration drama, emphasizing that they are fresh and natural and available for male consumption. In the georgic poetry of the eighteenth century, however, apples, and the cider they produce, are constructed as masculine. They are a hardy fruit yeomanry and this metaphor is dramatized in the characters of Thomas Appletree and Costar Pearmain in Farquhar's eighteenth-century play. In the novel, the apple is traditionally an object of childish desire, but with the growing preoccupation with hothouse fruits in the works of the Romantic period, the apple increasingly accrues the "Masculine Qualities" identified within mercantilist writings and georgic, as a simple and honest alternative not only to the produce of foreign countries but also to the exotic fruits being cultivated at home.[5]

Yet, although georgic seeks to elevate the apple as a symbol of masculinity that is appropriate to all, in drama and the novel this celebration, while acknowledged, is largely relegated to the realm of myth. Like country life within court pastoral, the apple is enlisted as a means of exposing the corruptions of contemporary society, rather than as a realistic alternative to it. Sir Charles Meriwill is not going to court a simple country girl; Desmond is not going to live on a diet of brown bread and cider, even though he may appreciate them as a change from his usual breakfast. This literary fruit hypocrisy is exposed and satirized in the sophisticated fruit banter of Restoration drama and forms the central theme of Gay's mock-georgic *Wine*, where cider causes melancholy, marital disharmony, and sexual dysfunction. Home-produced apples and cider may sound good in theory, but ideas of the organic community are presented as out of touch with the realities of a sophisticated and cosmopolitan metropolitan society in which fruit is fungible and commercialized. This internationalist perspective is manifested in the importance of the orange within Restoration drama at a time when, as this study has shown, dessert fruits were not being produced in British orangeries. Unlike the exotic fruits found in the island paradises of seventeenth-century poetry, the oranges consumed by theater audiences and presented on the stage are not symbols of the distant tropics and colonial territories but are imports from European rivals to the British economy and British power. They are not plucked from the trees by the land-owner or farmer but are purchased from hucksters who signify prostitution through a synechdochal identification with the commodification and sexual resonances of their wares. But the distinction here is primarily generic rather than temporal.

While the oranges eaten in the theater are characterized as fungible fruits and symbols of the modern metropolis, the poetry produced in the Restoration and the eighteenth century continues to identify tropical and semitropical fruits with the distant shores of colonially subjugated lands. The oranges, pineapples, and melons growing on Caribbean islands are celebrated in divine verse as well as in georgic as evidence of the hand of God who supplies every part of the world with the fruits that grow best and are most appropriate to the constitutions of the people. Yet this representation of providential ordering does not necessarily imply acceptance. The terms of the portrayal of exotic fruit and its distribution are used to legitimate British colonial power through the representation of the moral and physical superiority of hardy orchard fruits over weaker more luxurious tropical fruits, which reinforces the idea that different parts of the world contain goods that are needed by the colonial center and therefore must have been intended to come under British colonial control. While many of the fruit georgics and religious poems of the eighteenth century are grounded in explicit opposition to colonialist and expansionist rhetoric, their fruit iconography provides an implicit validation of ideas of national superiority that can inform other texts and genres, as shown in the passage from *Jane Eyre* cited at the beginning of this chapter.

Although most oranges, as well as many grapes and pineapples, continued to be imported in the eighteenth century, the development of hothouse technology, and the identification of the pineapple as a domestic product, leads to a reorientation not only of the fruit metaphor but also of the trope of labor, as the work required to produce fruit acquires different connotations. The healthful toil of the yeoman farmer described within georgic ensures a plentiful harvest of the apples which are primarily intended for his own consumption and profit. The affluent owner of the hothouse, in contrast, requires the efforts of a host of artisans and wage laborers in a range of occupations to produce pineapples for his table. Thus, Walker's Lord B—— represents pineapple production in a parodic version of Adam Smith's description of the division of labor; Smith's Bethel laments the construction of forcing houses as a movement from a prelapsarian landscape of agriculture to a postlapsarian industrial scene; Austen's account of the hothouses at Northanger Abbey appropriates the language and images of the enclosure and displacement that have disrupted the rural community. Hothouse enthusiasts are concerned with controlling and subverting, rather than adapting to, the patterns of nature and they do so using the labor of others rather than their own efforts.

The resultant fruit can be portrayed as the object of desire to the diseased or luxurious appetites of an emergent social class that is presented as having no experience or understanding of nature and the land. The technological developments that facilitate the domestic production of exotic fruit destabilize a repertoire of representational conventions. They challenge literary concepts of natural fecundity and divine providence, the identification of domestic produce, and the associated labor, with health, the binary opposition of native and foreign, and the biblical and classical connection of fruit with feminine sexuality. The medical orthodoxy that tropical fruit was unhealthy because of its foreign origins was absorbed into the discourse of luxury, to reinforce the association of the unnaturalness of the production methods with the unhealthiness of the product and the debased nature of the desire. A craving for exotic fruit could be portrayed as a disruption or distortion of nature, which could signify effeminacy, tyranny, the unnatural aspirations of the new commercial class, or a combination of these. These shifts show the impact of historical, or, in this case, horticultural changes on literary iconography, and it is significant that these changes are first felt within the more fluid conventions of the most recently established genre, the novel.

While the apple continues to symbolize health and naturalness and maintains its significance as an object of desire within children's fiction,[6] exotic fruit becomes a metonym for the decadence of consumer culture and the sickness of society. Drawing on the associations with luxury and weakness in poetic representations of foreign fruit but planting these in the manure of the British hothouse, the pineapple acquires especially strong negative inflections. It is identified with slavery through its association with the Caribbean, and as a fruit which is itself subject to confinement and oppressive heat. It is simultaneously a symbol and product of enslavement and provides an apt metonym for imperialist power at a time when Britain was expanding its influence in the Caribbean, a major pineapple-growing region, and in Brazil, the home of the pineapple.[7] Rachel Crawford has argued that confined space and horticultural enclosure become increasingly important in the gardening treatises and lyric poetry of the late eighteenth and early nineteenth centuries.[8] Yet the novels of this period contain a counter discourse, in which the enclosed space of the hothouse and the greenhouse connotes tyranny, slavery, and oppression. Rather than denying the labor involved in the production of tropical fruits, the novel emphasizes both the economic and human costs to construct a symbol of artifice and confinement that is the direct opposite of the trope of bounty and pastoral images of abundance.

The owners of the hothouses producing these fruits are tyrannical and oppressive because of their lack of respect for nature and the natural processes of production, and this relates to their characterization as social climbers. They are aspiring after objects that symbolize pretension but which also represent a disruption of the natural order that replicates their own social promiscuity. They are like hothouse plants that cannot naturally survive in the environment in which they are growing and, like Sir Edward Clarendon in *Angelina*, will ultimately fail to thrive. Their obsessiveness is also satirized, since the object of their preoccupation is inconsequential, drawing on fruit's role as a form of confectionary appropriate to infantile tastes as well as on the ambivalent status of the forbidden fruit as simultaneously trivial and vital.[9] The ambivalence is manifested in the novel in the juxtaposition of a preoccupation with hothouse fruit that appears in itself rather demeaning, with the use of fruit cultivation as a metaphor for the serious issues of the oppression of slavery and the repression of women. The latter draws on the biblical and classical resonances of fruit and its connection to ideas of female frailty, but it also has more direct antecedents in the seventeenth- and eighteenth-century deployment of fruit and its consumption to symbolize sexual consummation.

King and Lynch have emphasized the importance of floral imagery in fiction of the Romantic period, with Lynch showing how Austen presents the dangers of female education through the depiction of hothouse blooms.[10] But while the hothouses used for the forcing of flowers have been seen as female spaces, the orangeries and pineries in the novels discussed here are clearly identified as male, and associated with a male desire to control and dominate nature, in the form of the feminized fruits that are forced within. The male proprietors attempt to display their status by showing off the size of their pineries, although in doing so they tend to expose their lack of true gentility. While both hothouse flowers and hothouse fruits are natural products raised within an artificial environment, the comestibility of fruit makes its symbolic function fundamentally different. Flowers can be admired and plucked, and their fragrance savored, but they are not normally eaten. Just as the portrayal of adolescent girls through the language of hothouse flowers draws on a literary tradition of floral imagery, the representation of hothouse fruits is informed by a rather different tradition in which consumption is central and inherently sexual. This has roots in the Song of Solomon and biblical and classical myth and is influenced by medical discourse and fruticultural practice, but it is also informed by the iconographic tradition developed within drama, with its deployment of fruit to articulate anxieties about the consequences of increasingly commercialized production. This furnishes a range of images of the dangers of fruit consumption, which can be appropriated within fiction to explore female sexuality. While women who have reached the point of perfect ripeness can be portrayed as the ideal food for the healthy male appetite, young girls may be green fruit, suggesting naïveté but also a potential danger to health. This metaphor combines the contemporary enthusiasm for producing out-of-season fruit with anxieties about the perils of a prematurely sexualized society. At the same time, older women who manifest symptoms of sexual desire can be characterized as overripe, rotten, or rivelled fruits. At best they are unappetizing, at worst they are hazardous, but above all they provide a source of comedy as a manifestation of the unnatural that is again linked to developments in horticultural practice and the need to extend the harvest to satisfy the demands of the market.

The identification of women as fruits that are part of the commercial system and available to be eaten by men is accompanied by condemnation of women who see themselves as active consumers of fruit, rather than as items of consumption. This links to the story of the fall, and particularly to those retellings of the medieval and early modern period which flesh out the biblical core to stress female culpability. Despite the revisionist readings by recent critics of *Paradise Lost*, stressing the ecological awareness and progressive ideology of Milton's Eve, she ultimately succumbs to female appetite. The association of fruit consumption with physical desire in stories of Eve and Proserpine is developed in the literary forms of the early modern period to elicit comedy and disgust, articulating a social rejection of active female sexuality, particularly when manifested in an appetite for green fruit. The emphasis on commercial and artificial mechanisms of production enhances the moral resonances of the celebration of simple orchard fruit at the same time as it confines it to the realm of nostalgic myth.

Thus, attitudes toward fruit, and attitudes toward sexuality, are fundamentally ambivalent. A fruit, like sexual experience, is simultaneously valuable and nugatory; in some respects, a luxury item but one that is transitory; a natural product but one that is enmeshed in a capitalist system. Individual fruits are invested with a range of symbolic associations. The apple embodies female frailty through its mythic connotations, but it also embodies hardy masculinity or childish simplicity. The orange is a recognized token of love, a metaphor for theatrical attendance, and a symbol of popular protest. Its prominence within the comedy of the Restoration emphasizes the preoccupation with a sophisticated urban culture that is bound by acts of commercial exchange, but it also exposes the misogyny that challenges critical readings which have identified the libertine philosophy of Restoration comedy as sexually liberating for women. Fictional depictions of the pineapple in terms of artificiality, vapidity, weakness, unnaturalness, and extravagance provide a flexible metaphor for the representation of women. It can be used as an indictment of women as costly and affected triflers, but it can also function to criticize the society that is attempting to force them into this distorted character through its system of cultivation. Where men are obsessed with fruit or experience the cravings that conventionally connote pregnancy, they are identified as showing unnatural effeminacy that is a consequence of commodification and a rejection of traditional roles and practices.

The analysis of the depiction of fruit highlights the complexity of the process of representation and the range of factors mediating relationships between the sign and the signified, whether in poetry, drama, the novel, or the horticultural treatise. Ecocriticism has developed the historicist approach to emphasize the extent to which literary texts engage with the environmental issues and scientific innovations of their time, challenging older readings based on symbolic and iconographic interpretations of the representation of nature. Formalist approaches have stressed the significance of genre in providing a series of codes and conventions that shape the way cultural change and ideology are represented. This study has highlighted the fundamental role of genre in influencing the kinds of fruits that are presented in literary texts and how they are portrayed. Yet it suggests that genre functions more like a Venn diagram than a bar chart, with overlaps between the representational zones. To use a fruit analogy, if genres are different varieties of tree within the orchard of literature, this analysis has indicated the extent to which their slips can be grafted onto one another, while they all have common ancestors in the pervasive myths derived from biblical and classical sources. Discoursing with fruit trees can therefore provide a case study in the nature of representation, exposing the relationships among practical, economic change, the inherited symbolic repertoire, and genre conventions, showing how these are manifested and interact in individual literary iterations.

NOTES

≈

Introduction

1. Ralph Austen, "Epistle to the Reader," in *A Dialogue (or familiar discourse) and Conference between the Husbandman and Fruit-Trees in his Nurseries, Orchards and Gardens* (Oxford, 1676), n.p.

2. On translations, see Alexandra Lianeri and Vanda Zajko, eds., *Translation and the Classic: Identity as Change in the History of Culture* (Oxford: Oxford University Press, 2008).

3. Robert Appelbaum, *Aguecheek's Beef, Belch's Hiccup, and Other Gastronomic Interjections: Literature, Culture, and Food Among the Early Moderns* (Chicago: University of Chicago Press, 2012), 118–54.

4. See Joan Thirsk, "Making a Fresh Start: Sixteenth-Century Agriculture and the Classical Inspiration," in *Culture and Cultivation in Early Modern England: Writing and the Land*, ed. Michael Leslie and Timothy Raylor (Leicester: Leicester University Press, 1992), 15–34, 19.

5. Ken Albala, *Eating Right in the Renaissance* (Berkeley: University of California Press, 2002), 8; Thomas Austin, ed., *Two Fifteenth-Century Cookery Books*, Harleian MS, 279; *This is the Boke of Cokery* [London, 1500]; *A Propre New Booke of Cokery* [London, 1545]; John Partridge, *The Treasurie of Commodious Conceits, & Hidden secrets and may be called, the Huswives Closet, of Healthfull Provision* (London, 1573); Thomas Dawson, *A Booke of Cookerie and the Order of Meates to bee Serued to the table, both for Flesh and Fish Dayes* (London, 1620), 42–46, 58, 62–70, 84. For a fascinating analysis of early modern cookbooks, see Appelbaum, *Aguecheek's Beef*, 66–117.

6. Patsy Dallas, Gerry Barnes, and Tom Williamson, "Orchards in the Landscape: A Norfolk Case Study," *Landscapes* 16, no. 1 (2015): 26–43, 28–29.

7. John Parkinson, *Paradisi in Sole Paradisus Terrestris* (London, 1629), reprinted (London: Methuen, 1904), 557–612, describes the culinary and medicinal uses of different kinds of fruit. Subsequent references will be to this edition and included in parentheses.

8. The works of the second-century Greek physician Galen were still influential in the early modern period, notably through Galen and Nicholas Culpeper's *Galen's Art of Physick*. Galen suggests that, in contrast to most other fruits, pears are "quite nourishing" and describes how his neighbors chop them up and "make wafer-thin cakes out of them which they dry and store for the winter," Galen and Nicholas Culpeper, *Galen's Art of Physick* (London, 1653). See also Joan Fitzpatrick, "Body and Soul," in *A Cultural History of Food in the Renaissance*, ed. Ken Albala (London: Bloomsbury, 2016), 151–70, 152–53; Albala, *Eating Right in the Renaissance*, 21; Mark Grant, *Galen on Food and Diet* (London: Routledge, 2000), 130.

9. See, for example, John Taverner, *Certain Experiments concerning Fish and Fruit* (London, 1600), 29; John Evelyn, "Preface," in *Pomona: or, An Appendix Concerning Fruit Trees in Relation to Cider in Sylva, or A Discourse of Forest-Trees and the Propagation of Timber in His Majesty's*

Dominions (London, 1664), 1; Moses Cook, *The Manner of Raising, Ordering, and Improving Forest and Fruit-Trees* (London, 1679), 14.

10. John Beale, *Herefordshire Orchards: A Pattern for all England* (London, 1657), 3.

11. See, for example, N. F., "Epistle to the Reader," in *The Fruiterers Secrets* (London, 1604); Beale, *Herefordshire Orchards*, 3.

12. Harriet Ritvo, "At the Edge of the Garden: Nature and Domestication in Eighteenth- and Nineteenth-Century Britain," *Huntington Library Quarterly* 55, no. 3 (Summer, 1992): 363–78, 368; see also Amy King, *Bloom: The Botanical Vernacular in the English Novel* (Oxford: Oxford University Press, 2003), 74; Amy L. Tigner, *Literature and the Renaissance Garden from Elizabeth I to Charles II* (Farnham: Ashgate, 2012), 17.

13. G. R. Hibbard identifies the genre with poems by Jonson, Carew, Herrick, and Marvell in "The Country House Poem of the Seventeenth Century," *Journal of the Warburg and Courtauld Institutes* 19 (1956): 159–74. Further discussion can be found in Raymond Williams, *The Country and the City* (Oxford: Oxford University Press, 1973), 27–34; William A. McClung, *The Country House in English Renaissance Poetry* (Berkeley: University of California Press, 1977); Alastair Fowler, "The Country House Poem: The Politics of a Genre," *Seventeenth Century* 1, no. 1 (1986): 1–14.

14. For detailed analysis of the significance of fruit imagery in *Paradise Lost*, see Robert Appelbaum, "Eve's and Adam's 'Apple': Horticulture, Taste, and the Flesh of the Forbidden Fruit in *Paradise Lost*," *Milton Quarterly* 36, no. 4 (2002): 221–39.

15. Anthony Low summarizes his concept of the georgic revolution in "Agricultural Reform and the Love Poems of Thomas Carew" in Leslie and Raylor, *Culture and Cultivation*, 63–80, 63; Alastair Fowler, "Georgic and Pastoral: Laws of Genre in the Seventeenth Century," in Leslie and Raylor, *Culture and Cultivation*, 81–88, 83–84.

16. Caroline Levine, *Forms: Whole, Rhythm, Hierarchy, Network* (Princeton, N.J.: Princeton University Press, 2015), 20.

17. On agrarian discourse, see Leslie and Raylor, *Culture and Cultivation*, and Andrew McRae, *God Speed the Plough: The Representation of Agrarian England, 1500–1660* (Cambridge: Cambridge University Press, 1996).

18. John Dixon Hunt, *Greater Perfections: The Practice of Garden Theory* (Philadelphia: University of Pennsylvania Press, 2000), 180–206; Rachel Crawford, *Poetry, Enclosure and the Vernacular Landscape, 1700–1830* (Cambridge: Cambridge University Press, 2002), 16.

19. Rebecca Bushnell, *Green Desire: Imagining Early Modern English Gardens* (Ithaca, N.Y.: Cornell University Press, 2003).

20. Jennifer Munroe, "Shakespeare and Ecocriticism Reconsidered," *Literature Compass* 12, no. 9 (2015): 461–70, 461; see also Karen Raber, "Recent Ecocritical Studies of English Renaissance Literature," *English Literary Renaissance* 37, no. 1 (2007): 151–71; Christopher Hitt, "Ecocriticism and the Long Eighteenth Century," *College Literature* 31, no. 3 (2004): 123–47; Erin Drew and John Sitter, "Ecocriticism and Eighteenth-Century English Studies," *Literature Compass* 8, no. 5 (2011): 227–39.

21. Munroe, "Shakespeare and Ecocriticism," 461.

22. Ken Hiltner, "Introduction," in *Renaissance Ecology: Imagining Eden in Milton's England*, ed. Ken Hiltner (Pittsburgh: Duquesne University Press, 2008), 1–14, 1; Tigner, *Literature and the Renaissance Garden*, 195.

23. Diane Kelsey McColley, *Milton's Eve* (Urbana: University of Illinois Press, 1983), 126; Ken Hiltner, *Milton and Ecology* (Cambridge: Cambridge University Press, 2003), 29.

24. Robert N. Watson, *Back to Nature: The Green and the Real in the Late Renaissance* (Philadelphia: University of Pennsylvania Press, 2006); Tigner, *Literature and the Renaissance Garden*.

25. Michel Foucault, *The Order of Things: An Archaeology of the Human Sciences* (London: Vintage, 1994); Ritvo, "At the Edge of the Garden," 371; Alan Bewell, "'On the Banks of the South Sea': Botany and Sexual Controversy in the Late Eighteenth Century," in *Visions of Empire: Voyages, Botany, and Representations of Nature*, ed. David Miller and Peter Hannis Reill (Cambridge: Cambridge University Press, 1996), 173–96; King, *Bloom*; Sam George, *Botany, Sexuality and Women's Writing, 1760–1830: From Modest Shoot to Forward Plant* (Manchester: Manchester University Press, 2007); Deidre Lynch, "'Young Ladies are Delicate Plants': Jane Austen and Greenhouse Romanticism," *ELH* 77 (2010): 689–729.

26. Levine, *Forms*, xii–xiii, 17.

27. Richard H. Grove, *Green Imperialism: Colonial Expansion, Tropical Island Edens and the Origins of Environmentalism, 1600–1860* (Cambridge: Cambridge University Press, 1995), 474, 7; Graham Huggan and Helen Tiffin, *Postcolonial Ecocriticism: Literature, Animals, Environment*, 2nd ed. (Abingdon: Routledge, 2015), 2–5.

28. Beth Fowkes Tobin, *Colonizing Nature: The Tropics in British Arts and Letters, 1760–1820* (Philadelphia: University of Pennsylvania Press, 2004), 168–97. The literary technique identified by Tobin could be described as a topos rather than a trope, but I will follow Tobin's wording hereafter.

29. Albala, *Eating Right in the Renaissance*; Appelbaum, *Aguecheek's Beef*; Joan Fitzpatrick, *Renaissance Food from Rabelais to Shakespeare: Culinary Readings and Culinary Histories* (London: Routledge, 2010); Ken Albala, ed., *A Cultural History of Food in the Renaissance* (London: Bloomsbury, 2012).

30. Albala, *Eating Right in the Renaissance*, 184–85.

31. Tom Carter, *The Victorian Garden* (London: Harper Collins, 1984); John Dixon Hunt, *Garden and Grove: The Italian Renaissance Garden in the English Imagination 1600–1750* (London: Dent, 1986); Tom Williamson, *Polite Landscapes: Gardens and Society in Eighteenth-Century England* (Stroud: Alan Sutton, 1995); Chris Ridgeway and Robert Williams, eds. *Sir John Vanbrugh and Landscape Architecture in Baroque England, 1690–1730* (Stroud: Alan Sutton, 2000); Stephen Bending, ed., *A Cultural History of Gardens in the Age of Enlightenment* (London: Bloomsbury, 2013); David Brown and Tom Williamson, *Lancelot Brown and the Capability Men: Landscape Revolution in Eighteenth-Century England* (London: Reaktion, 2016).

32. For a history of the pineapple, see Fran Beauman, *The Pineapple: King of Fruits* (London: Vintage, 2006); Appelbaum, "Eve's and Adam's 'Apple,'" 221–39, and Appelbaum, *Aguecheek's Beef*, 187–200; G. S. Rousseau, "Pineapples, Pregnancy, Pica, and *Peregrine Pickle*," in *Tobias Smollett: Bicentennial Essays Presented to Lewis M. Knapp*, ed. G. S. Rousseau and P.-G. Boucé, (New York: Oxford University Press, 1971), 79–109; Carol Howard, "'The Story of the Pineapple': Sentimental Abolitionism and Moral Motherhood in Amelia Opie's *Adeline Mowbray*," *Studies in the Novel* 30, no. 3 (1998): 355–76. See also Crawford, *Poetry, Enclosure and the Vernacular Landscape* for the significance of the apple in georgic poetry.

33. Anthony Low, *The Georgic Revolution* (Princeton, N.J.: Princeton University Press, 1985); Rachel Crawford, "English Georgic and British Nationhood," *ELH* 65, no. 1 (1998): 123–58; Crawford, *Poetry, Enclosure*; David Fairer, "Persistence, Adaptation and Transformations in Pastoral and Georgic Poetry," in *The Cambridge History of English Literature, 1660–1780*, ed. John J. Richetti

(Cambridge: Cambridge University Press, 2005), 259–86; Robert Irvine, "Labor and Commerce in Locke and Early Eighteenth-Century English Georgic," *ELH* 76 (2009): 963–88; Clare Bucknell, "The Mid-Eighteenth-Century Georgic and Agricultural Improvement," *Journal for Eighteenth-Century Studies* 36, no. 3 (2013): 335–52.

34. Chris Jones, *Radical Sensibility: Literature and Ideas in the 1790s* (London: Routledge, 1993); Nicola Watson, *Revolution and the Form of the British Novel 1780–1852* (Oxford: Oxford University Press, 1994); Adriana Craciun and Kari Lokke, eds., *Rebellious Hearts: British Women Writers and the French Revolution* (Albany: State University of New York Press, 2001).

35. Levine, *Forms*, 14.

Chapter 1

Note to epigraph: Genesis 3:6. All quotations from the Bible are from the Authorized King James Version unless otherwise indicated, using the Oxford World's Classics edition with introduction and notes by Robert Carroll and Stephen Prickett (Oxford: Oxford University Press, 2008).

1. Thirsk, "Making a Fresh Start," 15–34, 18–28.

2. Ritvo, "At the Edge of the Garden," 364.

3. Leah S. Marcus, "Ecocritical Milton," in *Ecological Approaches to Early Modern English Texts: A Field Guide to Reading and Teaching*, ed. Jennifer Munroe, Edward J. Geisweidt, and Lynne Bruckner (Farnham: Ashgate, 2015), 131–41, 131.

4. John Milton, *Paradise Lost*, ed. Alastair Fowler (Harlow: Pearson, 2007), note to Book 8, lines 320–22.

5. William Lawson, *A New Orchard and Garden* (London, 1618), 32–33.

6. "Adam Lay Ybounden," British Library, Sloane 2593, ff.10v-11.

7. Diane McColley, *A Gust for Paradise* (Chicago: University of Illinois Press, 1993), 21, 56–57.

8. Norman Tanner, "Religious Practice," in *Medieval Norwich*, ed. Richard Wilson and Carole Rawcliffe (London: Palgrave Macmillan, 2004), 137–56, 154.

9. *OED Online*, 3a. For discussion of the development of the definition of the apple and the identity of the forbidden fruit in Genesis and Milton, see Appelbaum, "Eve's and Adam's 'Apple,'" 224, 227; Crawford, *Poetry, Enclosure*, 130.

10. Henry Butts, *Dyets Dry Dinner* (London: William Wood, 1599), n.p., B2; Georg Andreas Agricola, *Philosophical Treatise of Husbandry and Gardening* (London, 1721), reprinted as *The Experimental Husbandman and Gardener* (London, 1726), 91–92.

11. Song of Solomon, 2:3. For clarity, the King James version is here referred to as The Song of Solomon and the Vulgate version as the Song of Songs. References are to the Song of Solomon unless otherwise indicated and are incorporated in parentheses. For the Vulgate text, see E. Ann Matter, *The Voice of My Beloved: The Song of Songs in Western Medieval Christianity* (Philadelphia: University of Pennsylvania Press, 1990).

12. Phyllis Trible, *God and the Rhetoric of Sexuality* (Philadelphia: Fortress Press, 1978), 144–66.

13. See, for example, Edmund Spenser, *Amoretti* (1595), sonnet 64, in *Spenser: Poetical Works*, ed. J. C. Smith and E. de Selincourt (Oxford: Oxford University Press, 1970), 573; Thomas Campion, "There is a Garden in her Face" (1617) , in *The Works of Thomas Campion*, ed. Walter R. Davis and

J. Max Patrick (London: Norton, 1970), 174; Shakespeare parodies this tradition in *A Midsummer Night's Dream* in Demetrius's declaration of love to Helena in act 3, scene 2, 139–44, and Flute's speech in the Pyramus and Thisbe play, act 5, scene 1, 317–19, as well as in Sonnet 130. All references to Shakespeare are to *The Norton Shakespeare*, ed. Stephen Greenblatt (London: Norton, 2008).

14. Song of Songs, 4:12; Matter, *Voice of My Beloved,* 162–63, 33–35, 86, 138.

15. Matter, *Voice of My Beloved,* 138.

16. See, for example, Laura Howes, *Chaucer's Gardens and the Language of Convention* (Gainesville: University Press of Florida, 1997); Terry Comito, *The Idea of the Garden in the Renaissance* (New Brunswick, N.J.: Rutgers University Press, 1978).

17. For the use of the vine as a symbol of Israel, see Isaiah 5:1–7 discussed above; Jeremiah 2:21; 5:10; 6:9.

18. Alastair Fowler, *The Country House Poem: A Cabinet of Seventeenth-Century Estate Poems and Related Items* (Edinburgh: Edinburgh University Press, 1994), 76–79; 404–6.

19. See, e.g., Alexander Pope, *The Odyssey of Homer, translated by Alexander Pope* (London: Suttaby, Evance and Co. and Crosby and Co., 1811), Book 7, lines 142–75, 146–47; Homer, *The Odyssey,* translated by Walter Shewring (Oxford: Oxford University Press, 2008), 78.

20. Homer, *The Odyssey* in *Chapman's Homer: The Iliad and The Odyssey,* trans. George Chapman, ed. Jan Parker (Ware: Wordsworth editions, 2002), book 7, line 155; compare Homer, *The Odyssey,* trans. Shewring, 78. Subsequent references will be to Chapman's edition unless otherwise indicated.

21. Fowler, *Country House Poem: A Cabinet,* 78, note to lines 153–74.

22. Eclogues 1 and 9 are usually identified as the lyrics which particularly emphasize the theme of agrarian protest, although elements of this have been identified throughout the work. See, e.g., Leendert Weeda, *Vergil's Political Commentary: In the Eclogues, Georgics and Aeneid* (Warsaw: De Gruyter, 2015), 54–84.

23. Virgil, *Georgics,* in *The Works of Virgil containing his Pastorals, Georgics and Aeneis: adorn'd with a hundred sculptures, translated into English verse by Mr. Dryden* (London: Printed for Jacob Tonson, 1697), Book 2, lines 46–50 in *The Works of John Dryden,* vol. 5, *Poems: The Works of Virgil in English,* ed. William Frost (Berkeley: University of California Press, 1987), 182. The Latin text can be found in *Virgil: Eclogues, Georgics, Aeneid 1–6* (London: Loeb Classical Library, 1978), Book 2, lines 35–38. Subsequent references will be to the Latin text, in the form of book and line numbers, and references to translated passages will be to Dryden's version.

24. David Ross, *Virgil's Elements: Physics and Poetry in the* Georgics (Princeton, N.J.: Princeton University Press, 1987), 109; Richard Thomas, "Tree Violation and Ambivalence in Virgil," *Transactions of the American Philological Association* 118 (1988): 261–73, 271.

25. Dunstan Lowe, "The Symbolic Value of Grafting in Ancient Rome," *Transactions of the American Philological Association* 140, no. 2 (Autumn 2010): 461–88, 463, 482.

26. See discussion in Chapter 3.

27. Virgil, *Georgics,* 2:458–71; Dryden, *Works of Virgil,* 2: 639–60.

28. Virgil, *Georgics,* 2: 490; Dryden, *Works of Virgil,* 2: 698–99.

29. Virgil, *Georgics,* 2: 527–31; Dryden, *Works of Virgil,* 2: 767–72.

30. Henry Rider, *All the Odes and Epodes of Horace: Translated into English Verse* (London, 1638), 114. Subsequent references to English versions of Horace will be to this translation unless otherwise indicated. References to the Latin will be to *Horace: Odes and Epodes* (London: Loeb Classical Library, 2004).

31. See, e.g., Fowler, *Country House Poem: A Cabinet*, 70–74, 149–52.

32. Abraham Cowley, "Of Agriculture" (1650) in *Prose works of Abraham Cowley*, ed. Thomas Sprat (London: William Pickering, 1826), 142–69, lines 159–61; Paul Davis, *Translation and the Poet's Life: The Ethics of Translating in English Culture, 1646–1726* (Oxford: Oxford University Press, 2008), 106–7.

33. Ovid, *Metamorphoses*, trans. Arthur Golding (London, 1567), Book 1, lines 107, 100, 102–5. Accessed via Perseus Digital Library.

34. Ovid, *Fasti*, 4: 417–620, in *Ovid's Fasti*, trans. Sir James George Frazer (London: Loeb Classical Library, 1959), 220–35.

35. In the *Fasti*, she is picking crocuses and white lilies: "ipsa crocos tenues liliaque alba legit," 4: 442.

36. The etiological function is more obvious in the *Fasti* version, where Proserpine only eats three seeds, representing the three winter months: Ovid, *Fasti*, 4: 607–8.

37. Virgil, *Georgics*, 2: 367; Horace, *Odes*, 2, 15: 4 and 4, 5: 30; Ovid, *Metamorphoses*, 14: 661–66.

38. Sir Walter Raleigh, *The History of the World* (1614) in *The Works of Sir Walter Ralegh*, 8 vols. (Oxford: Oxford University Press, 1829), 2: 167.

39. Colluthus, "The Rape of Helen," in *Oppian, Colluthus, Tryphiodorus*, trans. A. W. Mair for the Loeb Classical Library, vol. 219 (London: Heinemann, 1989), line 59; Hesiod, *Theogony*, lines 215 ff.

40. Geoffrey Chaucer, "The Merchant's Tale," in *The Riverside Chaucer*, ed. Larry D. Benson and F. N. Robinson (Oxford: Oxford University Press, 2008), 154–68, Fragment 4, lines 1245–2418, lines 1782, 1932, 1955. Subsequent parenthetical references are to lines within this fragment.

41. Compare Song of Solomon, 1:14; 2:10–12; 4:1, 7–12.

42. Howes, *Chaucer's Gardens*, 83.

43. Tory Vandeventer Pearman, "'O Sweete Venym Queynte!': Pregnancy and the Disabled Female Body in the *Merchant's Tale*," in *Disability in the Middle Ages: Reconsiderations and Reverberations*, ed. Joshua Eyler (London: Routledge, 2010), 25–37, 35.

44. Pearman, in "O Sweete Venym," 35, suggests that it is not clear whether May's pregnancy is genuine, but the representation of Januarie's sexual performance, combined with the incorporation of the reference to May's condition in the account of her deception, seem to place this beyond doubt.

45. Athenaeus, *Deipnosophistae*, 3, cited in *The Seven Books of Paulus Aegineta*, translated from the Greek by Francis Adams, 3 vols. (London: Sydenham Society, 1844), Commentary on Section 81, 1: 134; Compare Grant, *Galen on Food and Diet*, 126.

46. Tigner, *Literature and the Renaissance Garden*, 15.

47. "I Have a New Garden," *Middle English Lyrics*, ed. R. T. Davies (London: Faber and Faber, 1963), 158; reproduced in *The Oxford Book of Garden Verse*, ed. John Dixon Hunt (Oxford: Oxford University Press, 1994), 7–8.

48. Bruce A. Rosenberg, "The 'Cherry-Tree Carol' and the 'Merchant's Tale,'" *Chaucer Review* 5, no. 4 (Spring 1971): 264–76, 270.

49. Howes, *Chaucer's Gardens*, 99.

50. Sir Thomas Malory, *The Morte Darthur or The Hoole Book of Kyng Arthur and of his Noble Knyghtes of the Rounde Table*, ed. Stephen H. A. Shepherd (London: Norton, 2004), 590.

51. Grant, *Galen on Food and Diet*, 125.

52. Athenaeus, *Deipnosophistae*, 1: 134.

53. *The Universal Family Physician and Surgeon* (Blackburn, 1798), 519. This material is incorporated into the seventh and subsequent editions of William Buchan's *Domestic Medicine* (1800) as well Lewis Mansey's *The Practical Physician or Medical Instructor* (1800).

Chapter 2

1. Taverner, *Certain Experiments*, 29; Evelyn, "Preface" to *Pomona*, 1; Cook, *Manner of Raising, Ordering, and Improving*, 14.

2. See Jennifer Potter, *Strange Blooms: The Curious Lives and Adventures of the John Tradescants* (London: Atlantic, 2006); Harold Love, "Early Modern Print Culture," in *The Book History Reader*, ed. Alistair Finkelstein and David McCleery (London: Routledge, 2006), 74–86; Jason Peacey, *Print and Public Politics in the English Revolution* (Cambridge: Cambridge University Press, 2013), 35; Bushnell, *Green Desire*, 35.

3. See, e.g., Lawson, *New Orchard and Garden*, 56, Preface.

4. Bushnell, *Green Desire*, 50–51; William Eamon, *Science and the Secrets of Nature: Books of Secrets in Medieval and Modern Culture* (Princeton, N.J.: Princeton University Press, 1994).

5. Bushnell, *Green Desire*, 51.

6. Ibid., 190.

7. John Evelyn, *Elysium Britannicum, or The Royal Gardens*, ed. John E. Ingram (Philadelphia: University of Pennsylvania Press, 2001), 42; Hunt, *Greater Perfection*, 192.

8. Crawford, *Poetry, Enclosure*, 37–64, 65–87, 194–223.

9. On agrarian discourse, see Leslie and Raylor, *Culture and Cultivation*, and McRae, *God Speed the Plough*.

10. Albala, *Eating Right in the Renaissance*, 224–31.

11. Taverner, *Certain Experiments*; N.F., *Fruiterers Secrets*; Gervase Markham, *The English Husbandman* (London: John Browne, 1613); Parkinson, *Paradisi in Sole*; Walter Blith, *The English Improver, or, A New Survey of Husbandry* (London, 1649); Samuel Hartlib, *A Designe for Plentie, by an Universall Planting of Fruit-Trees: tendred by some wel-wishers to the Publick* (London, 1652); Ralph Austen, *A Treatise of Fruit Trees*, 1st ed. (Oxford: Thomas Robinson, 1653); Evelyn, *Pomona*; John Rea, *Flora, seu, de Florum Cultura* (London, 1665); Joseph Blagrave, *The Epitome of the Whole Art of Husbandry* (London, 1669); Charles Cotton, *The Planters Manual* (London, 1675); John Worlidge, *Vinetum Britannicum* (London, 1676); Cook, *Manner of Raising, Ordering, and Improving*.

12. F. A. Roach, *Cultivated Fruits of Britain: Their Origin and History* (Oxford: Blackwell, 1985), 42–43; Vittoria di Palma, "Drinking Cider in Paradise: Science, Improvement, and the Politics of Fruit Trees," in *A Pleasing Sinne: Drink and Conviviality in Seventeenth-Century England*, ed. Adam Smyth (Woodbridge: Boydell and Brewer, 2004), 161–77, 163.

13. Joan Thirsk, "Agricultural Innovations and Their Diffusion," in *The Agrarian History of England and Wales: Volume 5, 1640–1750, Part 2, Agrarian Change*, ed. Joan Thirsk (Cambridge: Cambridge University Press, 1985), 533–89, 562–65.

14. Thirsk, "Making a Fresh Start," 18–28.

15. Graham Parry, "John Evelyn as Hortulan Saint," in Leslie and Raylor, *Culture and Cultivation*, 130–50, 142; Tigner, *Literature and the Renaissance Garden*, 194.

16. Markham, "Epistle to the General and Gentle Reader," in *English Husbandman*, unpaginated, A3.

17. Andrew McRae, "Husbandry Manuals and the Language of Agrarian Improvement," in Leslie and Raylor, *Culture and Cultivation*, 35–62, 47.

18. Roach, *Cultivated Fruits*, 180.

19. Geoffrey Parker, *Global Crisis: War, Climatic Change and Catastrophe in the Seventeenth Century* (New Haven, Conn.: Yale University Press, 2013), 5–6; Tigner, *Literature and the Renaissance Garden*, 204.

20. Tigner, *Literature and the Renaissance Garden*, 17–18; Lynch, "Young Ladies," 691.

21. Ritvo, "At the Edge of the Garden," 368–69.

22. Lawson, *New Orchard and Garden*, 3; Blagrave, *Epitome of the Whole Art of Husbandry*, 240. See also Parkinson, *Paradisi in Sole*, 537; Cotton, *Planters Manual*, 23.

23. Abraham Cowley, *Plantarum*, trans. Nahum Tate, 6 vols. (London, 1708), 5: 132.

24. Dallas, Barnes, and Williamson, "Orchards in the Landscape," 28–29.

25. Michael Leslie, "'Bringing Ingenuity into Fashion': The 'Elysium Britannicum' and the Reformation of Husbandry" in *John Evelyn's "Elysium Britannicum" and European Gardening*, ed. Therese O'Malley and Joachim Wolschke-Bulmahn (Washington, D.C.: Dumbarton Oaks, 1998), 131–52, 139–40; Hunt, *Greater Perfections*, 181–89; Michelle DiMeo, "Openness vs. Secrecy in the Hartlib Circle: Revisiting 'Democratic Baconianism' in Interregnum England," in *Secrets and Knowledge in Medicine and Science, 1500–1800*, ed. Alisha Rankin and Elaine Leong (Farnham: Ashgate, 2011), 105–21, 116. See also Anthony Low, *Georgic Revolution*.

26. Taverner, *Certain Experiments*, 29; Lawson, *New Orchard and Garden*, 10; Hartlib, *Designe for Plentie*, 4.

27. Austen, "Epistle Dedicatory," in *Treatise of Fruit Trees*, n.p.

28. Ralph Austen, *A Treatise of Fruit-Trees*, 2nd ed. (Oxford: Thomas Robinson, 1657), 113–40. The number of propositions is increased from twenty to one hundred and the number of pages expanded from 51 (out of 172) in 1653, to 227 (out of 390) in the second edition, thus becoming the main component of the book.

29. Michael Leslie, "The Spiritual Husbandry of John Beale," in Leslie and Raynor, *Culture and Cultivation*, 151–72, 157.

30. Austen, *Treatise of Fruit-Trees* (1653), 64–65; Austen, *Treatise of Fruit-Trees* (1657), 69–70; Ralph Austen, *A Treatise of Fruit-Trees*, 3rd ed. (Oxford: Amos Curteyne, 1665), 130–32.

31. Austen, *Treatise of Fruit-Trees* (1657), 132, 134.

32. Ibid., 120.

33. Austen, *Observations*, in *Treatise of Fruit-Trees* (1665), 16–17.

34. John Evelyn, *Kalendarium Hortense, or, The Gard'ner's Almanac*, 9th ed. (1699), 112.

35. Austen, "Epistle Dedicatory," in *Treatise of Fruit-Trees* (1653), n.p.

36. Ibid., 1665, n.p.

37. Taverner, *Certaine Experiments*, 30, 36, 30, 29; Ann Kussmaul, *Servants in Husbandry in Early Modern England* (Cambridge: Cambridge University Press, 1981), 4.

38. Austen, "A Preface to the Reader," in *Spirituall Use*, in *Treatise of Fruit-Trees*, 1653 and 1657, n.p.

39. Austen, "To the Reader," in *Treatise of Fruit Trees* (1653), n.p.

40. J. F., "To my deare Friend and Brother" in Austen, *Spirituall Use* in *Treatise of Fruit-Trees* (1657), n.p.

41. Lawson, *New Orchard and Garden*, 32–33; see also Bushnell, *Green Desire*, 95.

42. Tigner, *Literature and the Renaissance Garden*, 219.

43. Austen, "To the Reader," in *Treatise of Fruit Trees* (1653), n.p.

44. John Salkeld, *A Treatise of Paradise* (London: 1617), 145–46.

45. N. F., "Epistle to the Reader," *Fruiterers Secrets*, n.p.; Appelbaum, *Aguecheek's Beef*, 104.

46. N. F., "Epistle to the Reader," *Fruiterers Secrets*, n.p.

47. Markham, *English Husbandman*, 41; Parkinson, *Paradisi in Sole*, 538.

48. Blagrave, *Epitome of the Whole Art of Husbandry*, 240.

49. Dallas, Barnes, and Williamson, "Orchards in the Landscape," 29.

50. Jane Austen, *Mansfield Park*, ed. John Wiltshire (Cambridge: Cambridge University Press, 2005), 63.

51. John Laurence, "Preface" in *The Clergyman's Recreation: Shewing the Pleasure and Profit of the Art of Gardening*, 3rd ed. (London: 1715), n.p.

52. Billie S. Britz, "Environmental Provisions for Plants in Seventeenth-Century Northern Europe," *Journal of the Society of Architectural Historians* 33, no. 2 (1974): 133–44, 139.

53. Low, "Agricultural Reform," 63; Fowler, "Georgic and Pastoral," 83–84.

54. Compare T. C. Barnard, "Gardening, Diet and 'Improvement' in Later Seventeenth-Century Ireland," *Journal of Garden History* 10 (1990): 71–85, 71–72.

55. Bushnell, *Green Desire*, 52.

56. Austen, *Observations upon . . . Sir Francis Bacon's Naturall History*, in *Treatise of Fruit-Trees* (1665), 2.

57. Austen, *Observations upon some part of Sir Francis Bacon's Naturall History as it concerns Fruit-trees, Fruits and Flowers* (Oxford, 1658), 1, 2.

58. Giovanni Boccaccio, *The Decameron*, trans. Guido Waldman (Oxford: Oxford World's Classics, 2008), day 10, ch. 5, 619–20; Giovanni Boccaccio, *Filocolo*, trans. Victoria Kirkham. (Baltimore: Johns Hopkins University Press, 1971), book 4.

59. Christopher Marlowe, *Dr. Faustus: The A- and B-Texts*, ed. David Bevington and Eric Rasmussen (Manchester: Manchester University Press, 2013), A text, act 4, scene 2, 19–20.

60. John Baptista Porta, *Natural Magick by John Baptista Porta, a Neapolitane; in twenty books . . . wherein are set forth all the riches and delights of the natural sciences* (London, 1658), 3, 73–79. Accessed via EEBO. See Eamon, *Science and the Secrets of Nature*, 205–21 for an account of the scientific basis for della Porta's natural magic.

61. Porta, *Natural Magick*, 3, 74; Tigner, *Literature and the Renaissance Garden*, 15.

62. Roach, *Cultivated Fruits*, 180.

63. Malcolm Thick, "Market Gardening in England and Wales," in *Agrarian History*, ed. Joan Thirsk, vol. 5, part 2, 233–62; see also John Harvey, *Early Nurserymen* (London: Phillimore, 1974).

64. Waverley Root, *Food: An Authoritative and Visual History and Dictionary of the Foods of the World* (New York: Simon and Schuster, 1980), 303–4.

65. John Evelyn, *The Diary of John Evelyn*, ed. William Bray, 2 vols. (London, 1901), 1:325; see also Virginia Black, "Beddington—'The Best Orangery in England,'" *Journal of Garden History* 3, no. 2 (1983): 113–20.

66. See, for example, Sir John Vanbrugh and Colley Cibber, *The Provoked Husband* (1727) act 2, scene 1; Sheridan, *The Rivals*, act 1, scene 2, 206, and act 3, scene 3, 20–21.

67. Gillian Riley, "Food in Painting," in *A Cultural History of Food in the Renaissance*, ed. Ken Albala (London: Bloomsbury, 2016), 171–82, 175.

68. Nicholas de Bonnefons, *The French Gardiner* (London, 1658), 25.

69. "A short Account of several Gardens near London, with remarks on some particulars wherein they excel, or are deficient, upon a view of them in December 1691. Communicated to the Society by the Reverend Dr. Hamilton, Vice President, from an original Manuscript in his possession," in *Archaeologia or Miscellaneous Tracts Relating to Antiquity* 12 (1796), 181–92, 184. The "Account" is also reproduced in *The New Annual Register or General Repository of History, Politics and Literature, for the Year 1796*, ed. George Robinson, William Godwin, and Andrew Kippis (London: 1797) 122–27, and as an appendix to William Carew Hazlitt's *Gleanings in Old Garden Literature* (London, 1887), 225–41, where it is attributed to John Gibson, 66–68.

70. Black, "Beddington," 118; Britz, "Environmental Provisions," 133–44.

71. Samuel Pepys, *The Diary of Samuel Pepys*, ed. Robert Latham and William Matthews, 11 vols. (Berkeley: University of California Press, 2000), 7:182.

72. Britz, "Environmental Provisions," 136.

73. "Short Account," *Archaeologia* 12, 182; Britz, "Environmental Provisions," 133–44, 136; Black, "Beddington," 115, attributes the passage to John Evelyn.

74. Philip Miller, *The Gardeners and Florists Dictionary, or A Complete System of Horticulture* (London, 1724), 2, Section 20, G4.

75. Hazlitt, *Gleanings*, 58.

76. Dawson, *A Booke of Cookerie*, 12, 53, 56.

77. A. Bettesworth and C. Hitch, *The Complete Family-piece: and, Country Gentleman, and Farmer's, Best Guide*, 2nd ed. (London, 1737), 1: 92.

78. Miller, *Gardeners and Florists Dictionary*, 2, Section 20.

79. Markham, *English Husbandman*, 67, 87.

80. *Calendar of State Papers Venetian, 1628–29*, 21: 553, cited in Robert Brenner, *Merchants and Revolution: Commercial Change, Political Conflict, and London's Overseas Traders, 1550–1653* (Princeton, N.J.: Princeton University Press, 1993), 43.

81. See William Congreve, *The Old Bachelor: A Comedy* (1693), in *The Works of William Congreve*, Volume 1, 5–123, act 4, scene 8; see also E. M. Foster, *Miriam: A Novel*, 2 vols. (London: Minerva, 1800), 1:127–28.

82. Albala, *Eating Right in the Renaissance*, 212.

83. Britz, "Environmental Provisions," 138.

84. Rea, *Flora*, 20; Cowell, *Curious and Profitable Gardener*, 22.

85. George Martine, "The Various Degrees of Heat in Bodies," in *Essays Medical and Philosophical* (London, 1740), 297. Accessed via ECCO.

86. Britz, "Environmental Provisions," 136.

87. Jan Woudstra, "The Re-Instatement of the Greenhouse Quarter at Hampton Court Palace," *Garden History* 37, no. 1 (Summer 2009): 80–110.

88. Richard Bradley, *General Treatise of Husbandry and Gardening* (London, 1726), 2: 394–408. Accessed via ECCO. References are to the 1726 edition unless otherwise indicated. Miller, *Gardeners and Florists Dictionary*, 2, Section 20, n.p.

89. *Oxford English Dictionary*, online edition 2015.

90. Henrik van Oosten, *The Dutch Gardener, translated from the Dutch* (London: D. Midwinter and T. Leigh, 1703), 242. Accessed via ECCO.

91. Thomas Fairchild, *The City Gardener* (London, 1722), 64.

92. Natasha Korda, "Gender at Work in the Cries of London," in *Oral Traditions and Gender in Early Modern Literary Texts*, ed. Mary Ellen Lamb and Karen Bamford (Aldershot: Ashgate, 2008), 117–35; Marion Wynne-Davies, "Orange Women, Female Spectators, and Roaring Girls: Women and Theatre in Early Modern England," *Medieval and Renaissance Drama in England* 22 (2009): 19–26.

93. Miller, *Gardeners and Florists Dictionary*, unpaginated.

94. Cowell, *Curious and Profitable Gardener*, 27; John Giles, *Ananas: Or, A Treatise on the Pine-Apple* (London, 1767), 1.

95. See, in particular, Root, *Food*; Beauman, *The Pineapple*; Ruth Levitt, "'A Noble Present of Fruit': A Transatlantic History of Pineapple Cultivation," *Garden History* 42, no. 1 (2014): 106–19.

96. Root, *Food*, 354; Beauman, *The Pineapple*, 2–23; Levitt, "Noble Present," 106–7.

97. Evelyn, *Diary*, 1: 348.

98. See Beauman, *The Pineapple*, 34–38.

99. Evelyn, *Diary*, 2, 43.

100. Richard Ligon, *A True and Exact History of Barbados* (London, 1657), 82. Accessed via EEBO.

101. Beauman, *The Pineapple*, 46–49.

102. Henry Phillips, *The Companion for the Orchard* (London, 1831), 294. The claim is repeated on numerous modern websites, such as *The American Gardener*.

103. Tigner, *Literature and the Renaissance Garden*, 160.

104. Johann Beckmann, *A History of Inventions and Discoveries* (London, 1797), 169.

105. Ibid., 169–71.

106. Bradley, *General Treatise*, 2: 276; See also Cowell, *Curious and Profitable Gardener*, 27–33; John Abercrombie, *The Hot-House Gardener* (London, 1789).

107. Adam Fitz-Adam [Edward Moore, Lord Chesterfield, R. O. Cambridge et al.], *The World* 162, Thursday 28th November 1755, in *The World*, 6 vols. (London, 1757), 5: 103–4.

108. Tobias Smollett, *The Adventures of Peregrine Pickle*, ed. James Clifford and Paul-Gabriel Boucé (Oxford: Oxford University Press, 1983), 22–23; Amelia Opie, *Adeline Mowbray*, ed. Shelley King and John B. Pierce (Oxford: Oxford University Press, 1999), 135.

109. *The Gentleman's Magazine and Historical Chronicle* 34 (1764): 477; Edward Copeland, *Women Writing About Money: Women's Fiction in England, 1790–1820* (Cambridge: Cambridge University Press, 2004), 25–28.

110. Giles, *Ananas*, v.

111. Levitt, "Noble Present," 112.

Chapter 3

1. Ben Jonson, "To Penshurst," in *Ben Jonson: The Complete Poems*, ed. George Parfitt (Harmondsworth: Penguin, 1980), 95–98, lines 41–44.

2. J. C. A. Rathmell, "Jonson, Lord Lisle, and Penshurst," *English Literary Renaissance*, 1 (1971): 250–60, 253; Amy Tigner, "The Ecology of Eating in Jonson's 'To Penshurst,'" in *Ecological Approaches*, ed. Munroe, Geisweidt, and Bruckner, 109–19, 116–17.

3. Tigner, "Ecology of Eating," 110; Don E. Wayne, *Penshurst: The Semiotics of Place and the Poetics of History* (London: Methuen, 1984), 3; G. R. Hibbard identifies the genre with poems by Jonson, Carew, Herrick, and Marvell in "The Country House Poem," 159–74. Further discussion can be found in Williams, *Country and the City*, 27–34; McClung, *Country House*; Fowler, "Georgic and Pastoral, 81–88, 86; Fowler, "Country House Poem: The Politics," 1–14; Tigner, "Ecology of Eating," 111.

4. Tigner, "Ecology of Eating," 109; Appelbaum, *Aguecheek's Beef*, 119.

5. Wayne, *Penshurst*, 18–19, 154; McRae, "Husbandry Manuals," 35–62, 57.

6. Wayne, *Penshurst*, 120; Tigner, "Ecology of Eating," 109.

7. Alastair Fowler, "The 'Better Marks' of Jonson's 'To Penshurst,'" *Review of English Studies* 24, no. 95 (1973): 266–82, 272.

8. For the Renaissance division of the seasons, see Albala, *Eating Right in the Renaissance*, 129. This division persisted into the nineteenth century, as shown in Wilkie Collins, *The Woman in White*, ed. John Sutherland (Oxford: Oxford University Press, 1998), 6.

9. *Husband Mans*, 5.

10. Levine, *Forms*, 74–77.

11. Joshua Scodel, "Allusions and Distinctions: Pentameter Couplets in Ben Jonson's Epigrams and Forest," in *The Work of Form: Poetics and Materiality in Early Modern Culture*, ed. Ben Burton and Elizabeth Scott-Baumann (Oxford: Oxford University Press, 2014), 39–55, 49–50.

12. Austen, *Treatise of Fruit Trees*, 1657, 120.

13. Dallas, Barnes, and Williamson, "Orchards in the Landscape," 28–29.

14. Parkinson, *Paradisi in Sole*, 590.

15. Ibid., 567.

16. Markham, *English Husbandman*, 87.

17. Tigner, "Ecology of Eating," 116; Wayne, *Penshurst*, 85.

18. Wayne, *Penshurst*, 42.

19. Susan Broomhall and Jacqueline Van Gent, *Dynastic Colonialism: Gender, Materiality and the Early Modern House of Orange-Nassau* (London: Routledge, 2016), 169–222. Broomhall and Van Gent analyze the use of oranges in early modern portraits as symbols of the power network of the Orange-Nassau dynasty. Yet the artists discussed also use other fruits, such as the peach or apple in Abraham van den Tempel's *Portrait of a Lady Holding Fruit* and the assorted fruits in his *Portrait of Jan van Amstel and Anna Boxhoorn*. While the fruit in *Albertine Agnes with Her Children* (1668) may be an orange and may thus reference the House of Orange-Nassau, it could also function as a traditional symbol of fecundity because the tree can bear flowers and fruit at the same time. See also Oliver Goldsmith, *The Vicar of Wakefield* (1766), ch. 16.

20. Alastair Fowler, *The Mind of the Book: Pictorial Title Pages* (Oxford: Oxford University Press, 2017), 107.

21. Watson, *Back to Nature*, 111; Diane McColley notes in *Poetry and Ecology in the Age of Milton and Marvell* (Abingdon: Routledge, 2007) that "nothing is known of the gardener except that he contrived the herbal sundial," 131.

22. Nigel Smith, *Andrew Marvell: The Chameleon* (London: Yale University Press, 2010), 3.

23. John Dixon Hunt, *Andrew Marvell: His Life and Writings* (Ithaca, N.Y.: Cornell University Press, 1978), 37; Smith, *Andrew Marvell*, 54, 219; Andrew Marvell, *The Poems of Andrew Marvell*, ed. Nigel Smith (Harlow: Longman, 2007), 152–55; Mildmay Fane, "To Retiredness," in *Otia Sacra* (London, 1648), ed. Donald M. Friedman (New York: Scholars Facsimiles and Reprints, 1975).

24. Andrew Marvell, *Complete English Poems*, ed. Elizabeth Story Donno (London: Allen Lane, 1972), 255; Smith, *Andrew Marvell*, 219; Marvell, *Poems*, 152–53; Abraham Cowley, "The Garden" (1668) in *The Poetical Works of Abraham Cowley*, 4 vols. (Edinburgh: Apollo Press, 1784) 4: 254–62; Katherine Philips, "Upon the Graving of Her Name upon a Tree in Barnelmes Walks," *Printed Poems* (London, 1667), 137.

25. Watson, *Back to Nature*, 325–26, 333.

26. McColley, *Poetry and Ecology*, 129–30, 128; A. D. Cousins, *Andrew Marvell: Loss and Aspiration, Home and Homeland* (Abingdon: Routledge, 2016), 85, 6.

27. Marvell, *Poems*, 153.

28. Andrew Marvell, "The Garden" in *Poems*, 155–59, lines 34–40.

29. Timothy Raylor, "The Instability of Marvell's *Bermudas*," *Marvell Society Newsletter* 6, no. 4 (2014): 3–12, 8.

30. Robert Watson, "Tell Inconvenient Truths, but Tell Them Short," in *Ecological Approaches*, ed. Munroe, Geisweidt, and Bruckner, 17–28, 22.

31. Andrew Marvell, "The Mower Against Gardens," in *Poems of Andrew Marvell*, 133–34, lines 1–6.

32. Christopher Hill, "Society and Andrew Marvell," in John Carey, ed. *Andrew Marvell: A Critical Anthology* (Harmondsworth: Penguin, 1969), 83–85; McColley, *Poetry and Ecology*, 130–31.

33. Cousins, *Andrew Marvell*, 23–24.

34. Parkinson, *Paradisi in Sole*, 67; Tigner, *Literature and the Renaissance Garden*, 187–88.

35. Donno in Marvell, *Complete English Poems*, 261, note 30; Smith in Marvell, *Poems*, 134, notes 29–30. See Gervase Markham, *Maison rustique, or The countrey farme*, 7 vols. (London, 1616), a translation of Charles Estienne, *Maison Rustique*, 3:375.

36. Lynch, "Young Ladies," 698; see also George, *Botany, Sexuality*, 110.

37. William Badley, "A New Reading of Andrew Marvell's Mower Poems" (unpublished PhD diss., Middle Tennessee State University, 1994), cited in Marvell, *Poems*, 133; McColley, *Poetry and Ecology*, 131.

38. Grove, *Green Imperialism*, 32–33.

39. William Strachey, "A true reportory of the wracke, and redemption of Sir Thomas Gates Knight; upon, and from the Ilands of the Bermudas . . . July 15. 1610" in *Purchas his Pilgrimage*, 4, ch. 6; Lewis Hughes, *A Letter Sent into England from the Summer Islands* (1615); John Smith, *A Generall Historie of Virginia, New England and the Summer Isles* (1624); Cousins, *Andrew Marvell*, 75.

40. Edmund Waller, "The Battle of the Summer Islands," in Edmund Waller, *Poems, &c. written upon several occasions, and to several persons* (London: Printed for Henry Herringman, 1664), lines 5–7, accessed via Early English Books Online.

41. Tobin, *Colonizing Nature*, 35.

42. Edmund Waller, "To the King upon His Majesties Happy Return," in Waller, *Poems, &c.*, 174, lines 48–51.

43. David Armitage, "Literature and Empire" in *The Oxford History of the British Empire, Volume 1: The Origins of Empire. British Overseas Enterprise to the Close of the Seventeenth Century*, ed. Nicholas Canny (Oxford: Oxford University Press, 1998), 98–123; Bridget Orr, *Empire on the English Stage, 1660–1714* (Cambridge: Cambridge University Press, 2001), 272–74.

44. Andrew Marvell, "Bermudas" in *Poems*, 56–58, line 37; Cousins, *Andrew Marvell*, 74.

45. C. B. Hardman, "Row Well Ye Mariners," *Review of English Studies* 51 (2000), 80–82; Cousins, *Andrew Marvell*, 75–76; Marvell, *Poems*, 55–56.

46. Cousins, *Andrew Marvell*, 80.

47. Raylor, "Instability," 6.

48. Marvell, *Complete English Poems*, 266, n. 23; Marvell, *Poems*, 57.

49. Cousins, *Andrew Marvell*, 84; Grove, *Green Imperialism*, 41–42, 45.

50. Eric Song, "The Country Estate and the Indies (East and West): The Shifting Scene in Eden in *Paradise Lost*," *Modern Philology* 108, no. 2 (2010): 199–223, 203–4.

51. Raylor dates the poem to early 1653, and connects it to the "Eleuthera project," a plan by Bermudan Puritans to settle in the Bahamas. Raylor, "Instability," 6–7.

52. Tigner, *Literature and the Renaissance Garden*, 228, 219.

53. Appelbaum, "Eve's and Adam's 'Apple,'" 221–39; Appelbaum, *Aguecheek's Beef*, 187–200. See also, Crawford, *Poetry, Enclosure*, 130; Karen L. Edwards, *Milton and the Natural World: Science and Poetry in* Paradise Lost (Cambridge: Cambridge University Press, 1999), 144–49.

54. John Milton, *Paradise Lost*, Book 4, line 143. Subsequent references will be given as book and line numbers.

55. Barbara Lewalski, "Milton's Paradises," in Hiltner, *Renaissance Ecology*, 15–30, 17; Jeffrey S. Theis, "'The purlieus of heaven': Milton's Eden as a Pastoral Forest," in Hiltner, *Renaissance Ecology*, 229–57, 234–35, 247.

56. Edwards, *Milton and the Natural World*, 154–56.

57. John Evelyn, *Fumifugium: or, The Inconveniencie of the Aer and Smoak of London Dissipated* (London, 1661), 24; Edwards, *Milton and the Natural World*, 196; McColley, *Poetry and Ecology*, 83–85; Tigner, *Literature and the Renaissance Garden*, 206.

58. McRae, "Husbandry Manuals," 47.

59. Lewalski, "Milton's Paradises," 16.

60. John R. Knott, "Milton's Wild Garden," *Studies in Philology* 102, no. 1 (Winter, 2005): 66–82, 69.

61. Hiltner, *Milton and Ecology*; Stella Revard, "Eve and the Language of Love in *Paradise Lost*," in Hiltner, *Renaissance Ecology*, 31–44, 33; Ann Torday Gulden, "A Walk in the Paradise Garden: Eve's Influence in the 'Triptych' of Speeches, *Paradise Lost* 4.610–88,' in Hiltner, *Renaissance Ecology*, 45–62; Tigner, *Literature and the Renaissance Garden*, 227.

62. McColley, *Milton's Eve*, 154.

63. Tigner, *Literature and the Renaissance Garden*, 219.

64. Tigner suggests that "fermentation . . . is only necessary in a post-lapsarian world where one does not have direct access to the abundant and perpetually growing fruits of the Garden," *Literature and the Renaissance Garden*, 220–21.

65. Henry Fielding, *The History of Tom Jones, A Foundling*, ed. Martin C. Battestin and Fredson Bowers, 2 vols. (Oxford: Clarendon Press, 1974), 2: 510–13.

66. Barbara Lewalski, "Innocence and Experience in Milton's Eden," in *New Essays on* Paradise Lost, ed. Thomas Kranidas (Berkeley: University of California Press, 1970), 86–117. See also Song, "The Country Estate and the Indies," 202–3; John Knott, *Milton's Pastoral Vision* (Chicago: University of Chicago Press, 1971); Knott, "Milton's Wild Garden," 66.

67. Low, *Georgic Revolution*, 316–22.

68. Dennis Danielson, "The Fall and Milton's Theodicy," in *The Cambridge Companion to Milton*, ed. Dennis Danielson (Cambridge: Cambridge University Press, 1999), 144–59, 156; McColley, *Gust for Paradise*, 58.

69. McColley, *Milton's Eve*, 166–81; Gulden, "A Walk," 58–59.

70. Edwards, *Milton and the Natural World*, 18–28.

71. Appelbaum, "Eve's and Adam's 'Apple,'" 235; Appelbaum, *Aguecheek's Beef*, 192–200.

72. McColley, *Gust for Paradise*, 26, 36–47.

73. Christina Rossetti, *Goblin Market*, lines 134–36.

74. Ritvo, "At the Edge of the Garden," 361–65; King, *Bloom*, 6, 15, 38–43; Lynch, "Young Ladies," 690–91.

Chapter 4

1. Philip H. Highfill, Kalman A. Burnum, and Edward A. Langhans, eds., *A Biographical Dictionary of Actors, Actresses, Musicians, Dancers, Managers and Other Stage Personnel in London, 1660–1800* (Carbondale: Southern Illinois University Press, 2006), 166. The ensuing account of Mary Meggs draws on this source.

2. Edward A. Langhans, "The Theatre," in *The Cambridge Companion to English Restoration Theatre*, ed. Deborah Payne Fisk (Cambridge: Cambridge University Press, 2000), 1–18, 2–4; Peter Holland, *The Ornament of Action: Text and Performance in Restoration Comedy* (Cambridge: Cambridge University Press, 2000).

3. Hillary M. Nunn, "Playing with Appetite in Early Modern Comedy," in *Shakespearean Sensations: Experiencing Literature in Early Modern England*, ed. Katharine A. Craik and Tanya Pollard (Cambridge: Cambridge University Press, 2013), 110–17, 116.

4. Ibid., 117. Compare Michael Dobson, "'His Banquet Is Prepared': Onstage Food and the Permeability of Time in Shakespearean Performance," in *Shakespeare Jahrbuch* 145 (2009): 62–73. Dobson argues that Renaissance audiences would have eaten before the performance, so dramatic representations of food might precipitate nausea rather than hunger. See also Elisabeth Angel-Perez and Alexandra Poulain, "Introduction" in *Hunger on the Stage*, ed. Elisabeth Angel-Perez and Alexandra Poulain (Newcastle: Cambridge Scholars Publishing, 2008), ix–xii, ix.

5. Susan Owen, *Restoration Theatre and Crisis* (Oxford: Clarendon Press, 1996), 158–62; Anna Bryson, *From Courtesy to Civility: Changing Codes of Conduct in Early Modern England* (Oxford: Clarendon Press, 1998), 271; Jeremy Webster, *Performing Libertinism in Charles II's Court: Politics, Drama, Sexuality* (Basingstoke: Palgrave Macmillan, 2005), 5–6.

6. Webster, *Performing Libertinism*, 19.

7. John Downes, *Roscius Anglicanus, or, an Historical Review of the Stage, with Additions by the late Mr. Thomas Davies* (London, 1789), 52.

8. Pilar Cuder-Domínguez, *Stuart Women Playwrights, 1613–1713* (Farnham: Ashgate, 2010), 65; Aphra Behn, "Prologue," *The Young King, or, The Mistake* in *The Works of Aphra Behn*, ed. Janet Todd, 7 vols., *Volume 7: The Plays, 1682–1696* (London: Pickering and Chatto, 1996), 79-151, 86; Charles Sedley, *The Mulberry-Garden, A Comedy* (London, 1668), in *Four Restoration Comedies*, ed. Dennis Davison (Oxford: Oxford University Press, 1970), 69–134, act 1, scene 2, 73. Subsequent references will be to this edition and included in parentheses in the form of act, scene, and line numbers.

9. Robert D. Hume, "The Economics of Culture in London, 1660–1740," *Huntington Library Quarterly* 69: 4 (2006): 487–533, 487–88, 497.

10. Peter Earle, *The Making of the English Middle Class: Business, Society, and Family Life in London, 1660–1730* (Berkeley: University of California Press, 1989), 55–56. Earle cites Tobias Smollett, *The Adventures of Roderick Random* (Oxford: Oxford University Press, 1979), 66.

11. Wynne-Davies, "Orange Women," 22–23.

12. Ibid., 20.

13. Korda, "Gender at Work," 117–35, 125, 131–32, 118.

14. Owen, *Restoration Theatre*, 14.

15. Susanna Centlivre, "Epilogue," *The Platonick Lady* (London, 1707). Accessed via ECCO.

16. Thomas Shadwell, *A True Widow* (London, 1678), act 4, 49, 52. Accessed via EEBO.

17. Thick, "Market Gardening," 233–62.

18. Joseph Addison, *The Spectator*, no. 454, Monday, August 11, 1712.

19. John Dryden, *All for Love; or, The World Well Lost*, in *The Works of John Dryden*, vol. 13, *Plays*, ed. Maximillian E. Novak (Berkeley: University of California Press, 1984), 1–111. Prologue, lines 37–41.

20. Laura Rosenthal, *Playwrights and Plagiarists in Early Modern England: Gender, Authorship, Literary Property* (Ithaca, N.Y.: Cornell University Press, 1996), 50; Paulina Kewes, *Authorship and Appropriation: Writing for the Stage in England, 1660–1710* (Oxford: Clarendon, 1998), 58.

21. Dryden, *The Works of John Dryden*, vol. 13, 363.

22. See 62–63 on the importation of grapes.

23. Nicholas Venette, *The Art of Pruning Fruit Trees* (London, 1685), 51. Accessed via EEBO.

24. N. F., *Fruiterers Secrets*, Epistle to the Reader, 24.

25. William Shakespeare, *Henry IV, Part 1*, act 3, scene 3, 4; *The Sedan: A Novel* (London: R. Baldwin, 1757) in Blackwell, *British It-Narratives, 1750–1830*, vol. 3, *Clothes and Transportation*, ed. Christina Lupton, 79–110, 93.

26. N. F., *Fruiterers Secrets*, 9–10.

27. John Dryden, *The Wild Gallant: A Comedy* (London, 1669), in *Works*, vol. 8, *Plays*, ed. John Harrington Smith and Dougald MacMillan (Berkeley: University of California Press, 1962), 1–91, act 5, scene 5, 84–87.

28. Holland, *Ornament of Action*, 15.

29. Pepys, *Diary of Samuel Pepys*, January 15, 1668, 9:415; Matthew J. Kinservik, "Theatrical Regulation During the Restoration Period," in *A Companion to Restoration Drama*, ed. Susan J. Owen (Oxford: Blackwell, 2001), 36–52, 48–49; Deborah Payne Fisk, "The Restoration Actress," in *A Companion to Restoration Drama*, 69–91, 79.

30. Thomas Shadwell, *The Virtuoso*, ed. Marjorie Hope Nicolson and David Stuart Rose (Lincoln and London: University of Nebraska Press, 1966), act 5, scene 2, 109–15.

31. George Etherege, *She Would If She Could*, in *The Plays of George Etherege*, ed. Michael Cordner (Cambridge: Cambridge University Press, 1982), 107–208, act 5, scene 1, 219–22, 183–90. Subsequent references will be to this edition and will be included in parentheses in the text in the form of act, scene, and line numbers.

32. William Wycherley, *The Country Wife*, ed. James Ogden (London: Bloomsbury Methuen, 2014), act 1, scene 1, 7.

33. Aparna Gollapudi, *Moral Reform in Comedy and Culture, 1696–1747* (Farnham: Ashgate, 2011), 136.

34. John Crowne, *The Country Wit* (1676), in *The Dramatic Works of John Crowne*, ed. James Maidment and William Logan (Charleston: Nabu Press, 2013), act 2, scene 3.

35. Robert Markley, *Two-Edg'd Weapons: Style and Ideology in the Comedies of Etherege, Wycherley and Congreve* (Oxford: Clarendon, 1988), 172–73; Harold Weber, *The Restoration Rake-Hero: Transformations in Sexual Understanding in Seventeenth-Century England* (Madison: University of Wisconsin Press, 1986), 53.

36. Markley, *Two-Edg'd Weapons*, 173; see, for example, the poem by J. Marsh, "To Mr Congreve," in *The Old Bachelor*, in *The Works of William Congreve*, ed. D. F. McKenzie, 3 vols. (Oxford: Oxford University Press, 2011), 1: 10–11; Henry Fielding, *Love in Several Masques* (1728) in *Plays, Volume One, 1728–1731*, ed. Thomas Lockwood (Oxford: Oxford University Press, 2004), 17–96, act 5, scene 1, 79.

37. Susanna Centlivre, *The Busybody* (1709), in *Eighteenth-Century Women Dramatists*, ed. Melinda C. Finberg (Oxford: Oxford University Press, 2001), 75–143, act 4, scene 5, 95–96.

38. Markley, *Two-Edg'd Weapons*, 177; Webster, *Performing Libertinism*, 97.

39. Webster, *Performing Libertinism*, 103, 109–10; Weber, *Restoration Rake-Hero*, 81–82; Markley, *Two-Edg'd Weapons*, 132–35.

40. Susan Staves, *Players' Scepters: Fictions of Authority in the Restoration* (Lincoln: University of Nebraska Press, 1979), 160.

41. Sir George Etherege, *The Man of Mode*, in *The Plays of George Etherege*, 209–333, act 1, scene 1, 25–187. Subsequent references will be to this edition and will be included in parentheses in the form of act, scene, and line numbers.

42. Markley, *Two-Edg'd Weapons*, 124.

43. Webster, *Performing Libertinism*, 111.

44. Pepys, *Diary of Samuel Pepys*, August 22, 1667, 8: 365; December 30, 1667, 8: 598–99.

45. Compare Tobias Smollett, *The Expedition of Humphry Clinker*, ed. Lewis M. Knapp and Paul-Gabriel Boucé (Oxford: Oxford University Press, 1998), 121–22.

46. Norman Holland, *The First Modern Comedies* (Cambridge: Harvard University Press, 1959), 88–95; Laura Brown, *English Dramatic Form: 1660–1760* (New Haven, Conn.: Yale University Press, 1981); Webster, *Performing Libertinism*, 114–22; Markley, *Two-Edg'd Weapons*, 132–37.

47. Markley, *Two-Edg'd Weapons*, 135; Webster, *Performing Libertinism*, 122.

48. Webster, *Performing Libertinism*, 122; Markley, *Two-Edg'd Weapons*, 136.

49. See, e.g., Sir John Vanbrugh, *The Relapse* (1696), a sequel to Colley Cibber's *Love's Last Shift* (1696) and George Farquhar, *Sir Harry Wildair* (1701), in *The Complete Works of George Farquhar*, ed. Charles Stonehill, 2 vols. (New York: Gordian Press, 1967), 1: 155–210, a sequel to his *The Constant Couple* (1700), *Complete Works*, 1: 77–154.

50. Owen, *Restoration Theatre*, 157, 177.

51. Aphra Behn, *The City Heiress* (1682) in *Works*, 7: 6–77, act 1, scene 1, 415–20. Subsequent references are to this edition and are in the form of act, scene, and line numbers.

52. Henry Fielding, *The Temple Beau* in *Plays, Volume One, 1728–1731*, 109–83.

53. See di Palma, "Drinking Cider in Paradise," 161–77, 161–62.

54. Owen, *Restoration Theatre*, 177.

55. N. F., *Fruiterers Secrets*, 5–6, Compare 24.

56. Grant, *Galen on Food and Diet*, 111, 116, 126.

57. See Lesel Dawson, "'A Thirsty Womb': Lovesickness, Green Sickness, Hysteria, and Uterine Fury," in *Lovesickness and Gender in Early Modern English Literature*, ed. Lesel Dawson (Oxford: Oxford University Press, 2008), 46–90; Helen King, *The Disease of Virgins: Green Sickness, Chlorosis, and the Problems of Puberty* (London: Psychology Press, 2004).

58. Centlivre, *The Busybody*, 75–143, act 4, scene 5, 92–93; Aphra Behn, *The Rover* (1677), in *Works, Volume 5: Plays, 1671–1677* (1996), 445–521, act 3, scene 1, 34; John Vanbrugh, *The Relapse* (1697), in *Restoration Drama*, 595–645, act 3, scene 2, 325.

59. Albala, *Eating Right in the Renaissance*, 153.

60. See, e.g., Daniel Tauvry, *A New Rational Anatomy* (London: Midwinter and Leigh, 1701), 8; Monsieur d'Ablancourt, *Health Restor'd, or, the Triumph of Nature, over Physick, Doctors, and Apothecaries. In Twelve Entertaining Conversations* (London: Torbuck, Boydell and Noble, 1740), a translation of Nicolas Fremont d'Ablancourt, *Dialogue de la santé* (Paris, 1683), 121; James Adair, *Commentaries on the Principles and Practice of Physic* (London: T. Becket and Co., 1772), 160, 321, 549.

61. Congreve, *The Old Bachelor*, act 4, scene 5, 10–13.

62. Weber, *Restoration Rake-Hero*, 102–3, 52.

63. Owen, *Restoration Theatre*, 171.

64. Congreve, *The Way of the World*, in *Works*, 2: 95–225, act 2, scene 7, 22.

65. Parkinson, *Paradisi in Sole*, 560–61.

66. Susanna Centlivre, *The Gamester* (London: William Turner, [1705]), act 1, scene 1.

67. Markley, *Two-Edg'd Weapons*, 223; Weber, *Restoration Rake-Hero*, 114.

68. Markley, *Two-Edg'd Weapons*, 222.

69. William Congreve, *Love for Love*, in *Works*, vol. 1, 247–391, act 5, scene 2, lines 17–19.

70. Mark S. Dawson, *Gentility and the Comic Theatre of Late Stuart London* (Cambridge: Cambridge University Press, 2005), 97; Centlivre, *The Busybody*, act 1, scene 1, line 130.

71. Edward A. Langhans, "The Post-1660 Theatres as Performance Spaces," in *A Companion to Restoration Drama*, ed. Susan J. Owen (Oxford: Blackwell, 2001), 3–18, 15.

72. A similar comparison is evident in the verses prefixed to Henry Higden, *The Wary Widow or Sir Noisy Parrot* (London, 1693), sig. A5.

73. Michael Cordner, "Playwright Versus Priest: Profanity and the Wit of Restoration Comedy," in Fisk, *Cambridge Companion to English Restoration Theatre*, 209–25, 212.

74. Gollapudi, *Moral Reform*, 2, 20–30.

75. Colley Cibber, *Love's Last Shift*, in *Restoration Drama: An Anthology*, ed. David Womersley (Oxford: Blackwell, 2000), 553–93, act 1, scene 1, 59–63. Subsequent references in parentheses are to this edition in the form of act, scene, and line numbers.

76. Langhans, "The Theatre," 5; Brian Corman, "Comedy," in Fisk, *Cambridge Companion to English Restoration Theatre*, 52–69, 65; Gollapudi, *Moral Reform*.

77. George Farquhar, *The Recruiting Officer*, in *Complete Works*, 2:33–111, act 2, scene 3, p. 64.

78. Richard Brinsley Sheridan, *The Rivals*, in *The School for Scandal and Other Plays*, ed. Michael Cordner (Oxford: Oxford University Press, 2008), 3–86, act 1, scene 2, 205–8.

79. See 66–75, 162–70, 175–78.

80. Kewes, *Authorship and Appropriation*, 12–31.

Chapter 5

1. John Philips, *Cider: A Poem in Two Books* (London, 1708) ed. Charles Dunster (London: T. Cadell, 1791), 1, 5. Subsequent references, unless otherwise specified, will be to this edition and will be in the form of book and line numbers. The first edition used the spelling *Cyder*, but in the Dunster edition this was modernized to *Cider* and the latter has been used throughout this account. Philips was from a Herefordshire family and refers to the county as his native soil, even though he was born in Oxfordshire.

2. For an account of the significance of georgic tradition within Philips's work, see Fairer, "Persistence, Adaptation and Transformations in Pastoral and Georgic Poetry," in *The Cambridge History of English Literature, 1660–1780*, ed. John J. Richetti (Cambridge: Cambridge University

Press, 2005), 259–86, 278; Pat Rogers, "John Philips, Pope and Political Georgic," *Modern Language Quarterly* 66, no. 4 (December 2005): 411–42, 411.

3. Low, *Georgic Revolution*, 12, 118, 221.

4. Chris Mounsey, "Christopher Smart's *The Hop-garden* and John Philips's *Cider*: A Battle of the Georgics? Mid-Eighteenth-Century Poetic Discussions of Authority, Science and Experience," *British Journal for Eighteenth-Century Studies* 22 (1999): 67–84, 72–73.

5. Crawford, "English Georgic," 123–58, 137; Crawford, *Poetry, Enclosure*, 126.

6. Fairer, "Persistence, Adaptation and Transformations," 275, 276–77.

7. Irvine, "Labor and Commerce," 963–88, 979, 963.

8. Bucknell, "Mid-Eighteenth-Century Georgic," 335–52, 349.

9. Dustin Griffin, "The Bard of Cyder-Land: John Philips and Miltonic Imitation," *Studies in English Literature* 24 (1984): 441–60, 458.

10. Michael Drayton, *Poly-Olbion* (1612) in *The Complete Works of Michael Drayton*, ed. Richard Hooper (London: John Russell Smith, 1876), 3 vols, 2: 280, The Eighteenth Song, lines 677–82.

11. Albala, *Eating Right in the Renaissance*, 128–29.

12. J. G. A. Pocock, *The Machiavellian Moment: Florentine Political Thought and the Atlantic Republican Tradition* (Princeton, N.J.: Princeton University Press, 1975), 406–9.

13. Crawford, *Poetry, Enclosure*, 133.

14. Parkinson, *Paradisi in Sole*, 588.

15. Appelbaum, "Eve's and Adam's 'Apple,'" 226.

16. Milton, "The Verse," *Paradise Lost*, 54–55.

17. Dustin Griffin has focused on the form and content of Philips's poetry in general, and *Cider* in particular, to show how he adapts Milton's "myth of a garden paradise" to an early eighteenth-century context so that the poem makes "both Milton's style and myth more available for creative use." Griffin, "Bard of Cyder-Land," 441, 457.

18. Thomson, "Autumn" in *The Seasons*, line 639; compare James Thomson, "Autumn" in *The Seasons* (London: printed by [Henry Woodfall] for A. Millar in the Strand, 1744), line 654; James Grainger, *The Sugar-Cane: A Poem, in Four Books* (London: R. and J. Dodsley, 1764), 1, line 12. Accessed via ECCO. For information on Thomson's revisions to *The Seasons*, see Sandro Jung, "Thomson's 'Winter,' the Ur-Text, and the Revision of *The Seasons*," *Papers on Language and Literature* 45, no. 1 (2009): 60–81.

19. John Gay, *Wine: A Poem* (London, 1708) in *John Gay: Poetry and Prose*, ed. Vinton A. Dearing and Charles Beckwith, 2 vols. (Oxford: Clarendon Press, 1974), 1:21–29, lines 15, 3. Subsequent references will be to this edition and will be included in the text in the form of line numbers.

20. Albala, *Eating Right in the Renaissance*, 51. See Tobias Venner, *Via Recta ad Vitam Longam* (London: Edward Griffen, 1620), 43.

21. David Nokes, *John Gay: A Profession of Friendship* (Oxford: Oxford University Press, 1995), 57.

22. Juan Christian Pellicer, "John Gay, *Wine* (1708) and the Whigs," *British Journal for Eighteenth-Century Studies* 27 (2004): 245–55, 246; compare Milton, *Paradise Lost* 1:22–23.

23. J. A. Downie, "Gay's Politics," in *John Gay and the Scriblerians*, ed. Peter Lewis and Nigel Wood (London: Palgrave Macmillan, 1988), 41–61; Nokes, *John Gay*, 56–60; Pellicer, "John Gay," 245–55.

24. Nokes, *John Gay*, 58–59; Downie, "Gay's Politics," 45–48.

25. Pellicer, "John Gay," 248–50.

26. Ibid., 250.

27. Nokes, *John Gay*, 57.

28. David Fairer, "'Where Fuming Trees Refresh the Thirsty Air': The World of Eco-Georgic," *Studies in Eighteenth-Century Culture* 40 (2011): 201–18, 212; for analysis of the scientific significance of Armstrong's poem, see the introduction to Adam Budd, ed., *John Armstrong's The Art of Preserving Health: Eighteenth-Century Sensibility in Practice* (London: Ashgate, 2013).

29. John Armstrong, *The Art of Preserving Health: A Poem*, 4 vols. (London, 1744), 3: line 122. Accessed via ECCO. Subsequent references will be to this edition and will be included in the text in the form of volume and line numbers.

30. David Armitage, *The Ideological Origins of the British Empire* (Cambridge: Cambridge University Press, 2000), 194; John Shovlin, "War and Peace: Trade, International Competition, and Political Economy," in *Mercantilism Reimagined: Political Economy in Early Modern Britain and Its Empire*, ed. Philip J. Stern and Carl Wennerlind (Oxford: Oxford University Press, 2014), 305–27, 319.

31. In later editions, the adjective used for the ananas is changed from "soft" to "crisp," perhaps suggesting that Armstrong received more accurate information in relation to the sensation of eating a pineapple.

32. Marvell, "Bermudas," lines 17–18, and "The Garden," lines 34–48, in *Poems*.

33. Grainger, *Sugar-Cane*, 1: lines 416–26; Sophia Burrell, "The Enamoured Moor" in *Poems Dedicated to the Right Honourable Earl of Mansfield*, 2 vols. (London: 1793), 2: 154. See also T. Archer, *The Triumph of Agriculture* (London, 1797), 6. Accessed via ECCO.

34. Christopher Smart, *On the Goodness of the Supreme Being: A Poetical Essay* (Cambridge, 1756), 11. Accessed via ECCO.

35. James Thomson, "Summer," in *The Poetical Works of James Thomson, Esq; with his last corrections and additions. Containing, The Seasons. Spring, Summer, Autumn, Winter*, 2. vols. (London: printed for J. Thomson, in the Strand, 1768), 1, lines 685–89.

36. Thomson, "Summer," in *Poetical Works*, 1768 edition, 1: line 865; Tobin, *Colonizing Nature*, 53–55.

37. Richard Graves, "The Rural Deities, or, The New-Bath-Ride" in *Euphrosyne: or, Amusements on the Road of Life*, 2 vols. (3rd ed., 1783), 2: 109.

38. Graves, "Rural Deities," in *Euphrosyne*, 110.

Chapter 6

1. Sarah Fielding, *The Governess: Or, The Little Female Academy*, ed. Candace Ward (Peterborough, Ontario: Broadview, 2005), 51. Subsequent references are to this edition.

2. Thomas Holcroft, *Anna St. Ives* (Teddington: Echo, 2006), Letter 13, 41; *The Adventures of a Whipping-Top* (London: J. Marshall, [1786]) in Blackwell, *British It-Narratives, 1750–1830*, vol. 4, *Toys, Trifles and Portable Furniture*, ed. Mark Blackwell, 109–28, 126, 122.

3. See, e.g., [Richard Johnson], *The Adventures of a Silver Penny* (London: E. Newbery, [1786]) in Blackwell, *British It-Narratives*, vol. 1 *Money*, ed. Liz Bellamy (London: Pickering and Chatto, 2012), 73–93, 91, 92.

4. John Sekora, *Luxury: The Concept in Western Thought, Eden to Smollett* (Baltimore: Johns Hopkins University Press, 1977); Liz Bellamy, *Commerce, Morality and the Eighteenth-Century*

Novel (Cambridge: Cambridge University Press, 1998); Deidre Shauna Lynch, *The Economy of Character: Novels, Market Culture and the Business of Inner Meaning* (Chicago: University of Chicago Press, 1998); E. J. Clery, *The Feminization Debate in Eighteenth-Century England: Literature, Commerce and Luxury* (Basingstoke: Palgrave Macmillan, 2004); Mary Poovey, *Genres of the Credit Economy: Mediating Value in Eighteenth- and Nineteenth-Century Britain* (Chicago: University of Chicago Press, 2008); Liz Bellamy, "Money's Productivity in Narrative Fiction," in *The Cambridge History of the English Novel*, ed. Robert L. Caserio and Clement Hawes (Cambridge: Cambridge University Press, 2012), 180–95; Paul Keen, *Literature, Commerce, and the Spectacle of Modernity, 1750–1800* (Cambridge: Cambridge University Press, 2012).

5. Bellamy, *Commerce, Morality*, 119–28; Mark Blackwell, ed., *The Secret Life of Things* (Lewisburg, Pa.: Bucknell University Press, 2007); Blackwell, *British It-Narratives*; Mark Blackwell, "Extraordinary Narrators: Metafiction and It-Narratives," in Caserio and Hawes, *Cambridge History of the English Novel*, 230–45.

6. Ritvo, "At the Edge of the Garden," 361–65; King, *Bloom*, 6, 15, 38–43; Lynch, "Young Ladies," 690–91.

7. Sir Harry Beaumont [Joseph Spence], *Crito: or, A Dialogue on Beauty* (London, 1752), 43. Accessed via ECCO. The description was extensively reproduced in eighteenth-century prose anthologies. For analysis of Spence's own garden, see Peter Martin, "Joseph Spence's Garden in Byfleet: Some New Descriptions," *Journal of Garden History* 3, no. 2 (1983): 121–29.

8. For contemporary discussions of pica, see, e.g., John Maubray, *The Female Physician, Containing all the Diseases Incident to that Sex, in Virgins, Wives and Widows* (London, 1724), 81–84. This view was challenged in works such as James Augustus Blondel, *The Strength of Imagination in Pregnant Women Examin'd and the Opinion that Marks and Deformities in Children Arise from thence Demonstrated to be a Vulgar Error* (London, 1727). George Rousseau explores the debate in "Pineapples, Pregnancy, Pica," in Rousseau and Boucé, *Tobias Smollett*, 79–109, 83–85.

9. For the incident described in this passage, see Smollett, *The Adventures of Peregrine Pickle*, 21–23, 21.

10. Maubray, *Female Physician*, 75.

11. Albala, *Eating Right in the Renaissance*, 151–52

12. John Webster, *The Duchess of Malfi*, ed. Brian Gibbons (London: Bloomsbury Methuen, 2014), act 2, scene 1, 127–46.

13. Paul-Gabriel Boucé, "Imagination, Pregnant Women and Monsters in Eighteenth-Century England and France," in *Sexual Underworlds of the Enlightenment*, ed. G. S. Rousseau and Roy Porter (Manchester: Manchester University Press, 1987), 86–100, 98; Jennifer Buckley, *Gender, Pregnancy and Power in Eighteenth-Century Literature: The Maternal Imagination* (London: Palgrave Macmillan, 2017).

14. Smollett, *The Adventures of Peregrine Pickle*, 21.

15. Maubray, *Female Physician*, 83.

16. Henry Fielding, *The History of the Adventures of Joseph Andrews*, ed. Martin Battestin (Oxford: Oxford University Press, 1967), 225.

17. See Albala, *Eating Right in the Renaissance*, 96.

18. John Giles, *Ananas*, Preface, v.

19. See 73, 153.

20. Rousseau, "Pineapples, Pregnancy, Pica," 79–109.

21. Nicholas Culpeper, *The English Physitian Enlarged* (London, 1684), 189–90, cited in Rousseau, "Pineapples, Pregnancy, Pica," 104–5. Rousseau cites it as *The English Physitian*, gives the date as 1674 and spells the name Culpepper.

22. Nicholas Culpeper, *The English Physitian* (London, 1652), 195.

23. Evelyn, *Diary*, 1: 348.

24. Culpeper, *English Physitian Enlarged*, 195. See also Nicholas Culpeper, *The English Physitian Enlarged* (London, 1653), 299.

25. Sekora, *Luxury*.

26. Smollett, *Humphry Clinker*, 118–19.

27. Fielding, *Joseph Andrews*, 226.

28. Unless otherwise indicated, the quotations here are taken from Smollett, *Humphry Clinker*, 121–23.

29. Charles Burney, *The Present State of Music in France and Italy* (1771) and *The Present State of Music in Germany, the Netherlands and United Provinces* (1773).

30. The work has been attributed to various hands, including Thomas Day, Alexander Bicknell, and Peter Beckford, with the British Library identifying John Bicknell as the author. This incident is included in the revised second edition, [John Bicknell] *Musical Travels through England by the late Joel Collier, licentiate in Music*, second edition (London, 1775), 24–25. The aldermen are described as having pockets full of melons and pineapples, which substantiates the argument proposed in Chapter 2 that these fruits were still relatively small in this period.

31. [John Bicknell] *Musical Travels through England by the late Joel Collier, licentiate in Music*, fourth edition (London, 1776), 24.

32. See Clare le Corbeiller, "James Cox: A Biographical Review," *Burlington Magazine* 112 (June 1970): 351–58; Marcia Pointon, "Dealer in Magic: James Cox's Jewelry Museum and the Economics of Luxurious Spectacle in Late-Eighteenth-Century London," in *Economic Engagements with Art*, ed. Neil de Marchi and Craufurd D. W. Goodwin, Annual Supplement to Volume 31, *History of Political Economy* (London: Duke University Press, 1999), 423–51; Roger Smith, "James Cox (c. 1723–1800): A Revised Biography," *Burlington Magazine* 142 (June 2000): 353–61.

33. Frances Burney, *Evelina: or the History of a Young Lady's Entrance into the World*, ed. Edward A. Bloom and Lillian D. Bloom (Oxford: Oxford University Press, 1984), 76–77.

34. Mrs. Cullum, *Charlotte: Or One Thousand Seven Hundred and Seventy Three: A Play* (1775), 64.

35. James Cox, *Descriptive catalogue of the several superb and magnificent pieces of mechanism and jewellery, exhibited in the museum, at Spring-Gardens* (London, 1772), 28–29.

36. Pointon, "Dealer in Magic," 426 and passim.

37. Marilyn Butler, *Jane Austen and the War of Ideas* (Oxford: Oxford University Press, 1975); Gary Kelly, *The English Jacobin Novel, 1780–1805* (Oxford: Oxford University Press, 1976); M. O. Grenby, *The Anti-Jacobin Novel: British Conservatism and the French Revolution* (Cambridge: Cambridge University Press, 2001).

38. See, e.g., the range of articles included in the special issue of *Novel: A Forum on Fiction* 34, no. 2 (March 2001), devoted to the Romantic-era novel, edited by Amanda Gilroy and Wil Verhoeven. Gilroy and Verhoeven's "Introduction," 147–62, addresses the history of the genre and problems of definition.

39. Katherine Binhammer, "The Sex Panic of the 1790s," *Journal of the History of Sexuality* 6, no. 3 (1996): 410; Lynch, "Young Ladies," 699.

40. Edward Said, *Culture and Imperialism* (London: Vintage, 1994), 106; Armitage, *Ideological Origins*, 182–97.

41. Antje Blank and Janet Todd, "Introduction" to Charlotte Smith, *Desmond*, eds. Antje Blank and Janet Todd (Peterborough, Ontario: Broadview, 2001), 19; Craciun and Lokke, "Introduction" in *Rebellious Hearts*, 19; Tamara S. Wagner, *Longing: Narratives of Nostalgia in the British Novel, 1740–1890* (Lewisburg, Pa.: Bucknell University Press, 2004), 73. Anne Mellor has suggested that the positive reading of the novel's ending is undercut by the recognition that it represents an entirely male perspective. See Anne K. Mellor, *Mothers of the Nation: Women's Political Writing in England, 1780–1830* (Bloomington: University of Indiana Press, 2002), 119. More recently, Fuson Wang has argued that the political texture of the novel appears more complex if viewed in terms of transnational rather than purely domestic political debates. See Fuson Wang, "Cosmopolitanism and the Radical Politics of Exile in Charlotte Smith's *Desmond*," *Eighteenth-Century Fiction* 25, no. 1 (2012): 37–59. Subsequent references to *Desmond* are to the Broadview edition.

42. For analysis of Burke's architectural imagery, see Paul Fussell, *The Rhetorical World of Augustan Humanism: Ethics and Imagery from Swift to Burke* (Oxford: Clarendon Press, 1965); David Weiser, "The Imagery in Burke's *Reflections*," *Studies in Burke and His Time* 16, no. 3 (1975): 213–34; Amy Garnai, *Revolutionary Imaginings in the 1790s: Charlotte Smith, Mary Robinson, Elizabeth Inchbald* (Basingstoke: Palgrave Macmillan, 2009); Candice Smith, "'Fine Old Castles' and 'Pull-Me-Down Works': Architecture, Politics and Gender in the Gothic Novel of the 1790s" (PhD diss., University of Aberdeen, 2014).

43. E. J. Clery, *The Rise of Supernatural Fiction, 1762–1800* (Cambridge: Cambridge University Press, 1995), 125–26; on the significance of Blackstone's architectural metaphors in Gothic fiction, see also Wolfram Schmidgen, *Eighteenth-Century Fiction and the Law of Property* (Cambridge: Cambridge University Press, 2002), 168–72.

44. Wagner, *Longing*, 73.

45. Jacqueline M. Labbe, "Metaphoricity and the Romance of Property in *The Old Manor House*," *Novel: A Forum on Fiction* 34, no. 2 (March 2001): 216–31, 217, 228.

46. Darren Howard, "Necessary Fictions: The 'Swinish Multitude' and the Rights of Man," *Studies in Romanticism* 47, no. 2 (2008): 161–78.

47. Smith, "Fine Old Castles," 158–64; Stephanie Russo, "The Damsel of Brittany: Mary Robinson's *Angelina*, Tyranny and the 1790s," *English Studies* 97, no. 4 (2016): 397–411.

48. Smith, "Fine Old Castles," 165.

49. William Brewer, "Egalitarianism in Mary Robinson's *Metropolis*," *Wordsworth Circle* 41, no. 3 (2010): 146–50, 146; compare Adriana Craciun, "Mary Robinson, the *Monthly Magazine*, and the Free Press," in *Romantic Periodicals and Print Culture*, ed. Kim Wheatley (London: Routledge, 2003), 19–40, 28.

50. Diego Saglia, "Commerce, Luxury, and Identity in Mary Robinson's Memoirs," *SEL* 49, no. 3 (Summer 2009): 717–36, 717. For accounts of Robinson's relationship with the Prince of Wales, see Paula Byrne, *Perdita: The Life of Mary Robinson* (London: Harper Perennial, 2005), 110–42; Smith, "Fine Old Castles," 131; Russo, "The Damsel of Brittany," 398–99.

51. Mary Robinson, *Angelina: A Novel*, 3 vols. (London, 1796), 2: 24. Accessed via ECCO. Subsequent references are to this edition in the form of volume and page numbers.

52. Smith, "Fine old castles," 149.

53. *Ananas bracteatus,* the red pineapple, was known in the eighteenth century as the Penguin Pineapple or Wild Pine. John Cowell includes a section on "the *Penguin* or Wild-Pine, which some Authors call *Anana Sylvestris*" in *The Curious and Profitable Gardener* (London, 1730) 31.

54. This is one of a number of inconsistencies in the text since, as the owner of a pinery, Clarendon would presumably not need to purchase commercial pineapples. Elsewhere, Robinson seems to have forgotten the name of one of her characters: *Angelina,* 3: 112.

55. Said, *Culture and Imperialism,* 70.

56. Kari Winter, *Subjects of Slavery, Agents of Change: Women and Power in Gothic Novels and Slave Narratives, 1790–1865* (Athens: University of Georgia Press, 1995), 10–11.

57. Moira Ferguson, *Subject to Others: British Women Writers and Colonial Slavery, 1670–1834* (London: Routledge, 1992), 176; Winter, *Subjects of Slavery,* 11; See also William Stafford, "Narratives of Women: English Feminists of the 1790s," *History* 82, no. 265 (January 1997): 24–43, 34; Bridget Marshall, *The Transatlantic Gothic Novel and the Law, 1790–1860* (London: Routledge, 2016); Caroline Franklin, "Enlightenment Feminism and the Bluestocking Legacy," in *The Cambridge Companion to Women's Writing in the Romantic Period,* ed. Devoney Looser (Cambridge: Cambridge University Press, 2015), 115–28, 119–20.

58. bell hooks, *Ain't I a Woman: Black Women and Feminism* (London: Routledge, 2014), 8; Gayatri Spivak, "Can the Subaltern Speak?" in *Colonial Discourse and Post-Colonial Theory: A Reader,* ed. Laura Chrisman and Patrick Williams (Hemel Hempstead: Harvester Wheatsheaf, 1994), 66–101, 82–83.

59. Mary Hays, *The Memoirs of Emma Courtney* (Oxford: Oxford University Press, 2009); Mary Wollstonecraft, *Mary and the Wrongs of Woman* (Oxford: Oxford University Press, 2009)

60. Smith, "Fine old castles," 154.

61. See Barbara Benedict and Deirdre La Faye, "Introduction" to Jane Austen, *Northanger Abbey* (Cambridge: Cambridge University Press, 2006), xxv.

62. King, *Bloom,* 35, 76.

63. Lynch, "Young Ladies," 719.

64. Austen, *Northanger Abbey.* The account of General Tilney's hothouses is on 182–83 and references are to here unless otherwise indicated.

65. Lynch, "Young Ladies," 692.

66. Austen, *Northanger Abbey,* 220–21. The account of the parsonage is here unless otherwise indicated.

67. Eric C. Walker, *Marriage, Writing and Romanticism: Wordsworth and Austen After War* (Stanford, Calif.: Stanford University Press, 2009), 93; Lynch "Young Ladies," 710.

68. Lynch, "Young Ladies," 715.

69. Crawford, *Poetry, Enclosure,* 194–252.

70. George Walker, *The Vagabond: A Novel,* ed. W. M. Verhoeven (Plymouth: Broadview, 2004), 137. Subsequent references are to this edition.

71. Adam Smith, *An Inquiry into the Nature and Causes of the Wealth of Nations,* ed. R. H. Campbell and A. S. Skinner, textual editor W. B. Todd, 2 vols (Oxford: Clarendon Press, 1976), 1: 9.

72. The identification of the pineapple as artificial is indicated in the inclusion of a detailed account of techniques for raising the fruit in Johann Beckmann's *Inventions and Discoveries,* 166–73.

73. Tobin, *Colonizing Nature*, 32–55, 144–67.

74. Opie, *Adeline Mowbray*, 15.

75. Ibid., 135. The pineapple incident is described on 135–41 and references are from here unless otherwise indicated.

76. Elizabeth Steele [possibly a pseudonym for Alexander Bicknell], *The Memoirs of Mrs. Sophia Baddeley, late of Drury-Lane Theatre*, 6 vols. (London, 1787), 1:165.

77. Howard, "The Story of the Pineapple," 355–76, 366.

78. Ann Hamilton, *The Adventures of a Seven Shilling Piece* (1811) in Blackwell, *British It-Narratives*, 1: 206; compare Fielding, *Tom Jones*, 2:680–81; William Shakespeare, *The Merchant of Venice*, act 4, scene 1, 179–200.

79. William Buchan, *Domestic Medicine: or, a Treatise on the Prevention and Cure of Diseases by Regimen and Simple Medicines*, 2nd ed. (London, 1772), note to 230; Beckmann, *Inventions and Discoveries*, 167.

80. John Guy, *Miscellaneous Selections: or, the Rudiments of Useful Knowledge* (1796), 1, 92. Guy suggests the "danger" might be lessened by eating the sugar loaf variety.

81. Keats, "Eve of St. Agnes," stanza 30, lines 264–70; Byron, *The Corsair*, canto I, 70–71.

Conclusion

1. Charlotte Brontë, *Jane Eyre: An Autobiography*, ed. Sally Shuttleworth (Oxford: Oxford University Press, 2000), 308.

2. Jean Rhys, *Wide Sargasso Sea* (Harmondsworth: Penguin, 2000), 39–67.

3. Gayatri Spivak, "Three Women's Texts and a Critique of Imperialism," *Critical Inquiry* 12, no. 1 (1985): 243–61, 248, 251.

4. Terry Eagleton, *Myths of Power: A Marxist Study of the Brontës* (Basingstoke: Palgrave Macmillan, 2005).

5. Beale, *Herefordshire Orchards*, 3.

6. See, e.g., Fielding, *The Governess*, 51–54; [Johnson], *Adventures of a Silver Penny*, 1:91; *Adventures of a Whipping-Top*, 4: 122, 126.

7. Said, *Culture and Imperialism*, 106–7.

8. Crawford, *Poetry, Enclosure*, 169–250.

9. In addition to being sold in fruiterer's shops, fruit was also available in confectioner's shops, see *A Month's Adventures of a Base Shilling* (Bristol: J. Wansborough [1820]), in Bellamy, *British It-Narratives*, 1: 262. This fruit may have been in dried or preserved form rather than fresh.

10. King, *Bloom*; Lynch, "Young Ladies."

BIBLIOGRAPHY

Primary Sources

Abercrombie, John. *The Hot-House Gardener*. London: John Stockdale, 1789.

Adair, James. *Commentaries on the Principles and Practice of Physic*. London: T. Becket and Co., 1772.

"Adam Lay Ybounden." British Library, Sloane 2593, ff.10v–11.

Addison, Joseph, Steele, Richard, et al. *The Spectator*. London: Sam Buckley [1711–1714].

The Adventures of a Whipping-Top. London: J. Marshall, [1786]. In Blackwell, *British It-Narratives, 1750–1830*. Vol. 4, *Toys, Trifles and Portable Furniture*. Ed. Mark Blackwell, 109–28.

Agricola, Georg Andreas. *Philosophical Treatise of Husbandry and Gardening*. London: P. Valiant, 1721. Reprinted as *The Experimental Husbandman and Gardener*. London: W. Mears, 1726.

Archer, T. *The Triumph of Agriculture: A Poem*. London: W. Lane, 1797.

Armstrong, John. *The Art of Preserving Health: A Poem*. London: John Smith and William Powell, 1744.

Athenaeus, *Deipnosophistae*, in *The Seven Books of Paulus Aegineta*. Trans. Francis Adams.. London: Sydenham Society, 1844.

Austen, Jane. *Mansfield Park*. Ed. John Wiltshire. Cambridge: Cambridge University Press, 2005.

———. *Northanger Abbey*. Ed. Barbara Benedict and Deirdre La Faye. Cambridge: Cambridge University Press, 2006.

Austen, Ralph. *A Treatise of Fruit Trees*. 1st ed. Oxford: Thomas Robinson, 1653. 2nd ed. Oxford: Thomas Robinson, 1657. 3rd ed. Oxford: Amos Curteyne, 1665.

———. *Observations upon some part of Sir Francis Bacon's Naturall History as it concernes Fruit-trees, Fruits and Flowers*. Oxford: Thomas Robinson, 1658.

———. *A Dialogue (or familiar discourse) and Conference between the Husbandman and Fruit-Trees in his Nurseries, Orchards and Gardens*. Oxford: Thomas Bowman, 1676.

Austin, Thomas, ed. *Two Fifteenth-Century Cookery Books*, Harleian MS.

Beale, John. *Herefordshire Orchards: A Pattern for all England*. London: 1657.

Beckmann, Johann. *A History of Inventions and Discoveries*. London: J. Bell, 1797.

Behn, Aphra. *The Works of Aphra Behn*. Ed. Janet Todd. 7 vols. London: Pickering and Chatto, 1993–96.

Bettesworth A., and Hitch, C. *The Complete Family-piece: and, Country Gentleman, and Farmer's, Best Guide*, 2nd ed. London: 1737.

[Bicknell, John]. *Musical Travels through England by the late Joel Collier, licentiate in Music*. 2nd ed. London: 1775. 4th ed. London: 1776.

Blagrave, Joseph. *The Epitome of the Whole Art of Husbandry*. London: Ben Billingsley and Obadiah Blagrave, 1669.

Blith, Walter. *The English Improver, or, A New Survey of Husbandry*. London: J. Wright, 1649.

Blondel, James Augustus. *The Strength of Imagination in Pregnant Women Examin'd and the Opinion that Marks and Deformities in Children Arise from thence Demonstrated to be a Vulgar Error*. London: J. Peele, 1727.

Boccaccio, Giovanni. *Filocolo*. Trans. Victoria Kirkham. Baltimore: Johns Hopkins University Press, 1971.

———. *The Decameron*. Trans. Guido Waldman. Oxford: Oxford University Press, 2008.

Bradley, Richard. *General Treatise of Husbandry and Gardening*. London: T. Woodward, 1726.

British It-Narratives, 1750–1830. Ed. Mark Blackwell. 4 vols. London: Pickering and Chatto, 2012.

Brontë, Charlotte. *Jane Eyre: An Autobiography*. Ed. Sally Shuttleworth. Oxford: Oxford University Press, 2000.

Buchan, William. *Domestic Medicine: or, a Treatise on the Prevention and Cure of Diseases by Regimen and Simple Medicines*. 2nd ed. London: Strahan, 1772. 17th ed. London: Strahan, 1800.

Burney, Charles. *The Present State of Music in France and Italy*. London: T. Becket and Co., 1771.

———. *The Present State of Music in Germany, the Netherlands and United Provinces*. London: T. Becket and Co., 1773.

Burney, Frances. *Evelina: or the History of a Young Lady's Entrance into the World*. Ed. Edward A. Bloom and Lillian D. Bloom. Oxford: Oxford University Press, 1984.

Burrell, Sophia. *Poems Dedicated to the Right Honourable Earl of Mansfield*. 2 vols. London: 1793.

Butts, Henry. *Dyets Dry Dinner*. London: William Wood, 1599.

Byron, George Gordon. *The Major Works*. Ed. Jerome McGann. Oxford: Oxford University Press, 2008.

Campion, Thomas. *The Works of Thomas Campion*. Ed. Walter R. Davis and J. Max Patrick. London: Norton, 1970.

Centlivre, Susanna. *The Gamester*. London: William Turner, [1705].

———. *The Platonick Lady*. London: James Knapton, [1707].

———. *The Busybody*. 1709. In *Eighteenth-Century Women Dramatists*. Ed. Melinda C. Finberg, 75–143. Oxford: Oxford University Press, 2001.

Chapman, George. *Chapman's Homer: The Iliad and The Odyssey*. Ed. Jan Parker. Ware: Wordsworth editions, 2002.

Chaucer, Geoffrey. *The Riverside Chaucer*. Ed. Larry D. Benson and F. N. Robinson. Oxford: Oxford University Press, 2008.

Cibber, Colley. *Love's Last Shift*. In *Restoration Drama: An Anthology*. Ed. David Womersley, 553–93. Oxford: Blackwell, 2000.

Collins, Wilkie. *The Woman in White*. Ed. John Sutherland. Oxford: Oxford University Press, 1998.

Colluthus, "The Rape of Helen." In *Oppian, Colluthus, Tryphiodorus*. Trans. A. W. Mair for the Loeb Classical Library, vol. 219. London: Heinemann, 1989.

Congreve, William. *The Works of William Congreve*. Ed. D. F. McKenzie. 3 vols. Oxford: Oxford University Press, 2011.

Cook, Moses. *The Manner of Raising, Ordering, and Improving Forest and Fruit-Trees*. London: Peter Parker, 1679.

Cotton, Charles. *The Planters Manual*. London: Henry Brome, 1675.

Cowell, John. *The Curious and Profitable Gardener*. London: Weaver Bickerton, 1730.

Cowley, Abraham. *Plantarum*. Trans. Nahum Tate. London: 1708.

———. *The Poetical Works of Abraham Cowley*. Edinburgh: Apollo Press, 1784.

———. *Prose Works of Abraham Cowley*. Ed. Thomas Sprat. London: William Pickering, 1826.

Cox, James. *Descriptive catalogue of the several superb and magnificent pieces of mechanism and jewellery, exhibited in the museum, at Spring-Gardens*. London: 1772.

Crowne, John. *The Country Wit* (1676). In *The Dramatic Works of John Crowne*. Ed. James Maidment and William Logan. Charleston, SC: Nabu Press, 2013.

Cullum, Mrs. *Charlotte: Or One Thousand Seven Hundred and Seventy Three: A Play*. London: 1775.

Culpeper, Nicholas. *The English Physitian or An astrologo-physical discourse of the vulgar herbs of this nation being a compleat method of physick*. London, 1652.

———. *The English Physitian Enlarged*. London, 1653.

———. *The English Physitian Enlarged*. London: Hannah Sawbridge, 1684.

d'Ablancourt, Monsieur. *Health Restor'd, or, the Triumph of Nature, over Physick, Doctors, and Apothecaries. In Twelve Entertaining Conversations*. London: Torbuck, Boydell and Noble, 1740.

Dawson, Thomas. *A Booke of Cookerie and the Order of Meates to bee Serued to the table, both for Flesh and Fish Dayes*. London: 1620.

de Bonnefons, Nicholas. *The French Gardiner*. London: John Crooke, 1658.

Downes, John. *Roscius Anglicanus, or, an Historical Review of the Stage, with Additions by the late Mr. Thomas Davies*. London: 1789.

Drayton, Michael. *The Complete Works of Michael Drayton*. Ed. Richard Hooper. London: John Russell Smith, 1876

Dryden, John. *The Works of John Dryden*. 20 vols. Berkeley: University of California Press, 1956–90.

Etherege, George. *The Plays of George Etherege*. Ed. Michael Cordner. Cambridge: Cambridge University Press, 1982.

Evelyn, John. *Fumifugium: or, The Inconveniencie of the Aer and Smoak of London Dissipated*. London: 1661.

———. *Pomona: or, An Appendix Concerning Fruit Trees in Relation to Cider*. In *Sylva, or A Discourse of Forest-Trees and the Propagation of Timber in His Majesty's Dominions*. London: 1664.

———. *Kalendarium Hortense, or, The Gard'ner's Almanac*. 9th ed. 1699.

———. *Elysium Britannicum, or The Royal Gardens*. London: 1700. Ed. John E. Ingram. Philadelphia: University of Pennsylvania Press, 2001.

———. *The Diary of John Evelyn*. Ed. William Bray. 2 vols. London: M. Walter Dunn, 1901.

Fairchild, Thomas. *The City Gardener*. London: T. Woodward, 1722.

Fane, Mildmay. *Otia Sacra*. Ed. Donald M. Friedman. New York: Scholars Facsimiles and Reprints, 1975.

Farquhar, George. *The Complete Works of George Farquhar*. Ed. Charles Stonehill. 2 vols. New York: Gordian Press, 1967.

Fielding, Henry. *The History of the Adventures of Joseph Andrews*. Ed. Martin Battestin. Oxford: Oxford University Press, 1967.

———. *The History of Tom Jones, A Foundling*. Ed. Martin C. Battestin and Fredson Bowers. 2 vols. Oxford: Oxford University Press, 1974.

———. *Plays, Volume One, 1728–1731*. Ed. Thomas Lockwood. Oxford: Oxford University Press, 2004.

——. *Plays, Volume Two, 1731–1734*. Ed. Thomas Lockwood. Oxford: Oxford University Press, 2007.

Fielding, Sarah. *The Governess: Or, The Little Female Academy*. Ed. Candace Ward. Peterborough, Ontario: Broadview, 2005.

Fitz-Adam, Adam [Edward Moore, Lord Chesterfield, R. O. Cambridge et al.]. *The World*, 6 vols. London: 1757.

Foster, E. M. *Miriam: A Novel*. London: Minerva, 1800.

Galen and Nicholas Culpeper. *Galen's Art of Physick*. London: 1653.

Gay, John. *Wine: A Poem*. In *John Gay: Poetry and Prose*. Ed. Vinton A. Dearing and Charles Beckwith, 2 vols. Oxford: Clarendon Press, 1974. 1, 21–29.

Gentleman's Magazine and Historical Chronicle, vol. 34. London: E. Cave, 1764.

Giles, John. *Ananas: Or, A Treatise on the Pine-Apple*. London: 1767.

Golding, Arthur. *Ovid's Metamorphoses*. London: 1567.

Goldsmith, Oliver. *The Vicar of Wakefield* (1766). Ed. Arthur Friedman and Robert L. Mack. Oxford: Oxford University Press, 2008.

Grainger, James. *The Sugar-Cane: A Poem, in Four Books*. London: R. and J. Dodsley, 1764.

Graves, Richard. *Euphrosyne: or, Amusements on the Road of Life*. 3rd ed. 2 vols. London: J. Dodsley, 1783.

Guy, John. *Miscellaneous Selections: or, the Rudiments of Useful Knowledge*. London: 1796.

Hamilton, Ann. *The Adventures of a Seven Shilling Piece*. 1811. In Blackwell, *British It-Narratives*, vol. 1, *Money*. Ed. Liz Bellamy. 161–211.

Hartlib, Samuel. *A Designe for Plentie, by an Universall Planting of Fruit-Trees: tendred by some wel-wishers to the Publick*. London: Richard Wodenothe, [1652].

Hays, Mary. *The Memoirs of Emma Courtney*. Oxford: Oxford University Press, 2009.

Hazlitt, William Carew. *Gleanings in Old Garden Literature*. London: Elliot Stock, 1887.

Higden, Henry. *The Wary Widow or Sir Noisy Parrot*. London: 1693.

Hogg, Robert, and Bull, Henry Graves. *The Herefordshire Pomona*. Hereford: Jakeman and Carver, 1876–85.

Holcroft, Thomas. *Anna St. Ives*. Teddington: Echo, 2006.

Homer. *The Odyssey of Homer, translated by Alexander Pope*. London: Suttaby, Evance and Co and Crosby and Co., 1811.

——. *The Odyssey*. Trans. Walter Shewring. Oxford: Oxford University Press, 2008.

——. *Chapman's Homer: The Iliad and The Odyssey*. Trans. George Chapman. Ed. Jan Parker. Ware: Wordsworth editions, 2002.

Horace. *All the Odes and Epodes of Horace: Translated into English Verse*. Trans. Henry Rider. London: 1638.

Horace: Odes and Epodes. London: Loeb Classical Library, 2004.

Hughes, Lewis. *A Letter Sent into England from the Summer Islands*. London: 1615.

The Husband Mans Fruitfull Orchard. In William Lawson, *A New Orchard and Garden*. London: Roger Jackson, 1618.

"I Have a New Garden." In *Middle English Lyrics*. Ed. R. T. Davies. London: Faber and Faber, 1963. Reproduced in *The Oxford Book of Garden Verse*. Ed. John Dixon Hunt, 7–8. Oxford: Oxford University Press, 1994.

[Johnson, Richard]. *The Adventures of a Silver Penny*. London: E. Newbery, [1786]. In Blackwell, *British It-Narratives*. Vol. 1, *Money*. Ed. Liz Bellamy, 73–93.

Jonson, Ben. *Ben Jonson: The Complete Poems*. Ed. George Parfitt. Harmondsworth: Penguin, 1980.

Laurence, John. *The Clergyman's Recreation: Shewing the Pleasure and Profit of the Art of Gardening*. 3rd ed. London: Bernard Lintott, 1715.

Lawson, William. *A New Orchard and Garden*. London: Roger Jackson, 1618.

Ligon, Richard. *A True and Exact History of Barbados*. London: Humphrey Moseley, 1657.

Malory, Thomas. *The Morte Darthur or The Hoole Book of Kyng Arthur and of his Noble Knyghtes of the Rounde Table*. Ed. Stephen H. A. Shepherd. London: Norton, 2004.

Mansey, Lewis. *The Practical Physician or Medical Instructor*. London: J. Stratford, 1800.

Markham, Gervase. *The English Husbandman*. London: John Browne, 1613.

———. *Maison rustique, or The countrey farme*. 7 vols. London: John Bill, 1616.

Marlowe, Christopher. *Dr Faustus: The A- and B-Texts*. Ed. David Bevington and Eric Rasmussen. Manchester: Manchester University Press, 2013.

Marsh, J. "To Mr Congreve." In *The Works of William Congreve*. Ed. D. F. McKenzie. 3 vols. 1: 10–11. Oxford: Oxford University Press, 2011.

Martine, George. "The Various Degrees of Heat in Bodies." In *Essays Medical and Philosophical*. London: A. Millar, 1740.

Marvell, Andrew. *Complete English Poems*. Ed. Elizabeth Story Donno. London: Allen Lane, 1972.

———. *The Poems of Andrew Marvell*. Ed. Nigel Smith. Harlow: Longman, 2007.

Maubray, John. *The Female Physician, Containing all the Diseases Incident to that Sex, in Virgins, Wives and Widows*. London: James Holland, 1724.

Miller, Philip. *The Gardeners and Florists Dictionary, or A Complete System of Horticulture*. 2 vols. London: Charles Rivington, 1724.

Milton, John. *Paradise Lost*. Ed. Alastair Fowler. Harlow: Pearson, 2007.

A Month's Adventures of a Base Shilling. Bristol: J. Wansborough [1820]. In Blackwell, *British It-Narratives, 1750–1830*. Vol. 1, *Money*. Ed. Liz Bellamy, 257–65.

N. F., *The Fruiterers Secrets*. London: 1604.

Opie, Amelia. *Adeline Mowbray*. Ed. Shelley King and John B. Pierce. Oxford: Oxford University Press, 1999.

Ovid. *Metamorphoses*. Trans. Arthur Golding. London: 1567.

———. *Ovid's Fasti*. Trans. Sir James George Frazer. London: Loeb Classical Library, 1959.

Parkinson, John. *Paradisi in Sole Paradisus Terrestris*. London: 1629. Reprinted London: Methuen, 1904.

Partridge, John. *The Treasurie of Commodious Conceits, & Hidden secrets and may be called, the Huswives Closet, of Healthfull Provision*. London: 1573.

Paulus Aegineta. *The Seven Books of Paulus Aegineta*. Trans. Francis Adams. 3 vols. London: Sydenham Society, 1844.

Pepys, Samuel. *The Diary of Samuel Pepys*. Ed. Robert Latham and William Matthews. Berkeley: University of California Press, 2000.

Philips, John. *Cider: A Poem in Two Books*. London: 1708. Ed. Charles Dunster. London: T. Cadell, 1791.

Philips, Katherine. *Printed Poems*. London: 1667.

Phillips, Henry. *The Companion for the Orchard*. London: 1831.

Pope, Alexander. *The Odyssey of Homer, translated by Alexander Pope*. London: Suttaby, Evance and Co and Crosby and Co., 1811.

Porta, John Baptista. *Natural Magick by John Baptista Porta, a Neapolitane; in twenty books . . . wherein are set forth all the riches and delights of the natural sciences.* London: 1658.

A Propre New Booke of Cokery. London: Richard Lant and Richarde Bankes, 1545.

Ralegh, Sir Walter. *The Works of Sir Walter Ralegh.* 8 vols. Oxford: Oxford University Press, 1829.

Rea, John. *Flora, seu, de Florum Cultura.* London: 1665.

Rider, Henry. *All the Odes and Epodes of Horace: Translated into English Verse.* London, 1638.

Rhys, Jean. *Wide Sargasso Sea.* Harmondsworth: Penguin, 2000.

Robinson, Mary. *Angelina: A Novel.* 3 vols. London: 1796.

Robinson, George, Godwin, William and Kippis, Andrew. Eds. *The New Annual Register or General Repository of History, Politics and Literature, for the Year 1796.* London: 1797.

Salkeld, John. *A Treatise of Paradise.* London: 1617.

The Sedan: A Novel. London: R. Baldwin, 1757. In Blackwell, *British It-Narratives, 1750–1830.* Vol. 3, *Clothes and Transportation.* Ed. Christina Lupton, 79–110.

Sedley, Charles. *The Mulberry-Garden, A Comedy.* London: 1668. In *Four Restoration Comedies.* Ed. Dennis Davison, 69–134. Oxford: Oxford University Press, 1970.

Shadwell, Thomas. *A True Widow.* London: 1678.

———. *The Virtuoso.* Ed. Marjorie Hope Nicolson and David Stuart Rose. Lincoln: University of Nebraska Press, 1966.

Shakespeare, William. *The Norton Shakespeare.* Ed. Stephen Greenblatt. London: Norton, 2008.

Sheridan, Richard Brinsley. *The Rivals.* In *The School for Scandal and Other Plays.* Ed. Michael Cordner, 3–86. Oxford: Oxford University Press, 2008.

"A Short Account of Several Gardens near London, with remarks on some particulars wherein they excel, or are deficient, upon a view of them in December 1691. Communicated to the Society by the Reverend Dr. Hamilton, Vice President, from an original Manuscript in his possession." In *Archaeologia or Miscellaneous Tracts Relating to Antiquity* 12 (1796): 181–92.

Smart, Christopher. *On the Goodness of the Supreme Being: A Poetical Essay.* Cambridge: 1756.

Smith, Adam. *An Inquiry into the Nature and Causes of the Wealth of Nations.* Ed. R. H. Campbell, A. S. Skinner, and W. B. Todd. 2 vols. Oxford: Clarendon Press, 1976.

Smith, Charlotte. *Desmond.* Ed. Antje Blank and Janet Todd. Peterborough, Ontario: Broadview, 2001.

Smith, John. *A Generall Historie of Virginia, New England and the Summer Isles.* London: 1624.

Smollett, Tobias. *The Adventures of Roderick Random.* Oxford: Oxford University Press, 1979.

———. *The Adventures of Peregrine Pickle.* Ed. James Clifford and Paul-Gabriel Boucé. Oxford: Oxford University Press, 1983.

———. *The Expedition of Humphry Clinker.* Ed. Lewis M. Knapp and Paul-Gabriel Boucé. Oxford: Oxford University Press, 1998.

[Spence, Joseph]. *Crito: or, A Dialogue on Beauty by Sir Harry Beaumont.* London: 1752.

Spenser, Edmund. *Spenser: Poetical Works.* Ed. J. C. Smith and E. de Selincourt. Oxford: Oxford University Press, 1970.

Steele, Elizabeth [Bicknell, Alexander]. *The Memoirs of Mrs. Sophia Baddeley, late of Drury-Lane Theatre.* 6 vols. London: 1787.

Strachey, William. "A true reportory of the wracke, and redemption of Sir Thomas Gates Knight; upon, and from the Ilands of the Bermudas . . . July 15. 1610." In *Purchas his Pilgrimage.* Vol. 4, ch. 6. London: 1625.

Tauvry, Daniel. *A New Rational Anatomy.* London: Midwinter and Leigh, 1701.

Taverner, John. *Certain Experiments concerning Fish and Fruit*. London: 1600.

This is the Boke of Cokery. London: Richard Pynson, 1500.

Thomson, James. *The Seasons, A hymn, A poem to the memory of Sir Isaac Newton, and Britannia, a poem*. London: J. Millan, near Whitehall; and A. Millar, in the Strand, 1730.

———. *The Poetical Works of James Thomson, Esq; with his last corrections and additions. Containing, The Seasons. Spring, Summer, Autumn, Winter*. London: printed for J. Thomson, in the Strand, 1768.

The Universal Family Physician and Surgeon. Blackburn: Hemingway and Nuttall, 1798.

van Oosten, Henrik. *The Dutch Gardener, translated from the Dutch*. London: D. Midwinter and T. Leigh, 1703.

Vanbrugh, John. *The Relapse*. 1696. In *Restoration Drama: An Anthology*. Ed. David Womersley, 595–645. Oxford: Blackwell, 2000.

——— and Cibber, Colley. *The Provoked Husband*. London: 1727.

Venette, Nicholas. *The Art of Pruning Fruit Trees*. London: 1685.

Venner, Tobias. *Via Recta ad Vitam Longam*. London: Edward Griffen, 1620.

Virgil. *The Works of Virgil containing his Pastorals, Georgics and Aeneis: adorn'd with a hundred sculptures, translated into English verse by Mr. Dryden*. London: Printed for Jacob Tonson, 1697. In *The Works of John Dryden*, vol. 5, *Poems: The Works of Virgil in English*. Ed. William Frost. Berkeley: University of California Press, 1987.

———. *Virgil: Eclogues, Georgics, Aeneid 1–6*. London: Loeb Classical Library, 1978.

Walker, George. *The Vagabond: A Novel*. Ed. W. M. Verhoeven. Plymouth: Broadview, 2004.

Waller, Edmund. *Poems, &c. written upon several occasions, and to several persons*. London: Henry Herringman, 1664.

Webster, John. *The Duchess of Malfi*. Ed. Brian Gibbons. London: Bloomsbury Methuen, 2014.

Wollstonecraft, Mary. *Mary and the Wrongs of Woman*. Oxford: Oxford University Press, 2009.

Worlidge, John. *Systema Agriculturae*. London: 1669.

———. *Vinetum Britannicum*. London: 1676.

———. *Systema Horticulturae*. London: 1677.

———. *A Compleat System of Husbandry and Gardening; or, The Gentleman's Companion, in the Business and Pleasures of a Country Life*. London: 1716.

Wycherley, William. *The Country Wife*. Ed. James Ogden. London: Bloomsbury Methuen, 2014.

Secondary Sources

Albala, Ken. *Eating Right in the Renaissance*. Berkeley: University of California Press, 2002.

———, ed. *A Cultural History of Food in the Renaissance*. London: Bloomsbury, 2012.

Angel-Perez, Elisabeth, and Poulain, Alexandra, eds. *Hunger on the Stage*. Newcastle: Cambridge Scholars Publishing, 2008.

Appelbaum, Robert. "Eve's and Adam's 'Apple': Horticulture, Taste, and the Flesh of the Forbidden Fruit in *Paradise Lost*." *Milton Quarterly* 36, no. 4 (Dec. 2002): 221–39.

———. *Aguecheek's Beef, Belch's Hiccup, and Other Gastronomic Interjections: Literature, Culture, and Food Among the Early Moderns*. Chicago: University of Chicago Press, 2012.

Armitage, David. *The Ideological Origins of the British Empire*. Cambridge: Cambridge University Press, 2000.

———"Literature and Empire." In *The Oxford History of the British Empire, Volume 1: The Origins of Empire. British Overseas Enterprise to the Close of the Seventeenth Century.* Ed. Nicholas Canny, 98–123. Oxford: Oxford University Press, 1998.

Badley, William. "A New Reading of Andrew Marvell's Mower Poems." Unpublished PhD diss., Middle Tennessee State University, 1994.

Barnard, T. C. "Gardening, Diet and 'Improvement' in Later Seventeenth-Century Ireland." *Journal of Garden History* 10 (1990): 71–85.

Beauman, Fran. *The Pineapple: King of Fruits.* London: Vintage, 2006.

Bellamy, Liz. *Commerce, Morality and the Eighteenth-Century Novel.* Cambridge: Cambridge University Press, 1998.

———. "Money's Productivity in Narrative Fiction." In *The Cambridge History of the English Novel.* Ed. Robert L. Caserio and Clement Hawes, 180–95. Cambridge: Cambridge University Press, 2012.

Bending, Stephen, ed. *A Cultural History of Gardens in the Age of Enlightenment.* London: Bloomsbury, 2013.

Bewell, Alan. "'On the Banks of the South Sea': Botany and Sexual Controversy in the Late Eighteenth Century." In *Visions of Empire: Voyages, Botany, and Representations of Nature.* Ed. David Miller and Peter Hannis Reill, 173–96. Cambridge: Cambridge University Press, 1996.

Binhammer, Katherine. "The Sex Panic of the 1790s." *Journal of the History of Sexuality* 6, no. 3 (Jan. 1996): 409–434.

Black, Virginia. "Beddington—'the best Orangery in England.'" *Journal of Garden History* 3, no. 2 (1983): 113–20.

Blackwell, Mark, ed. *The Secret Life of Things.* Lewisburg, Pa.: Bucknell University Press, 2007.

———. *British It-Narratives, 1750–1830.* London: Pickering and Chatto, 2012.

———. "Extraordinary Narrators: Metafiction and It-Narratives." In *Cambridge History of the English Novel.* Ed. Robert L. Caserio and Clement Hawes, 230–45. Cambridge: Cambridge University Press, 2012.

Boucé, Paul-Gabriel. "Imagination, Pregnant Women and Monsters in Eighteenth-Century England and France." In *Sexual Underworlds of the Enlightenment.* Ed. G. S. Rousseau and Roy Porter, 86–100. Manchester: Manchester University Press, 1987.

Brenner, Robert. *Merchants and Revolution: Commercial Change, Political Conflict, and London's Overseas Traders, 1550–1653.* Princeton, N.J.: Princeton University Press, 1993.

Brewer, William. "Egalitarianism in Mary Robinson's *Metropolis.*" *Wordsworth Circle* 41, no. 3 (2010): 146–50.

Britz, Billie S. "Environmental Provisions for Plants in Seventeenth-Century Northern Europe." *Journal of the Society of Architectural Historians* 33, no. 2 (1974): 133–44.

Broomhall, Susan, and Van Gent, Jacqueline. *Dynastic Colonialism: Gender, Materiality and the Early Modern House of Orange-Nassau.* London: Routledge, 2016.

Brown, David, and Williamson, Tom. *Lancelot Brown and the Capability Men: Landscape Revolution in Eighteenth-Century England.* London: Reaktion, 2016.

Brown, Laura. *English Dramatic Form: 1660–1760.* New Haven, Conn.: Yale University Press, 1981.

Bryson, Anna. *From Courtesy to Civility: Changing Codes of Conduct in Early Modern England.* Oxford: Clarendon Press, 1998.

Buckley, Jennifer. *Gender, Pregnancy and Power in Eighteenth-Century Literature: The Maternal Imagination.* London: Palgrave Macmillan, 2017.

Bucknell, Clare. "The Mid-Eighteenth-Century Georgic and Agricultural Improvement." *Journal for Eighteenth-Century Studies* 36, no. 3 (2013): 335–52.

Budd, Adam, ed. *John Armstrong's The Art of Preserving Health: Eighteenth-Century Sensibility in Practice*. London: Ashgate, 2013.

Bushnell, Rebecca. *Green Desire: Imagining Early Modern English Gardens*. Ithaca, N.Y.: Cornell University Press, 2003.

Butler, Marilyn. *Jane Austen and the War of Ideas*. Oxford: Oxford University Press, 1975.

Byrne, Paula. *Perdita: The Life of Mary Robinson*. London: Harper Perennial, 2005.

Carter, Tom. *The Victorian Garden*. London: Harper Collins, 1984.

Caserio, Robert L. and Hawes, Clement, eds. *The Cambridge History of the English Novel*. Cambridge: Cambridge University Press, 2012.

Clery, E. J. *The Rise of Supernatural Fiction, 1762–1800*. Cambridge: Cambridge University Press, 1995.

———. *The Feminization Debate in Eighteenth-Century England: Literature, Commerce and Luxury*. Basingstoke: Palgrave Macmillan, 2004.

Comito, Terry. *The Idea of the Garden in the Renaissance*. New Brunswick, N.J.: Rutgers University Press, 1978.

Copeland, Edward. *Women Writing About Money: Women's Fiction in England, 1790–1820*. Cambridge: Cambridge University Press, 2004.

Cordner, Michael. "Playwright Versus Priest: Profanity and the Wit of Restoration Comedy." In *The Cambridge Companion to English Restoration Theatre*. Ed. Deborah Payne Fisk, 209–25. Cambridge: Cambridge University Press, 2000.

Corman, Brian. "Comedy." In *Cambridge Companion to English Restoration Theatre*. Ed. Deborah Payne Fisk, 52–69. Cambridge: Cambridge University Press, 2000.

Cousins, A. D. *Andrew Marvell: Loss and Aspiration, Home and Homeland*. Abingdon: Routledge, 2016.

Craciun, Adriana. "Mary Robinson, the *Monthly Magazine*, and the Free Press." In *Romantic Periodicals and Print Culture*. Ed. Kim Wheatley, 19–40. London: Routledge, 2003.

Craciun, Adriana, and Lokke, Kari, eds. *Rebellious Hearts: British Women Writers and the French Revolution*. Albany: State University of New York Press, 2001.

Crawford, Rachel. "English Georgic and British Nationhood." *ELH* 65, no. 1 (1998): 123–58.

———. *Poetry, Enclosure and the Vernacular Landscape, 1700–1830*. Cambridge: Cambridge University Press, 2002.

Cuder-Domínguez, Pilar. *Stuart Women Playwrights, 1613–1713*. Farnham: Ashgate, 2010.

Dallas, Patsy; Barnes, Gerry; and Williamson, Tom. "Orchards in the Landscape: A Norfolk Case Study." *Landscapes* 16, no. 1 (2015): 26–43.

Danielson, Dennis. "The Fall and Milton's Theodicy." In *The Cambridge Companion to Milton*. Ed. Dennis Danielson, 144–59. Cambridge: Cambridge University Press, 1999.

Davis, Paul. *Translation and the Poet's Life: The Ethics of Translating in English Culture, 1646–1726*. Oxford: Oxford University Press, 2008.

Dawson, Lesel. "'A Thirsty Womb': Lovesickness, Green Sickness, Hysteria, and Uterine Fury." In *Lovesickness and Gender in Early Modern English Literature*. Ed. Lesel Dawson, 46–90. Oxford: Oxford University Press, 2008.

Dawson, Mark S. *Gentility and the Comic Theatre of Late Stuart London*. Cambridge: Cambridge University Press, 2005.

di Palma, Vittoria. "Drinking Cider in Paradise: Science, Improvement, and the Politics of Fruit Trees." In *A Pleasing Sinne: Drink and Conviviality in Seventeenth-Century England*. Ed. Adam Smyth, 161–77. Woodbridge: Boydell and Brewer, 2004.

DiMeo, Michelle. "Openness vs. Secrecy in the Hartlib Circle: Revisiting 'Democratic Baconianism' in Interregnum England." In *Secrets and Knowledge in Medicine and Science, 1500–1800*. Ed. Alisha Rankin and Elaine Leong, 105–121. Farnham: Ashgate, 2011.

Dobson, Michael. "'His Banquet Is Prepared': Onstage Food and the Permeability of Time in Shakespearean Performance." *Shakespeare Jahrbuch* 145 (2009): 62–73.

Downie, J. A. "Gay's Politics." In *John Gay and the Scriblerians*. Ed. Peter Lewis and Nigel Wood, 41–61. London: Palgrave Macmillan, 1988.

Drew, Erin, and Sitter, John. "Ecocriticism and Eighteenth-Century English Studies." *Literature Compass* 8, no. 5 (2011): 227–39.

Eagleton, Terry. *Myths of Power: A Marxist Study of the Brontës*. Basingstoke: Palgrave Macmillan, 2005.

Eamon, William. *Science and the Secrets of Nature: Books of Secrets in Medieval and Modern Culture*. Princeton, N.J.: Princeton University Press, 1994.

Earle, Peter. *The Making of the English Middle Class: Business, Society, and Family Life in London, 1660–1730*. Berkeley: University of California Press, 1989.

Edwards, Karen L. *Milton and the Natural World: Science and Poetry in* Paradise Lost. Cambridge: Cambridge University Press, 1999.

Fairer, David. "Persistence, Adaptation and Transformations in Pastoral and Georgic Poetry." In *The Cambridge History of English Literature, 1660–1780*. Ed. John J. Richetti, 259–86. Cambridge: Cambridge University Press, 2005.

———. "'Where Fuming Trees Refresh the Thirsty Air': The World of Eco-Georgic." *Studies in Eighteenth-Century Culture* 40 (2011): 201–18.

Ferguson, Moira. *Subject to Others: British Women Writers and Colonial Slavery, 1670–1834*. London: Routledge, 1992.

Fisk, Deborah Payne. "The Restoration Actress." In *A Companion to Restoration Drama*. Ed. Susan J. Owen, 69–91. Oxford: Blackwell, 2001.

Fitzpatrick, Joan. *Renaissance Food from Rabelais to Shakespeare: Culinary Readings and Culinary Histories*. London: Routledge, 2010.

———. "Body and Soul." In *A Cultural History of Food in the Renaissance*. Ed. Ken Albala, 151–70. London: Bloomsbury, 2016.

Foucault, Michel. *The Order of Things: An Archaeology of the Human Sciences*. London: Vintage, 1994.

Fowler, Alastair. "The 'Better Marks' of Jonson's 'To Penshurst.'" *Review of English Studies* 24, no. 95 (1973): 266–82.

———. "The Country House Poem: The Politics of a Genre." *Seventeenth Century* 1, no. 1 (1986): 1–14.

———. "Georgic and Pastoral: Laws of Genre in the Seventeenth Century." In *Culture and Cultivation in Early Modern England: Writing and the Land*. Ed. Michael Leslie and Timothy Raylor, 81–88. Leicester: Leicester University Press, 1992.

———. *The Country House Poem: A Cabinet of Seventeenth-Century Estate Poems and Related Items*. Edinburgh: Edinburgh University Press, 1994.

———. *The Mind of the Book: Pictorial Title Pages*. Oxford: Oxford University Press, 2017.

Franklin, Caroline. "Enlightenment Feminism and the Bluestocking Legacy." In *The Cambridge Companion to Women's Writing in the Romantic Period*. Ed. Devoney Looser, 115–28. Cambridge: Cambridge University Press, 2015.

Fussell, Paul. *The Rhetorical World of Augustan Humanism: Ethics and Imagery from Swift to Burke*. Oxford: Clarendon Press, 1965.

Garnai, Amy. *Revolutionary Imaginings in the 1790s: Charlotte Smith, Mary Robinson, Elizabeth Inchbald*. Basingstoke: Palgrave Macmillan, 2009.

George, Sam. *Botany, Sexuality and Women's Writing, 1760–1830: From Modest Shoot to Forward Plant*. Manchester: Manchester University Press, 2007.

Gilroy, Amanda, and Verhoeven, Wil. "Introduction." *Novel: A Forum on Fiction* 34, no. 2 (March 2001), 147–62.

Gollapudi, Aparna. *Moral Reform in Comedy and Culture, 1696–1747*. Farnham: Ashgate, 2011.

Grant, Mark. *Galen on Food and Diet*. London: Routledge, 2000.

Grenby, M. O. *The Anti-Jacobin Novel: British Conservatism and the French Revolution*. Cambridge: Cambridge University Press, 2001.

Griffin, Dustin. "The Bard of Cyder-Land: John Philips and Miltonic Imitation." *Studies in English Literature* 24 (1984): 441–60.

Grove, Richard H. *Green Imperialism: Colonial Expansion, Tropical Island Edens and the Origins of Environmentalism, 1600–1860*. Cambridge: Cambridge University Press, 1995.

Gulden, Ann Torday. "A Walk in the Paradise Garden: Eve's Influence in the 'Triptych' of Speeches, *Paradise Lost* 4.610–88." In *Renaissance Ecology: Imagining Eden in Milton's England*. Ed. Ken Hiltner, 45–62. Pittsburgh: Duquesne University Press, 2008.

Hardman, C. B. "Row Well Ye Mariners." *Review of English Studies*, 51 (2000), 80–82.

Harvey, John. *Early Nurserymen*. London: Phillimore, 1974.

Hibbard, G. R. "The Country House Poem of the Seventeenth Century." *Journal of the Warburg and Courtauld Institutes* 19 (1956): 159–74.

Highfill, Philip H.; Burnum, Kalman A.; and Langhans, Edward A., eds. *A Biographical Dictionary of Actors, Actresses, Musicians, Dancers, Managers and Other Stage Personnel in London, 1660–1800*. Carbondale: Southern Illinois University Press, 2006.

Hill, Christopher. "Society and Andrew Marvell." In *Andrew Marvell: A Critical Anthology*. Ed. John Carey, 83–85. Harmondsworth: Penguin, 1969.

Hiltner, Ken. *Milton and Ecology*. Cambridge: Cambridge University Press, 2003.

———. "Introduction." In *Renaissance Ecology: Imagining Eden in Milton's England*. Ed. Ken Hiltner, 1–14. Pittsburgh: Duquesne University Press, 2008.

Hitt, Christopher. "Ecocriticism and the Long Eighteenth Century." *College Literature* 31, no. 3 (2004): 123–47.

Holland, Norman. *The First Modern Comedies*. Cambridge: Harvard University Press, 1959.

Holland, Peter. *The Ornament of Action: Text and Performance in Restoration Comedy*. Cambridge: Cambridge University Press, 1979.

hooks, bell. *Ain't I a Woman: Black Women and Feminism*. London: Routledge, 2014.

Howard, Carol. "'The Story of the Pineapple': Sentimental Abolitionism and Moral Motherhood in Amelia Opie's *Adeline Mowbray*." *Studies in the Novel* 30, no. 3 (1998): 355–76.

Howard, Darren. "Necessary Fictions: The 'Swinish Multitude' and the Rights of Man." *Studies in Romanticism* 47, no. 2 (2008): 161–78.

Howes, Laura. *Chaucer's Gardens and the Language of Convention.* Gainesville: University Press of Florida, 1997.

Huggan, Graham, and Tiffin, Helen. *Postcolonial Ecocriticism: Literature, Animals, Environment.* 2nd ed. Abingdon: Routledge, 2015.

Hume, Robert D. "The Economics of Culture in London, 1660–1740." *Huntington Library Quarterly* 69, no. 4 (2006): 487–533.

Hunt, John Dixon. *Andrew Marvell: His Life and Writings.* Ithaca, N.Y.: Cornell University Press, 1978.

———. *Garden and Grove: The Italian Renaissance Garden in the English Imagination 1600–1750.* London: Dent, 1986.

———. *Greater Perfections: The Practice of Garden Theory.* Philadelphia: University of Pennsylvania Press, 2000.

Irvine, Robert. "Labor and Commerce in Locke and Early Eighteenth-Century English Georgic." *ELH* 76 (2009): 963–88.

Jones, Chris. *Radical Sensibility: Literature and Ideas in the 1790s.* London: Routledge, 1993.

Jung, Sandro. "Thomson's 'Winter,' the Ur-Text, and the Revision of *The Seasons.*" *Papers on Language and Literature* 45, no. 1 (2009): 60–81.

Keen, Paul. *Literature, Commerce, and the Spectacle of Modernity, 1750–1800.* Cambridge: Cambridge University Press, 2012.

Kelly, Gary. *The English Jacobin Novel, 1780–1805.* Oxford: Oxford University Press, 1976.

Kewes, Paulina. *Authorship and Appropriation: Writing for the Stage in England, 1660–1710.* Oxford: Clarendon, 1998.

King, Amy. *Bloom: The Botanical Vernacular in the English Novel.* Oxford: Oxford University Press, 2003.

King, Helen. *The Disease of Virgins: Green Sickness, Chlorosis, and the Problems of Puberty.* London: Psychology Press, 2004.

Kinservik, Matthew J. "Theatrical Regulation During the Restoration Period." In *A Companion to Restoration Drama.* Ed. Susan J. Owen, 36–52. Oxford: Blackwell, 2001.

Knott, John R. *Milton's Pastoral Vision.* Chicago: University of Chicago Press, 1971.

——— "Milton's Wild Garden." *Studies in Philology* 102, no. 1 (Winter, 2005): 66–82.

Korda, Natasha. "Gender at Work in the Cries of London." In *Oral Traditions and Gender in Early Modern Literary Texts.* Ed. Mary Ellen Lamb and Karen Bamford, 117–35. Aldershot: Ashgate, 2008.

Kussmaul, Ann. *Servants in Husbandry in Early Modern England.* Cambridge: Cambridge University Press, 1981.

Labbe, Jacqueline M. "Metaphoricity and the Romance of Property in *The Old Manor House.*" *Novel: A Forum on Fiction* 34, no. 2 (March 2001): 216–31.

Langhans, Edward A. "The Theatre." In *The Cambridge Companion to English Restoration Theatre.* Ed. Deborah Payne Fisk, 1–18. Cambridge: Cambridge University Press, 2000.

———. "The Post-1660 Theatres as Performance Spaces." In *A Companion to Restoration Drama.* Ed. Susan J. Owen, 3–18. Oxford: Blackwell, 2001.

Le Corbeiller, Clare. "James Cox: A Biographical Review." *Burlington Magazine* 112 (June 1970): 351–58.

Leslie, Michael. "The Spiritual Husbandry of John Beale." In *Culture and Cultivation in Early Modern England: Writing and the Land.* Ed. Michael Leslie and Timothy Raylor, 151–72. Leicester: Leicester University Press, 1992.

———. "'Bringing Ingenuity into Fashion': The 'Elysium Britannicum' and the Reformation of Husbandry." In *John Evelyn's "Elysium Britannicum" and European Gardening*. Ed. Therese O'Malley and Joachim Wolschke-Bulmann, 131–52. Washington, DC: Dumbarton Oaks, 1998.

—— and Raylor, Timothy, eds. *Culture and Cultivation in Early Modern England: Writing and the Land*. Leicester: Leicester University Press, 1992.

Levine, Caroline. *Forms: Whole, Rhythm, Hierarchy, Network*. Princeton, N.J.: Princeton University Press, 2015.

Levitt, Ruth. "'A Noble Present of Fruit': A Transatlantic History of Pineapple Cultivation." *Garden History* 42, no. 1 (2014): 106–19.

Lewalski, Barbara. "Innocence and Experience in Milton's Eden." In *New Essays on* Paradise Lost. Ed. Thomas Kranidas, 86–117. Berkeley: University of California Press, 1970.

———. "Milton's Paradises." In Hiltner, *Renaissance Ecology*, 15–30. Pittsburgh: Duquesne University Press, 2008.

Lianeri, Alexandra, and Zajko, Vanda, eds. *Translation and the Classic: Identity as Change in the History of Culture*. Oxford: Oxford University Press, 2008.

Love, Harold. "Early Modern Print Culture." In *The Book History Reader*. Ed. David Finkelstein and Alistair McCleery, 74–86. London: Routledge, 2006.

Low, Anthony. *The Georgic Revolution*. Princeton, N.J.: Princeton University Press, 1985.

———. "Agricultural Reform and the Love Poems of Thomas Carew." In *Culture and Cultivation in Early Modern England: Writing and the Land*. Ed. Michael Leslie and Timothy Raylor, 63–80. Leicester: Leicester University Press, 1992.

Lowe, Dunstan. "The Symbolic Value of Grafting in Ancient Rome." *Transactions of the American Philological Association* 140, no. 2 (Autumn 2010): 461–88.

Lowenthal, Cynthia. *Performing Identities on the Restoration Stage*. Carbondale: Southern Illinois University Press, 2002.

Lynch, Deidre Shauna. *The Economy of Character: Novels, Market Culture and the Business of Inner Meaning*. Chicago: University of Chicago Press, 1998.

———. "'Young Ladies Are Delicate Plants': Jane Austen and Greenhouse Romanticism." *ELH* 77 (2010): 689–729.

Marcus, Leah S. "Ecocritical Milton." In *Ecological Approaches to Early Modern English Texts: A Field Guide to Reading and Teaching*. Ed. Jennifer Munroe, Edward J. Geisweidt, and Lynne Bruckner, 131–41. Farnham: Ashgate, 2015.

Markley, Robert. *Two-Edg'd Weapons: Style and Ideology in the Comedies of Etherege, Wycherley and Congreve*. Oxford: Clarendon, 1988.

Marshall, Bridget. *The Transatlantic Gothic Novel and the Law, 1790–1860*. London: Routledge, 2016.

Martin, Peter. "Joseph Spence's Garden in Byfleet: Some New Descriptions." *Journal of Garden History* 3, no. 2 (1983): 121–29.

Matter, E. Ann. *The Voice of My Beloved: The Song of Songs in Western Medieval Christianity*. Philadelphia: University of Pennsylvania Press, 1990.

McClung, William A. *The Country House in English Renaissance Poetry*. Berkeley: University of California Press, 1977.

McColley, Diane *Milton's Eve*. Urbana: University of Illinois Press, 1983.

———. *A Gust for Paradise*. Urbana: University of Illinois Press, 1993.

———. *Poetry and Ecology in the Age of Milton and Marvell*. Abingdon: Routledge, 2007.

McRae, Andrew. "Husbandry Manuals and the Language of Agrarian Improvement." In *Culture and Cultivation in Early Modern England: Writing and the Land*. Ed. Michael Leslie and Timothy Raylor, 35–62. Leicester: Leicester University Press, 1992.

———. *God Speed the Plough: The Representation of Agrarian England, 1500–1660*. Cambridge: Cambridge University Press, 1996.

Mellor, Anne K. *Mothers of the Nation: Women's Political Writing in England, 1780–1830*. Bloomington: University of Indiana Press, 2002.

Mounsey, Chris. "Christopher Smart's *The Hop-garden* and John Philips's *Cider*: A Battle of the Georgics? Mid-Eighteenth-Century Poetic Discussions of Authority, Science and Experience." *British Journal for Eighteenth-Century Studies* 22 (1999): 67–84.

Munroe, Jennifer. "Shakespeare and Ecocriticism Reconsidered." *Literature Compass* 12, no. 9 (2015): 461–70.

Munroe, Jennifer, Geisweidt, Edward J. and Bruckner, Lynne, eds. *Ecological Approaches to Early Modern English Texts: A Field Guide to Reading and Teaching*. Farnham: Ashgate, 2015.

Nokes, David. *John Gay: A Profession of Friendship*. Oxford: Oxford University Press, 1995.

Nunn, Hillary M. "Playing with Appetite in Early Modern Comedy." In *Shakespearean Sensations: Experiencing Literature in Early Modern England*. Ed. Katharine A. Craik and Tanya Pollard, 110–17. Cambridge: Cambridge University Press, 2013.

O'Malley, Therese and Wolschke-Bulmahn, Joachim. *John Evelyn's "Elysium Britannicum" and European Gardening*. Washington, DC: Dumbarton Oaks, 1998.

Orr, Bridget. *Empire on the English Stage, 1660–1714*. Cambridge: Cambridge University Press, 2001.

Owen, Susan. *Restoration Theatre and Crisis*. Oxford: Clarendon Press, 1996.

———, ed. *A Companion to Restoration Drama*. Oxford: Blackwell, 2001.

Parker, Geoffrey. *Global Crisis: War, Climatic Change and Catastrophe in the Seventeenth Century*. New Haven, Conn.: Yale University Press, 2013.

Parry, Graham. "John Evelyn as Hortulan Saint." In *Culture and Cultivation in Early Modern England: Writing and the Land*. Ed. Michael Leslie and Timothy Raylor, 130–50. Leicester: Leicester University Press, 1992.

Peacey, Jason. *Print and Public Politics in the English Revolution*. Cambridge: Cambridge University Press, 2013.

Pearman, Tory Vandeventer. "'O Sweete Venym Queynte!'": Pregnancy and the Disabled Female Body in the *Merchant's Tale*." In *Disability in the Middle Ages: Reconsiderations and Reverberations*. Ed. Joshua Eyler, 25–37. London: Routledge, 2010.

Pellicer, Juan Christian. "John Gay, *Wine* (1708) and the Whigs." *British Journal for Eighteenth-Century Studies* 27 (2004): 245–55.

Pocock, J. G. A. *The Machiavellian Moment: Florentine Political Thought and the Atlantic Republican Tradition*. Princeton, N.J.: Princeton University Press, 1975.

Pointon, Marcia. "Dealer in Magic: James Cox's Jewelry Museum and the Economics of Luxurious Spectacle in Late-Eighteenth-Century London." In *Economic Engagements with Art*. Ed. Neil de Marchi and Craufurd D. W. Goodwin, Annual Supplement to vol. 31, *History of Political Economy*, 423–51. London: Duke University Press, 1999.

Poovey, Mary. *Genres of the Credit Economy: Mediating Value in Eighteenth- and Nineteenth-Century Britain*. Chicago: University of Chicago Press, 2008.

Potter, Jennifer. *Strange Blooms: The Curious Lives and Adventures of the John Tradescants*. London: Atlantic, 2006.

Raber, Karen. "Recent Ecocritical Studies of English Renaissance Literature." *English Literary Renaissance* 37, no. 1 (2007): 151–71.

Rathmell, J. C. A. "Jonson, Lord Lisle, and Penshurst." *English Literary Renaissance,* 1 (1971): 250–60.

Raylor, Timothy. "The Instability of Marvell's *Bermudas." Marvell Society Newsletter,* 6, no. 4 (2014): 3–12.

Revard, Stella. "Eve and the Language of Love in *Paradise Lost." In Renaissance Ecology: Imagining Eden in Milton's England.* Ed. Ken Hiltner, 31–44. Pittsburgh: Duquesne University Press, 2008.

Ridgeway, Chris, and Williams, Robert, eds. *Sir John Vanbrugh and Landscape Architecture in Baroque England, 1690–1730.* Stroud: Alan Sutton, 2000.

Riley, Gillian. "Food in Painting." In *A Cultural History of Food in the Renaissance.* Ed. Ken Albala, 171–82. London: Bloomsbury, 2016.

Ritvo, Harriet. "At the Edge of the Garden: Nature and Domestication in Eighteenth- and Nineteenth-Century Britain." *Huntington Library Quarterly* 55, no. 3 (Summer, 1992): 363–78.

Roach, F. A. *Cultivated Fruits of Britain: Their Origin and History.* Oxford: Blackwell, 1985.

Rogers, Pat. "John Philips, Pope and Political Georgic." *Modern Language Quarterly* 66, no. 4 (Dec. 2005): 411–42.

Root, Waverley. *Food: An Authoritative and Visual History and Dictionary of the Foods of the World.* New York: Simon and Schuster, 1980.

Rosenberg, Bruce A. "The 'Cherry-Tree Carol' and the 'Merchant's Tale.'" *Chaucer Review* 5, no. 4 (Spring 1971): 264–76, 270.

Rosenthal, Laura. *Playwrights and Plagiarists in Early Modern England: Gender, Authorship, Literary Property.* Ithaca, N.Y.: Cornell University Press, 1996.

Ross, David. *Virgil's Elements: Physics and Poetry in the* Georgics. Princeton, N.J.: Princeton University Press, 1987.

Rousseau, George S. "Pineapples, Pregnancy, Pica, and *Peregrine Pickle." In Tobias Smollett: Bicentennial Essays Presented to Lewis M. Knapp.* Ed. George S. Rousseau and Paul-Gabriel Boucé, 79–109. New York: Oxford University Press, 1971.

Rousseau, George S. and Boucé, Paul-Gabriel, eds. *Tobias Smollett: Bicentennial Essays Presented to Lewis M. Knapp.* New York: Oxford University Press, 1971.

Russo, Stephanie. "The Damsel of Brittany: Mary Robinson's *Angelina,* Tyranny and the 1790s." *English Studies* 97, no. 4 (2016): 397–411.

Saglia, Diego. "Commerce, Luxury, and Identity in Mary Robinson's Memoirs." *SEL* 49, no. 3 (Summer 2009): 717–36.

Said, Edward. *Culture and Imperialism.* London: Vintage, 1994.

Schmidgen, Wolfram. *Eighteenth-Century Fiction and the Law of Property.* Cambridge: Cambridge University Press, 2002.

Scodel, Joshua. "Allusions and Distinctions: Pentameter Couplets in Ben Jonson's Epigrams and Forest." In *The Work of Form: Poetics and Materiality in Early Modern Culture.* Ed. Ben Burton and Elizabeth Scott-Baumann, 39–55. Oxford: Oxford University Press, 2014.

Sekora, John. *Luxury: The Concept in Western Thought, Eden to Smollett.* Baltimore: Johns Hopkins University Press, 1977.

Shovlin, John. "War and Peace: Trade, International Competition, and Political Economy." In *Mercantilism Reimagined: Political Economy in Early Modern Britain and Its Empire.* Ed. Philip J. Stern and Carl Wennerlind, 305–27. Oxford: Oxford University Press, 2014.

Smith, Candice. "'Fine Old Castles' and 'Pull-Me-Down Works': Architecture, Politics and Gender in the Gothic Novel of the 1790s." Unpublished PhD diss., University of Aberdeen, 2014.

Smith, Nigel. *Andrew Marvell: The Chameleon.* London: Yale University Press, 2010.

Smith, Roger. "James Cox (c. 1723–1800): A Revised Biography." *Burlington Magazine* 142 (June 2000): 353–61.

Song, Eric. "The Country Estate and the Indies (East and West): The Shifting Scene in Eden in *Paradise Lost.*" *Modern Philology*, 108, no. 2 (2010): 199–223.

Spivak, Gayatri. "Can the Subaltern Speak?" In *Colonial Discourse and Post-Colonial Theory: A Reader.* Ed. Laura Chrisman and Patrick Williams, 66–101. Hemel Hempstead: Harvester Wheatsheaf, 1994.

———. "Three Women's Texts and a Critique of Imperialism." *Critical Inquiry* 12, no. 1 (1985): 243–61.

Stafford, William. "Narratives of Women: English Feminists of the 1790s." *History* 82, no. 265 (Jan. 1997): 24–43.

Staves, Susan. *Players' Scepters: Fictions of Authority in the Restoration.* Lincoln: University of Nebraska Press, 1979.

Tanner, Norman. "Religious Practice." In *Medieval Norwich.* Ed. Richard Wilson and Carole Rawcliffe, 137–56. London: Palgrave Macmillan, 2004.

Theis, Jeffrey S. "'The purlieus of heaven': Milton's Eden as a Pastoral Forest." In *Renaissance Ecology: Imagining Eden in Milton's England.* Ed. Ken Hiltner, 229–57. Pittsburgh: Duquesne University Press, 2008.

Thick, Malcolm. "Market Gardening in England and Wales." In *The Agrarian History of England and Wales: Volume 5, 1640–1750, Part 2, Agrarian Change.* Ed. Joan Thirsk, 233–262. Cambridge: Cambridge University Press, 1985.

Thirsk, Joan. "Agricultural Innovations and Their Diffusion." In *The Agrarian History of England and Wales: Volume 5, 1640–1750, Part 2, Agrarian Change.* Ed. Joan Thirsk, 533–89. Cambridge: Cambridge University Press, 1985.

——— *The Agrarian History of England and Wales: Volume 5, 1640–1750, Part 2, Agrarian Change.* Cambridge: Cambridge University Press, 1985.

———. "Making a Fresh Start: Sixteenth-Century Agriculture and the Classical Inspiration." In *Culture and Cultivation in Early Modern England: Writing and the Land.* Ed. Michael Leslie and Timothy Raylor, 15–34. Leicester: Leicester University Press, 1992.

Thomas, Richard. "Tree Violation and Ambivalence in Virgil." *Transactions of the American Philological Association* 118 (1988): 261–73.

Tigner, Amy L. *Literature and the Renaissance Garden from Elizabeth I to Charles II.* Farnham: Ashgate, 2012.

———. "The Ecology of Eating in Jonson's 'To Penshurst'." In *Ecological Approaches to Early Modern English Texts.* Ed. Jennifer Munroe, Edward J. Geisweidt, and Lynne Bruckner, 109–19. Farnham: Ashgate, 2015.

Tobin, Beth Fowkes. *Colonizing Nature: The Tropics in British Arts and Letters, 1760–1820.* Philadelphia: University of Pennsylvania Press, 2004.

Trible, Phyllis. *God and the Rhetoric of Sexuality.* Philadelphia, Pa.: Fortress Press, 1978.

Wagner, Tamara S. *Longing: Narratives of Nostalgia in the British Novel, 1740–1890.* Lewisburg, Pa.: Bucknell University Press, 2004.

Walker, Eric C. *Marriage, Writing and Romanticism: Wordsworth and Austen After War*. Stanford, Calif.: Stanford University Press, 2009.

Wang, Fuson. "Cosmopolitanism and the Radical Politics of Exile in Charlotte Smith's *Desmond*." *Eighteenth-Century Fiction* 25, no. 1 (2012): 37–59.

Watson, Nicola. *Revolution and the Form of the British Novel 1780–1852*. Oxford: Oxford University Press, 1994.

Watson, Robert N. *Back to Nature: The Green and the Real in the Late Renaissance*. Philadelphia: University of Pennsylvania Press, 2006.

———. "Tell Inconvenient Truths, but Tell Them Short." In *Ecological Approaches to Early Modern English Texts: A Field Guide to Reading and Teaching*. Ed. Jennifer Munro, Edward Geisweidt, and Lynne Bruckner, 17–28. Farnham: Ashgate, 2015.

Wayne, Don E. *Penshurst: The Semiotics of Place and the Poetics of History*. London: Methuen, 1984.

Weber, Harold. *The Restoration Rake-Hero: Transformations in Sexual Understanding in Seventeenth-Century England*. Madison: University of Wisconsin Press, 1986.

Webster, Jeremy. *Performing Libertinism in Charles II's Court: Politics, Drama, Sexuality*. Basingstoke: Palgrave Macmillan, 2005.

Weeda, Leendert. *Vergil's Political Commentary: In the Eclogues, Georgics and Aeneid*. Warsaw: de Gruyter, 2015.

Weiser, David. "The Imagery in Burke's *Reflections*." *Studies in Burke and His Time* 16, no. 3 (1975): 213–34.

Williams, Raymond. *The Country and the City*. Oxford: Oxford University Press, 1973.

Williamson, Tom. *Polite Landscapes: Gardens and Society in Eighteenth-Century England*. Stroud: Alan Sutton, 1995.

Winter, Kari. *Subjects of Slavery, Agents of Change: Women and Power in Gothic Novels and Slave Narratives, 1790–1865*. Athens: University of Georgia Press, 1995.

Woudstra, Jan. "The Re-Instatement of the Greenhouse Quarter at Hampton Court Palace." *Garden History* 37, no. 1 (Summer 2009): 80–110.

Wynne-Davies, Marion. "Orange Women, Female Spectators, and Roaring Girls: Women and Theatre in Early Modern England." *Medieval and Renaissance Drama in England* 22 (2009): 19–26.

INDEX

≈

ACKNOWLEDGMENTS

The ideas for this book have developed over a long period through discussions with successive cohorts of students at City College Norwich and the Open University, as well as with friends and colleagues at both institutions. Special thanks go to Philip Church, the late Cathy Davies, Chris Hudson, Margie Kemsley, and David-Lee Priest at City College, and to Stephen Bygrave, Michael Englard, Angela Eyre, Joanna Gondris, Peter Lawson, and Bob Owens at the Open University. John Dixon Hunt provided invaluable guidance on early drafts of the manuscript, and the project was further shaped by the kind and insightful comments from the two anonymous readers for Penn Press. I am grateful to all the staff at Penn Press who have helped to turn the manuscript into a physical object, particularly Jerome Singerman, Hannah Blake, and Noreen O'Connor-Abel, and to Tom Williamson, Matt Williamson, and Jess Bellamy who have all contributed in their different ways.